MAVERICKS
of
the MIND

MAVERICKS of the MIND

CONVERSATIONS FOR THE NEW MILLENNIUM

Interviews by
DAVID JAY BROWN &
REBECCA MCCLEN NOVICK

The Crossing Press, Freedom, CA 95019

To our Mothers
Arleen & Noreen

———

Copyright © 1993 by David Jay Brown & Rebecca McClen Novick
Cover art & design by AnneMarie Arnold
Book design by Amy Sibiga

Printed in the U.S.A.

Mavericks of the mind: conversations for the new millenium, interviews / by
David Jay Brown & Rebecca McClen Novick.
     p.   cm.
     Conversations with Terence McKenna, Riane Eisler & David Loye,
Robert Trivers, Nick Herbert, Ralph Abraham, Timothy Leary, Robert
Anton Wilson, Rupert Sheldrake, Carolyn Mary Kleefeld, Colin Wilson,
Oscar Janiger, John Lilly, Nina Graboi, Laura Huxley, Stephen
LaBerge, Allen Ginsberg.
     ISBN 0-89594-602-5 (cloth). -- ISBN 0-89594-601-7 (pbk.)
     1. Consciousness. 2. Mind and Body. I. Brown, David Jay.
II. Novick, Rebecca McClen.
BF311.M4267 1991 153--dc20   92-38992
                                            CIP

Acknowledgments

An important lesson that we learned from doing this book is that cooperation, patience, tolerance, and communication are the keys to solving most of the world's problems. We really worked as a team to put this book together, and it was a balancing act that required much delicate coordination. It took about four years to complete, and although there was a great deal of work involved we did have a lot of fun. The collaboration of many others made it possible. We would like to extend special thanks to Carolyn Kleefeld and Nina Graboi who both helped tremendously in arranging many of the interviews. We would also like to thank our favorite magazine editor Judy McGuire at *High Times* for her support, and Jeanne St. Peter, who helped conduct the interview with Oscar Janiger while Rebecca was in England.

In addition, we would like to express our sincere gratitude to Gabrielle Alberici, Randy Baker, Bob Banner, Debra Berger, Steven Brown, Allyn Brodsky, Brummbaer, Linda Capetillo-Cunliffe, Barbara Clarke-Lilly, Robin Christianson-Day, Elizabeth Gips, Deborah Harlow, Betsy Herbert, Larry Hughes, Dan Joy, Jeff Labno, Lisa Lyon-Lilly, Joe & Nina Matheny, Ronny Novick, Andrew Shachat, Douglas Trainer, Silvia Utiger, Victoria Vaughn, Nur Wesley, Arlen Wilson, and wonderful friends too numerous to mention, for their contributions and support during the development of this project. We would also like to express our deepest appreciation to all the people we interviewed for their invaluable time and energy.

Previously Published Excerpts from Interviews

Ralph Abraham—*International Synergy Journal* #9, Spring, 1990, pp. 38-51. *International Synergy Newsletter*, vol. 1, No. 2, 1990, p. 3, pp. 7-8. *Mondo 2000* #3, Winter, 1991, pp.150-154.

Nina Graboi—*High Times*, June, 1992, pp. 12-16.

John Lilly—*High Times*, May, 1992, pp. 12-16. *Magical Blend* #36, Summer/Fall, 1992, pp. 44-50, p. 82.

Terence McKenna—*Critique* #31, Summer/Fall, 1989, pp. 58-60. *High Times*, April, 1992, pp. 12-16, 60-62. *The Archaic Revival* (Harper/San Francisco,1991) pp. 204-216.

Robert Anton Wilson— *Critique* #32 Fall/Winter, 1989-90, pp. 77-81.

Table of Contents

Preface

The four "isms" of the apocalypse: chauvinism, sexism, racism and fundamentalism are riding roughshod over the gardens of civilization. When we take a long look around at the effects of the modern world, it's not a pretty sight. Blackened stumps of ancient forests smoulder in the mid-day sun, young children stare from (and at) television sets, stunned with hunger and lack of love; torture and cruelty are the trademark of governments throughout the world; and wars are raging all over the face of our planet.

For all the shimmering beauty of life, for all the exquisite potential waiting in the wings, when we take a long look around, we find ourselves none too sure about the future of our species, or for that matter, of any other. Perhaps we should be bidding our farewells to DNA, thanking it for having us and apologizing for being such sloppy guests. Or perhaps we should act "as if" there is going to be a future, because the alternative leads down an ever-darkening path to humorlessness, apathy, and despair.

So, if we believe there is hope for our future, we must then get a grip on what it is that's wrong with our present. At first thought this seems pretty obvious—our senses tell us so. You can *see* that the lower skyline of Los Angeles looks like the rim of a toilet bowl, you can *hear* the stories of battered women, you can touch the swollen stomach of a starving Somalian child, you can *smell* the choking fumes of Saddam Hussein's mustard gas and you can *taste* the fruits of our labors with that nasty after-tang of malathion.

To attempt to exorcise these problems externally, without exorcising the mytho-scientific perspective which creates them, ensures that we will gain only temporary relief. A friend of mine defined insanity as repeating the same actions over and over again while remaining convinced things will turn out differently. The human species is in danger of being committed. What we need is a fundamental change of heart and mind, to shift the gears of our consciousness, and escape the temporal gridlock which has formed in the collective psyche.

Why take responsibility for our actions when we know that God is separate from us, directing our destiny? Why treat the ecosystem with respect, when we know that the universe is a machine? Why help one another when we know that competition is the key to success? Why express our sexuality when we know that it is something to be ashamed of? For all their genius, Descartes, Newton, Darwin and Freud had only part of the equation. We need to move on.

Yet it is not in order to overthrow the existing governing belief systems, but to *reform* them, that the people in this book speak out. Their concern is the promotion of *evolution* rather than revolution. They have built upon the established foundations of knowledge but have each added a story of their own, connected by the spiral staircase of integrity, wisdom and compassion. The men and women in this book are not afraid of change. They have questioned the stone-carved rules, which have been handed down to us from the summits of orthodoxy and in choosing to climb the mountain for themselves they have come up an alternative set of revelations which begin, not with, "Thou Shalt," but with "Why Not?"

We are the protaganists and the authors of our own drama. It is up to us; there is no one left to blame. Neither the "system," nor our leaders, nor our parents. We can't go out and hang the first amoeba. Upon these pages are some alternative responses to those of despair and disillusionment in the face of our global crises. The purpose of this collection is not to convince you of any particular point of view, but to encourage a deeper exploration into the universe of your own mind, and the discovery of your own innate truths. Use what works, discard what doesn't and above all—enjoy the show!

Rebecca McClen Novick

Introduction

The term "paradigm shift" was coined by Thomas Kuhn in his book *The Structure of Scientific Revolutions* in 1961. It was an attempt to describe the changes that occur in the Belief Systems (BS for short) of scientists, concerning how they interpret their data, and how scientific models evolve. Paradigms are the glasses that one sees through which color how and what we see. When they shift, so does the world. Today it's almost a cliche to speak about new paradigm shifts occuring. Paradigms are shifting kaleidoscopically these days. This makes sense in light of the fact that—according to the latest reports from quantum physicists—we inhabit a universe that is composed of undulating vibrations, oscillating in continuously and infinitely varied rhythms and frequencies. The universe is filled with ambiguity and mystery. It is a shifting cascade of relativistic perspectives, where nothing is really quite solid, and we exist as mostly empty space and waves of possible probabilities. Our beliefs are the brain's attempt to freeze the flow of matter and energy into fixed states, so we can grasp onto something familiar and tangible in a shifting sea too grand for us to ever fully comprehend.

Paradigms originate from, and exist only within, the framework of the human mind, but they lead to technological progress and social transformation in the material world. In your hands is a collection of in-depth interviews with some of the extraordinary minds from whom these new world views, and ultimately new world and social structures, are emerging. Within these pages we meet with some of the most creative and controversial thinkers on the intellectual frontiers of art and science—the mavericks, those who have stepped outside the boundaries of consensus thought, sometimes risking their careers, always risking ridicule. These are experts from various fields who have seen beyond the normal and traditional view, who are concerned with the problems facing modern day society, and who have traveled beyond the edges of the established horizons to find their answers. In questioning old belief systems these remarkable individuals have gained revolutionary insights into the nature of consciousness, and with intelligence, clarity, and wit they offer some enlightening proposals for the potential future of humanity.

Inside these maverick minds we tiptoe along the fringes of reason, exploring the realms of morphic fields, chaos theory, virtual reality, quantum philosophy, the possibilities of time travel, extraterrestrials, nanotechnology, and out-of-body experiences. We discussed such general themes with them as technology, ecology, God, psychedelics, death, and the future evolution of consciousness. We learned a lot from doing these interviews, but most importantly we got a very strong sense of optimism and hope from these people. In a world infested with pessimism, fear, and doubt, these individuals offer fresh perspectives and possibilities. Taken together, common underlying holistic themes emerge in these interviews of new world views that are at once analytical and intuitive, compassionate and wise, practical and imaginative in their perspectives.

"Inspiration," Allen Ginsberg told us, "means to breath in." The original inspiration for this book partly grew out of our desire to meet with people whose writing had had a great impact on us. Wild late-night philosophical discussions that Rebecca McClen Novick and I had on the nature of reality and exploration of consciousness provided the alchemical ignition that got the fire burning. Why not, we thought in a grandiose moment of audacious innocent inspiration, seek out some of the most brilliant brains and illuminated luminaries around, and see what they have to say on the subject. We wanted to somehow tie them all together, into a larger, grander, more comprehensive view.

We figured that as a man/woman team we could interview these people from a more holistic perspective than any single person. It was very interesting that when Rebecca and I would collaborate on questions, we would usually brainstorm separately, then share ideas and mutually arrange the sequence of the questions later. Almost everytime we both thought that we had covered the spectrum of important points ourselves, and we were astonished to discover that we had relatively unique lists of questions with suprisingly very little overlap. This demonstrated to us the biases of our own perspectives, and could be suggestive of the inherent difference in how male and female brains differ in their thinking.

Our central source of fascination was the timeless mystery of consciousness. It is our very sense of self—the most mysterious and mundane aspect of existence, the most essential part of us—and yet we don't know what it is, where it comes from, or where it's going. It is all around us in many forms, and yet when we try to define it—that is, to draw a boundary around it and distinguish it from the rest of the universe—it suddenly becomes extremely elusive. Alan Watts told us that the paradox that we experience when trying to understand consciousness is like an eyeball trying to see itself (without a mirror), or teeth trying to bite themselves. We are our own blind spots.

How does consciousness arise? Can consciousness leave the body? Is it limited to human brains, or does it exist elsewhere in other forms? What is consciousness made of? What changes it? How and why? What happens to consciousness after physical death? What do quantum physics, chaos theory, sociobiology, neurophysiology, and morphic field resonance suggest to us about the nature and potentials of consciousness? Where are we when we're lucid dreaming? Do intelligent extraterrestrials exist? What is consciousness evolving into? How does the world change when consciousness changes? These are some of the questions we—with the help of some extremely gifted thinkers—try to take on in this ambitious book.

One thing for sure about consciousness is that—like matter and energy, time and space—it changes, flows, and there are varying degrees of it. Some people, neurobiologists for the most part, think consciousness is an emergent property of the brain, which evolved over a 4.5-billion-year evolutionary struggle to survive and reproduce. Others, dubbed mystical (or kooks) by the former, think consciousness creates the brain. Chicken or egg? Mind in body? Or body in mind? Some think consciousness is the brain. Behavioral psychologists, such as B.F. Skinner, have claimed that consciousness does not even exist, while others, Zen Buddhists for example, say that consciouness is all that exists.

Hundreds, perhaps thousands, of fascinating models for consciousness have sprung out of the human mind. Numerous esoteric mystical disciplines claim to have used techniques to alter and heighten consciousness since the beginning of written history. Lao-tzu reminded us that it all comes from and flows back into the great Tao. Buddha contributed one of the first maps of human psychology, and some of the most enduring methods for changing brain states. Aristotle believed that consciousness was not constrained by physical processes. Descartes divided the mind from the divine. Darwin gave us the evolutionary perspective, and the mechanism of natural selection.

Wundt tried to make the study of consciouness a science through disciplined introspective techniques. Pavlov taught us about the roles of excitation, inhibition, and associative learning in the nervous system. Konrad Lorenz revealed the biological secrets of neural imprinting. Freud pointed out that part of us is conscious, most of us is unconscious. Jung went further claiming that all of the human species share a common meta-cultural collective unconscious, full of genetic dreams, myths, and legendary archetypes. Does this imply the potential for a collective consciousness? Is the process of development and evolution one in which the unconscious is being made more conscious?

From William James we learned that consciousness is not a thing, but a process, and that there is a vast multitude of mostly uncharted, potential conscious states. Aleister Crowley integrated many of the esoteric mystical traditions of previous centuries with the scientific method, wedding them into a single system. Albert Hofmann discovered the explosive psychoactive effects of LSD in 1943, vastly multiplying the questions of spirit and matter. Neuroscientists, such as Roger Sperry and Michael Gazzaniga, are discovering that the brain is actually composed of many submodules, each like a miniature brain in itself, making each of us a multitude of potential personalities. Where these people leave off is where this book begins.

Charles Tart, a psychologist at UC Davis, has pointed out that the ways in which scientists theorize about the complex interplay between the brain and consciousness is highly flavored by the prevailing technology of a particular time in history. For instance, in the beginning of the century Freud built his model of consciousness in accordance with the technology that was popular in his day— the technology of the steam engine and the science of hydraulics. We can see this clearly in many of his concepts. There is reference to the idea of how drives build up pressure, which needs to be released, and how fluid-like energies such as the libido need to flow. The symbolic release of libidinal tension in a dream then, is seen as functioning like a safety valve for libidinal build-up—so the system doesn't explode—like the safety valve on the boiler of a steam engine. The safety valve is there so if the pressure reaches a certain threshold, it just bleeds steam off in a harmless hissing. When the biological drives of the id become too strong, then dreams bleed off that excess drive in the form of hallucinatory gratification.

Then when the telephone came along, with it came the switchboard operator models of consciousness. My first undergraduate psychology textbook had a full-page illustration of how the brain functions like a giant switchboard with telephone-like connections to all parts of the body. John Lilly was the first to apply the computer as a metaphor for understanding the brain in his book *Programming and Metaprogramming the Human Biocomputer*. When I was an undergraduate studying psychology, the computer metaphor was just beginning to be entertained on the fringes of academia. Our brains could be seen as the hardware, and our culturally conditioned BS, language, and other memes would be the software. Since then cognitive psychology and cognitive science have adopted the model of the computer as a metaphor for how the brain functions, and this has now become the standard and accepted model.

All of these models help to shed some light on how the mysteries of the brain and mind interact, but they are also quite limited, and can be dangerously misleading. The brain is not a hydraulic system, a telephone switchboard, or a computer. But, as models, these metaphors give us a partial grasp of something that is otherwise too complex to comprehend. When we interviewed John Lilly he told us that he thought a human brain can never fully understand itself, because a simulation that modeled and mapped the entire brain would take up all the space in the brain, filling it to capacity. It would take a larger brain to understand our brain, and then that brain couldn't fully understand itself.

The newest technology to act as a metaphor for the brain and consciousness is Virtual Reality technology. VR allows us to control the sensory input that channels into our nervous system and to determine what our experience of reality is. People like Timothy Leary, who prefers the term "Electronic Reality," and Charles Tart have begun to see VR technology as a metaphor for the brain. Computer-generated simulations in Virtual Reality become acceptable to the brain as reality. This leads to the understanding that all we ever really experience of reality are simulations created by our brain out of the influx of sensory signals that we receive from our senses. We already live in fabricated realities. We each live inside a reality-generating apparatus called the nervous system. Timothy Leary dubbed this understanding "neuro-electric awareness"—the understanding that we are creating reality out of the sensory signals that we perceive. Buddha called this understanding "enlightenment."

But to fully understand this concept we must actually experience it. We almost always forget that our perception of what we call the physical world is a simulation and not "reality itself." William Blake understood the concept that we create our own reality when he stated, "That which appears without, is within." When I had my first LSD trip at the age of 16, among other things I realized that the brain entirely creates what we experience as reality. I realized it by *experiencing* it. Everything that we think is the external world is actually a neurological simulation fabricated out of complex chains of sensory signals by the human brain. On that psychedelic experience it appeared to me as though all of reality was composed of points or monads, and that our perception of reality is like those connect-the-dots games that we play as children. The possible ways of connecting the dots are far more varied than I had thought, and can be done in countless different ways.

Carl Jung coined a term that helps to explain this called "Constellating Power," based on how we create constellations in the sky out of the massive tangle of stars. Once a pattern has organized itself in our mind's "I," it becomes hard then not to see it that way. Since the Virtual Reality created by the perceptual simulation process is one's "reality experience," it is difficult to not completely identify with the Virtual Reality as the "real" reality. Part of the motivation for putting this book together stemmed from our understanding that since we are responsible for creating reality—individually and jointly—what then are the most fabulous and interesting realities that we can experience?

Reality is defined as that which is real, and it is created through a blend of belief and experience. Several years ago, Virtual Reality pioneer Jaron Lanier told me that he thought that there were three levels at which one can change or create "reality": (1) at the neurological level of the brain through neurochemistry; (2) at the sensory level through Virtual Reality simulation; or (3) in the external world through the atomic reconstructional possibilities of nanotechnology. But we can also change our perception and interpretation of the world through intention and will. Intentionally changing one's attitude can dramatically shift one's perspective and social relationships. Dreams also open up a frontier for exploring the possibilities of reality fabrication. When we asked Stephen LaBerge, lucid dream researcher at Stanford University, about using VR as a metaphor for lucid dreaming, he said that lucid dreaming was like "high-resolution VR."

A basic premise that we had for this book was that—through cosmological time, biological evolution, personal development, and cultural transformations—consciousness evolves. From atoms to galaxies, amoebas to neurons, the evolution of consciousness seems an endless adventure. Terence McKenna told us that he thought the ultimate goal of human evolution was a "good party." One thing is for sure. It is on the expanding edge of the horizon, where reality intersects the imagination, that we will forever find our new beginnings.

David Jay Brown
Topanga, California

Kathleen Thormod Carr

Terence McKenna

"Drugs are part of the human experience, and we have got to create a more sophisticated way of dealing with them..."

Mushrooms, Elves and Magic
with Terence K. McKenna

Terence McKenna is one of the leading authorities on the ontological foundations of shamanism and the ethno-pharmacology of spiritual transformation. After graduating from UC Berkeley with a major in Ecology, Resource Conservation and Shamanism, he traveled through the Asian and New World Tropics and became specialized in the shamanism and ethno-medicine of the Amazon Basin. What he learned in these explorations is documented in The Invisible Landscape, *which he wrote with his brother Dennis.*

Born in 1946, Terence is the father of two children, a girl of eleven and a boy of fourteen. He is the founder of Botanical Dimensions—a tax-exempt, non-profit research botanical garden based in Hawaii. This project is devoted to collecting and propagating plants of ethno-pharmacological interest and preserving the shamanic lore which accompanies their use.

Living in California, Terence divides his time between writing and lecturing and he has developed a software program called Timewave Zero. *His hypnotic multi-syllabic drawl is captured on the audio-tape adventure series* True Hallucinations—*soon to be published in book form—which tells of his adventures in far-flung lands in various exotic states of consciousness. Terence is also the author of* Food of the Gods, *which is a unique study of the impact of psychotropic plants on human culture and evolution and* The Archaic Revival, *in which this interview appears. His latest book* Trialogues at the Edge of the West, *is a collection of "discursive chats" with mathematician Ralph Abraham and biologist Rupert Sheldrake.*

This was our first interview. It took place on November 30th, 1988 in the dramatic setting of Big Sur. Overlooking the Pacific Ocean we sat on the top floor of the Big House at the Esalen Institute, where Terence was giving a weekend seminar. He needed little provocation to enchant us with the pyrotechnic wordplay which is his trademark, spinning together the cognitive destinies of Gaia, machines, and language and offering a highly unorthodox description of our own evolution.

—RMN

DJB: It's a pleasure to be here with you again, Terence. We'd like to begin by asking you to tell us how you became interested in shamanism and the exploration of consciousness.

Terence: I discovered shamanism through an interest in Tibetan folk religion. Bon, the pre-Buddhist religion of Tibet is a kind of shamanism. In going from the particular to the general with that concern, I studied shamanism as a general phenomenon. It all started out as an art historical interest in the pre-Buddhist iconography of thankas.

DJB: This was how long ago?

Terence: This was in '67 when I was a sophomore in college. The interest in altered states of consciousness came simply from, I don't know whether I was a precocious kid or what, but I was very early into the New York literary scene, and even though I lived in a small town in Colorado, I subscribed to the *Village Voice*, and there I encountered propaganda about LSD, mescaline, and all these experiments that the late beatniks were involved in. Then I read *The Doors of Perception and Heaven and Hell*, and it just rolled from there. That was what really put me over. I respected Huxley as a novelist, and I was slowly reading everything he'd ever written, and when I got to *The Doors of Perception* I said to myself, "There's something going on here for sure."

DJB: To what do you attribute your increasing popularity, and what role do you see yourself playing in the social sphere?

Terence: Well, without being cynical, the main thing I attribute to my increasing popularity is better public relations. As far as what role I'll play, I don't know, I mean I assume that anyone who has anything constructive to say about our relationship to chemical substances, natural and synthetic, is going to have a social role to play, because this drug issue is just going to loom larger and larger on the social agenda until we get some resolution of it, and by resolution I don't mean suppression or just saying no. I anticipate a new open-mindedness born of desperation on the part of the Establishment. Drugs are part of

> *I anticipate a new open-mindedness born of desperation on the part of the Establishment.*

the human experience, and we have got to create a more sophisticated way of dealing with them than exhortations to abstinence, because that has failed.

RMN: You have said that the term "New Age" trivializes the significance of the next phase in human evolution and have referred instead to the emergence of an archaic revival. How do you differentiate between these two expressions?

Terence: The New Age is essentially humanistic psychology, eighties style, with the addition of neo-shamanism, channeling, crystal and herbal healing, and this sort of thing. The archaic revival is a much larger, more global phenomenon that assumes that we are recovering the social forms of the late neolithic. It reaches far back in the twentieth century to Freud, to surrealism, to abstract expressionism, even to a phenomenon like National Socialism which is a negative force. But the stress on ritual, on organized activity, on race/ancestor consciousness—these are themes that have been worked out throughout the entire twentieth century, and the archaic revival is an expression of that.

RMN: In the book you wrote with your brother Dennis, *The Invisible Landscape,* and in recent lectures and workshops, you've spoken of a new model of time and your efforts to model the evolution of novelty based on the ancient oriental system of divination, the *I-Ching.* Can you briefly explain how you developed this model, and how an individual can utilize this system to modulate their own perspective on the nature of time?

Terence: Ah, no. I think I'd rather send you a reprint of a recent paper in *Revision* than to try and cover that. It's not easily explained. If I were to give an extremely brief resume of it, I would say that the new view of time is that time is holographic, fractal, and moves toward a definitive conclusion, rather than the historical model of time which is open-ended, trendlessly fluctuating, and in practical terms endless. What's being proposed is a spiral model of history, that sees history as a process actually leading toward a conclusion. But the details of it are fairly complex.

DJB: According to your time-wave model, novelty reaches its peak expression and history appears to come to a close in the year 2012. Can you explain what you mean by this, and what the global or evolutionary implications are of what you refer to as the "end of time"?

Terence: What I mean is this. The theory describes time with what are called novelty waves, because waves have wavelengths, one must assign an end point to the novelty wave, so the end of time is nothing more than the point on the historical continuum that is assigned as the end point of the novelty wave. Novelty, is something which has been slowly maximized through the life of the universe, something which reaches infinite density, or infinite contraction at the point from which the wave is generated. Trying to imagine what time would be like near the temporal singularity is difficult because we are far from it, in another domain of physical law. There need to be more facts in play, before we will be able to correctly envisage the end of time, but what we can say concerning the singularity is this: it

> *Novelty is something which has been slowly maximized through the life of the universe.*

is the obviation of life in three-dimensional space, everything that is familiar comes to an end, everything that can be described in Euclidian space is superceded by modes of being which require a more complicated description which is currently unavailable.

DJB: From your writings I have gleaned that you subscribe to the notion that psilocybin mushrooms are a species of high intelligence, that they arrived on this planet as spores that migrated through outer space and are attempting to establish a symbiotic relationship with human beings. In a more holistic perspective, how do you see this notion fitting into the context of Francis Crick's theory of directed panspermia, the hypothesis that all life on this planet and it's directed evolution has been seeded, or perhaps fertilized, by spores designed by a higher intelligence?

Terence: As I understand the Crick theory of panspermia, it's a theory of how life spread through the universe. What I was suggesting, and I don't believe it as strongly as you imply, but I entertain it as a possibility, that intelligence—not life but intelligence—may have come here in this spore bearing life form. This is a more radical version of the panspermia theory of Crick and Ponampurama. In fact I think that theory will probally be vindicated. I think in a hundred years if people do biology they will think it quite silly that people once thought that spores could not be blown from one star system to another by cosmic radiation pressure. As far as the role of the psilocybin mushroom, or its relationship to us and to intelligence, this is something that we need to consider. It really isn't important that *I* claim that it's an extraterrestrial, what we need is a *body* of people claiming this, or a *body* of people denying it, because what we're talking about is the experience of the mushroom. Few people are in a position to judge its extraterrestrial potential because few people in the orthodox sciences have ever experienced the full spectrum of psychedelic effects that is unleashed. One cannot find out whether or not there's an extraterrestrial intelligence inside the mushroom unless one is willing to take the mushroom.

DJB: You have a unique theory about the role that psilocybin mushrooms play in the process of human evolution. Can you tell us about this?

Terence: Whether the mushrooms came from outer space or not, the presence of

...the presence of psilocybin in the diet of early humans created a number of changes in our evolutionary situation.

psychedelic substances in the diet of early human beings created a number of changes in our evolutionary situation. When a person takes small amounts of psilocybin their visual acuity improves. They can actually see slightly better, and this means that animals allowing psilocybin into their food chain would have increased hunting success, which means increased food supply, which means increased reproductive success, which is the name of the game in evolution. It is the organism that manages to propagate itself numerically that is successful. The presence of psilocybin in the diet of early pack-hunting primates caused the individuals that were ingesting the psilocybin to have increased visual acuity. At slightly higher doses of psilocybin there is sexual arousal and erection and everything that goes under the term arousal of the central nervous system. Again, a factor which would increase reproductive success is reinforced.

DJB: Isn't it true that psilocybin inhibits orgasm?

Terence: No. I've never heard that. Not at the doses I'm talking about. At a psychedelic dose it might, but at just slightly above the "you can feel it" dose, it acts as a stimulant. Sexual arousal means paying attention, it means jumpiness, it indicates a certain energy level in the organism. And then, of course, at still higher doses psilocybin triggers this activity in the language-forming capacity of the brain that manifests as song and vision. It is as though it is an enzyme which stimulates eyesight, sexual interest, and imagination. And the three of these going together produce language-using primates. Psilocybin may have synergized the emergence of higher forms of psychic organization out of primitive protohuman animals. It can be seen as a kind of evolutionary enzyme, or evolutionary catalyst.

DJB: During your shamanistic voyages how do you, or do you, differentiate between the literal and the metaphorical I/thou dialogue that appears to occur in certain states of consciousness? In other words how do you differentiate between the possibility that you are communicating with otherworldly independently existing entities and the possibility that you are communicating with isolated, unconscious neuron clusters in your own brain?

Terence: It's very hard to differentiate it. How can I make that same distinction right now? How do I know I'm talking to you? It's just provisionally assumed, at you are ordinary enough that I don't question that you're there. But if you had two heads, I *would* question whether you were there. I would investigate to see if you were really what you appear to be. It's very hard to tell what this I/thou relationship is about, because it's very difficult to define the "I" part of it, let alone the "thou" part of it. I haven't found a way to tell, to trick it as it were into showing whether it was an extraterrestrial or the back side of my own head.

DJB: But normally the way we can tell is we receive mutual verification from other people, and we get information from many senses. You can touch me. You can see me. You can hear me.

Terence: Well, this is simply a voice, you know, so it's the issue of the mysterious telephone call. If you're awakened in the middle of the night by a telephone call, and you pick up the phone, and someone says "Hello" it would not be your first inclination to ask "Is anybody there?" because they just said hello. That establishes that somebody is there, but you can't see them, maybe they're aren't there, maybe you've been called by a machine. I've been called by machines. You pick up the phone and it says, "Hello this is Sears, and we're calling to tell you that your order 16312 is ready for pick up," and you say, "Oh, thank you." "Don't mention it." No, so this issue of identifying the other with certainty is tricky, even in ordinary intercourse.

RMN: There is a lot of current interest in the ancient art of sound technology. In a recent article you said that in certain states of consciousness you're able to create a kind of visual resonance and manipulate a "topological manifold" using sound vibrations. Can you tell us more about this technique, it's ethnic origins, and potential applications?

Terence: Yes, it has to do with shamanism that is based on the use of DMT in plants. DMT is a near—or pseudo-neurotransmitter, that when ingested and allowed to come to rest in the synapses of the brain, allows one to see sound, so that one can use the voice to produce, not musical compositions, but pictorial and visual compositions. This, to my mind, indicates that we're on the cusp of some kind of evolutionary transition in the language-forming area, so that we are going to go from a language that is heard to a language that is *seen*, through a shift in interior processing. The language will still be made of sound, but it will be processed as the carrier of the visual impression. This is actually being done by shamans in the Amazon. The songs they sing sound as they do in order to look a certain way. They are not musical compositions as we're used to thinking of them. They are pictorial art that is caused by audio signals.

...we are going to go from a language that is heard to a language that is seen...

DJB: Terence, you're recognized by many as one of the great explorers of the twentieth century. You've trekked through the Amazonian jungles and soared through the uncharted regions of the brain, but perhaps your ultimate voyages lie in the future, when humanity has mastered space technology and time travel. What possibilities for travel in these two areas do you foresee, and how do you think these new technologies will affect the future evolution of the human species?

Terence: Some question. I suppose most people believe space travel is right around the corner. I certainly hope so. I think we should all learn Russian in anticipation of it, because apparently the U.S. government is incapable of sustaining a space program. The time travel question is more interesting. Possibly the world is experiencing a compression of technological novelty that is going to lead to developments that are very much like what we would imagine time travel to be. We may be closing in on the ability to transmit information forward into the future, and to create an informational domain of communication between various points in time. How this will be done is difficult to imagine, but things like fractal mathematics, superconductivity, and nanotechnology offer new and novel approaches to realization of these old dreams. We shouldn't assume time travel is impossible simply because it hasn't been done. There's plenty of latitude in the laws of quantum physics to allow for moving information through time in various ways. Apparently you can move information through time, as long as you don't move it through time faster than light.

DJB: Why is that?

Terence: I haven't the faintest idea. What am I Einstein?

DJB: What do you think the ultimate goal of human evolution is?

Terence: Oh, a good party.

DJB: Have you ever had any experiences with lucid dreaming—the process by which one can become aware and conscious within a dream that one is dreaming—and if so, how do they compare with your other shamanic experiences?

Terence: I really haven't had experiences with lucid dreaming. It's one of those things that I'm very interested in. I'm sort of skeptical of it. I hope it's true, because what a wonderful thing that would be.

DJB: You've never had one?

Terence: I've had lucid dreams, but I have no technique for repeating them on demand, the dream state is possibly anticipating this cultural frontier that we're moving toward. We're moving toward something very much like eternal dreaming, going into the imagination, and staying there, and that would be like a lucid dream that knew no end, but what a tight simple solution. One of the things that interests me about dreams is this: I have dreams in which I smoke DMT, and it works. To me that's extremely interesting because it seems to imply that one does not have to smoke DMT to have the experience. You only have to convince your brain that you have done this, and it then delivers this staggering altered state.

DJB: Wow!

Terence: How many people who have had DMT dream occasionally of smoking it and have it happen? Do people who have never had DMT ever have that kind of an experience in a dream? I bet not. I bet you have to have done it in life to have established the knowledge of its existence, and the image of how it's possible, then this thing can happen to you without any chemical intervention. It is more powerful than any yoga, so taking control of the dream state would certainly be an advantageous thing and carry us a great distance toward the kind of cultural transformation that we're talking about. How exactly to do it, I'm not sure. The psychedelics, the near death experience, the lucid dreaming, the meditational reveries... all of these things are pieces of a puzzle about how to create a new cultural dimension that we can all live in a little more sanely than we're living in these dimensions.

DJB: Do you have any thoughts on what happens to human consciousness after biological death?

Terence: I've thought about it. When I think about it I feel like I'm on my own. The logos doesn't want to help here, has nothing to say to me on the subject of biological death. What I imagine happens is that for the self time begins to flow backwards; even before death, the act of dying is the act of reliving an entire life, and at the end of the dying process, consciousness divides into the consciousness of ones parents and ones children, and then it moves through these modalities, and then divides again. It's moving forward into the future through the people who come after you, and backwards into the past through your ancestors. The further away from the moment of death it is, the faster it moves, so that after a period of time, the Tibetans say 42 days, one is reconnected to everything that ever lived, and the previous ego-pointed existence is defocused, and one is you know, returned to the ocean, the morphogenetic field, or the One of Plotinus, you choose your term. A person is a focused illusion of being, and death occurs when the illusion of being can be sustained no longer. Then everything flows out and away from this disequilibrium state that life is. It is a state of disequilibrium, and it is maintained for decades, but finally, like all disequilibrium states, it must yield to the Second Law of Thermodynamics, and at that point it runs down, its specific character disappears into the general character of the world around it. It has returned then to the void/plenum.

DJB: What if you don't have children?

Terence: Well, then you flow backward into the past, into your parents, and their parents, and their parents, and eventually all life, and back into the primal protozoa. No, it's a hard thing to face, but from the long-term point of view of nature, you have no relevance for the future whatsoever, unless you procreate. It's very interesting that in the celebration of the Eleusynian mysteries, when they took the sacrament, what the god said was, "Procreate, procreate." It is uncanny the way history is determined by who sleeps with whom, who gets born, what lines are drawn forward, what tendencies are accelerated. Most people experience what they call magic only in the dimension of mate-seeking, and this is where even the dullest people have astonishing coincidences, and unbelievable things go on —it's almost as though hidden strings were being pulled. There's an esoteric tradition that the genes, the matings, are where it's all being run from. It is how I think a super extraterrestrial would intervene. It wouldn't intervene at all, it would make us who it wanted us to be by controlling synchronicity and coincidence around mate choosing.

RMN: Rupert Sheldrake has recently refined the theory of the morphogenetic field—a non-material organizing collective memory field which affects all biological systems. This field can be envisioned as a hyper-spatial information reservoir which brims and spills over into a much larger region of influence when critical mass is reached—a point referred to as morphic resonance. Do you think this morphic resonance could be regarded as a possible explanation for the phenomena of spirits and other metaphysical entities, and can the method of evoking beings from the spirit world be simply a case of cracking the morphic code?

Terence: That sounds right. It's something like that. If what you're trying to get at is do I think morphogenetic fields are a good thing, or do they exist, yes I think some kind of theory like that is clearly becoming necessary, and that the next great step to be taken in the intellectual conquest of nature, if you will, is a theory about how, out of the class of possible things, some things actually happen.

RMN: Do you think it could be related to the phenomena of spirits?

Terence: Spirits are the presence of the past, specifically expressed. When you go to ruins like Angkor Wat, or Tikal, the presence is there. You have to be pretty dull to not see how it was, where the market stalls were, the people and their animals, and the trade goods. It's quite weird. We're only conventionally bound in the present by our linguistic assumptions, but if we can still our linguistic machinery, the mind spreads out into time, and behaves in very unconventional ways.

DJB: How do you view the increasing waves of designer psychedelics and brain enhancement machines in the context of Rupert Sheldrake's theory of morphogenetic fields?

Terence: Well, I'm hopeful, but somewhat suspicious. I think drugs should come from the natural world, and be use-tested by shamanically oriented cultures. Then they have a very deep morphogenetic field, because they've been used thousands and thousands of years in magical contexts. A drug produced in the laboratory and suddenly distributed worldwide simply amplifies the global noise present in the historical crisis. And then there's the very practical consideration that one cannot predict the longterm effects of a drug produced in a laboratory. Something like peyote, or morning glories, or mushrooms have been used for vast stretches of time without detrimental social consequences. We know that. As far as the technological question is concerned, brain machines and all, I wish them luck. I'm willing to test anything that somebody will send me, but I'm skeptical. I think it's somehow like the speech-operated typewriter. It will recede ahead of us. The problems will be found to have been far more complex than first supposed.

DJB: Don't you think it's true that the designer psychedelics and the brain machines don't have much of a morphic field yet, so in a sense one is carving a new morphic field with their use, so it's up for grabs, and there would consequently be more possibilities for new things to happen, unlike the psychoactive substances which you speak of that have ancient morphic fields, and are much more entrenched in predictability and pattern, and therefore not as free for new types of expression?

Terence: Possibly, although I don't know how you grab the morphic field of a new designer drug. For instance, I'll speak to my own experience, which is ketamine. My impression of ketamine was it's like a brand new skyscraper, all the walls, all the floors are carpeted in white, all the drinking fountains work, the elevators run smoothly, the fluorescent lights recede endlessly in all directions down the hallways. It's just that there's nobody there. There's no office machinery, there's no hurrying secretaries, there's no telephones, it's just this immense, empty structure waiting. Well, I can't move into a sixty-story office building, I have only enough stuff to fill a few small rooms, so it gives me a slightly spooked-out feeling to enter into these empty morphic fields. If you take mushrooms, you know, you're climbing on board a starship manned by every shaman who ever did it in front of you, and this is quite a crew, and they've really pulled some stunts over the millenia, and it's all there, the tapes to be played, but the designer things should be very cautiously dealt with.

DJB: It's interesting that John Lilly had very different experiences with ketamine. Do you think that there's any relationship between the self-transforming machine elves that you've encountered on your shamanic voyages and the solid state entities that John Lilly has contacted in his interdimensional travels?

Terence: I don't think there is much congruence. The solid state entities that he contacted seem to make him quite upset. The elf machine entities that I encounter are the embodiment of merriment and humor. I have had a thought about this recently which I will tell you. One of the science fiction fantasies that haunts the collective unconscious is expressed in the phrase "a world run by machines"; in the 1950s this was first articulated in the notion, "perhaps the future will be a terrible place where the world is run by machines." Well now, let's think about machines for a moment. They are extremely impartial, very predictable, not subject to moral suasion, value neutral, and very long lived in their functioning. Now let's think about what machines are made of, in the light of Sheldrake's morphogenetic field theory. Machines are made of metal, glass, gold, silicon, plastic; they are made of what the earth is made of. Now wouldn't it be strange if biology is a way for earth to alchemically transform itself into a self-reflecting thing.

> *...wouldn't it be strange if biology is a way for earth to alchemically transform itself into a self-reflecting thing.*

In which case then, what we're headed for inevitably, what we are in fact creating is a world run by machines. And once these machines are in place, they can be expected to manage our economies, languages, social aspirations, and so forth, in such a way that we stop killing each other, stop starving each other, stop destroying land, and so forth. Actually the fear of being ruled by machines is the male ego's fear of relinquishing control of the planet to the maternal matrix of Gaia.

DJB: It's interesting the way you anticipate each question. The recent development of fractal images seems to imply that visions and hallucinations can be broken down into a precise mathematical code. With this in mind, do you think the abilities of the human imagination can be replicated in a super computer?

Terence: Yes. Saying that the components of hallucinations can be broken down and duplicated by mathematical code isn't taking anything away from them. Reality can be taken apart and redublicated with this same mathematical code, that's what makes the fractal idea so powerful. One can type in half a page of code, and on the screen get river systems, mountain ranges, deserts, ferns, coral reefs, all being generated out of half a page of computer coding. This seems to imply that we are finally discovering really powerful mathmatical rules that stand behind visual appearances. And yes, I think supercomputers, computer graphics and simulated enviroments, this is very promising stuff. When the world's being run by machines, we'll be at the movies. Oh boy.

RMN: It seems that human language is evolving at a much slower rate than is the ability of human consciousness to navigate more complex and more profound levels of reality. How do you see language developing and evolving so as to become a more sensitive transceiving device for sharing conscious experience?

Terence: Actually, consciousness can't evolve any faster than language. The rate at which language evolves determines how fast consciousness evolves otherwise you're just lost in what Wittgenstein called the unspeakable. You can feel it, but you can't speak of it, so it's an entirely private reality. Have you noticed how we have very few words for emotions? I love you, I hate you, and then basically we run a dial between those. I love you a lot, I hate you a lot.

RMN: How do you feel? Fine.

Terence: Yes, how do you feel, fine, and yet we have thousands and thousands of words about rugs, and widgets, and this and that, so we need to create a much richer language of emotion. There are times—and this would be a great study for somebody to do—there have been periods in English when there were emotions which don't exist anymore, because the words have been lost. This is getting very close to this business of how reality is made by language. Can we recover a lost emotion, by creating a word for it? There are colors which don't exist any more because the words have been lost. I'm thinking of the word "jacinth." This is a certain kind of orange. Once you know the word "jacinth," you always can recognize it, but if you don't have it, all you can say is it's a little darker orange than something else. We've never tried to consciously evolve our language, we've just let it evolve, but now we have this level of awareness, and this level of cultural need where we really must plan where the new words should be generated. There are areas

> *Can we recover a lost emotion, by creating a word for it?*

where words should be gotten rid of that empower political wrong thinking. The propagandists for the fascists already understand this, they understand that if you make something unsayable, you've made it unthinkable. So it doesn't plague you anymore. So planned evolution of language is the way to speed it toward expressing the frontier of consciousness.

DJB: I've thought at times that what you view as a symbiosis forming between humans and psychoactive plants may in fact be the plants taking over control of our lives and commanding us to do their bidding. Have you any thoughts on this?

Terence: Well, symbiosis is not parasitism, symbiosis is a situation of mutual benefit to both parties, so we have to presume that the plants are getting as much out of this as we are. What we're getting is information from another spiritual level. Their point of view, in other words, is what they're giving us. What we're giving them is care, and feeding, and propagation, and survival, so they give us their elevated higher dimensional point of view. We in turn respond by making the way easier for them in the physical world. And this seems a reasonable trade-off. Obviously they have difficulty in the physical world, plants don't move around much. You talk about Tao, a plant has the Tao. It doesn't even chop wood and carry water.

> *...a plant has the Tao. It doesn't even chop wood and carry water.*

RMN: Future predictions are often based upon the study of previous patterns and trends which are then extended like the contours of a map to extrapolate the shape of things to come. The future can also be seen as an ongoing dynamic creative interaction between the past and the present—the current interpertation of past events actively serves to formulate these future patterns and trends. Have you been able to reconcile these two perspectives so that humanity is able to learn from its experiences without being bound by the habits of history?

Terence: The two are antithetical. You must not be bound by the habits of history if you want to learn from your experience. It was Ludwig von Bertallanfy, the inventor of general systems theory, who made the famous statement that "people are not machines, but in all situations where they are given the opportunity, they will act like machines," so you have to keep disturbing them, 'cause they always settle down into a routine. So, historical patterns are largely cyclical, but not entirely; there is ultimately a highest level of the pattern which does not repeat, and that's the part which is responsible for the advance into true novelty.

RMN: The part that doesn't repeat. Hmm. The positive futurists tend to fall into two groups. Some visualize the future as becoming progressively brighter every day and that global illumination will occur as a result of this progression; others envision a period of actual devolution, a dark age, through which human consciousness must pass before more advanced stages are reached. Which scenario do you see as being the most likely to emerge, and why do you hold this view?

Terence: I guess I'm a soft Dark Ager. I think there will be a mild dark age, I don't think it will be anything like the dark ages which lasted a thousand years, I think it will last more like five years, and will be a time of economic retraction, religious fundamentalism, retreat into closed communities by certain segments of the society, feudal warfare among minor states, and this sort of thing. But I think it will give way in the late Nineties to the actual global future that we're all yearning for, and then there will be basically a fifteen-year period where all these things are drawn together with progressively greater and greater sophistication, much in the way that modern science and philosophy have grown with greater and greater sophistication in a single direction since the Renaissance, and that sometime around the end of 2012 all of this will be boiled down into a kind of alchemical distillation of the historical experience that will be a doorway into the life of the imagination.

RMN: Rupert Sheldrake's morphic resonance, Ralph Abraham's chaos theory, and your time wave model all appear to contain complimentary patterns which operate on similar underlying principles—that energy systems store information until a certain level is reached and the information is then transduced into a larger frame of reference, like water in a tiered fountain. Have you worked these theories into an all encompasing metatheory of how the universe functions and operates?

Terence: Well, it is true that the three of us and I would add Frank Barr in there, who is less well known, but has a piece of the puzzle as well—we're all complimentary. Rupert's theory is, at this point a hypothesis. There are no equations, there's no predictive machinery, it's a way of speaking about experimental approaches. My time wave thing is like an extremely formal and specific example of what he's talking about in a general way. And then what Ralph's doing is providing a bridge from the kind of things Rupert and I are doing back into the frontier branch of ordinary mathematics called dynamic modeling. And Frank is an expert in the repetition of fractal process. He can show you the same thing happening on many, many levels, in many, many different expressions. So I have named us Compressionists, or Psychedelic Compressionists. A Compressionism holds that the world is growing more and more complex, compressed, knitted together, and therefore holographically complete at every point, and that's basically where the four of us stand, I think, but from different points of view.

DJB: Can you tell us about Botanical Dimensions, and any current projects that you're working on?

Terence: Botanical Dimensions is a non-profit foundation that attempts to rescue plants with a history of shamanic and human usage in the warm tropics, and rescue the information about how they're used, store the information in computers, and move the plants to a nineteen-acre site on the big island of Hawaii, in a rainforest belt that reasonably replicates the Amazon situation. There we are keeping them toward the day when someone will want to do serious research on them. As a non-profit foundation we solicit donations, publish a newsletter, and support a number of collectors in the field to carry on this work, which nobody else is really doing. There's a lot of rainforest conservation going on, but very little effort to conserve the folk-knowledge of native peoples. Amazonian people are going off to sawmills and repairingvb outboard motors, and this whole body of knowledge about plants is going to be lost in the next generation. We're saving it, and saving the plants in a botanical garden in Hawaii.

Riane Eisler & David Loye

"We see a world where the most highly valued work
will have the consciousness of caring."

Raising the Chalice
with Riane Eisler & David Loye

Riane Eisler has been described as a modern renaissance woman due to her far-reaching insights as a cultural historian. She is the author of The Chalice and the Blade, *which the eminant anthropologist, Ashley Montagu has hailed as "the most important book since Darwin's* Origin of Species." *Her latest work,* The Partnership Way—*written with her husband David Loye—is a handbook for applying the partnership model for which she has become renowned.*

Riane was born in Vienna, Austria, and at the age of six she found herself a refugee of Nazi Europe. She sailed to Cuba, on the last ship before the ill-fated St. Louis was refused sanctuary by the United States and she emigrated to North America when she was fourteen. Her early experiences with the dark side of human culture led her to pursue studies in sociology and anthropology and she went on to obtain a J.D. from the UCLA School of Law.

She has taught at the University of California and the Immaculate Heart College in Los Angeles, and she is a member of the General Evolution Research Group. She has pioneered legislation to protect the human rights of women and children and founded such organizations as the Los Angeles Women's Center Legal Program and the Center for Partnership Studies.

Riane's articles have appeared in many publications and journals. She has frequently appeared on television and addressed corporations such as DuPont and Disney. She has also spoken at universities such as UCLA and Harvard and keynoted many conferences worldwide.

Riane is an eloquent and dynamic speaker. Her ability to interweave a vast expanse of information allowed for a fascinating and highly revelatory discussion on the politics of anthropology, the roots of civilization, the lost aspects of religion and the cease-fire recipe to humanity's "war of the sexes."

David Loye is a social psychologist and systems theorist. He is the author of numerous books on the use of the brain and mind in prediction, political leadership and race relations. His psychohistory, The Healing of a Nation, *was called "a work of uncommon humanity and vision" by* Psychology Today *and received the Anisfield-Wolfe Award for the best scholarly book on race relations in 1971. His other works include* The Leadership Passion, The Sphinx and the

Rainbow *and* The Knowable Future, *which has been recognized as a pioneering work of unusual stature in the field of future studies.*

David is a former member of the psychology faculty of Princeton University and for almost ten years he was the Director of Research for the Program on Psychosocial Adaption and the Future at the UCLA School of Medicine. He is also a founding member of the General Evolution Research Group, a multidisciplinary think tank composed of scholars from various parts of the world. A member of the Editorial Board and Book Review Editor of The Journal of General Evolution, *David's articles have appeared in numerous publications. He is also a major contributor to the first multi-volume* World Encyclopedia of Peace.

During recent years, David's main research project has been the scientific study of moral sensitivity and he is completing two books on the subject. This has involved a re-evaluation of the work of many philosophers and psychologists in light of new discoveries in brain research, human prehistory, and the systems dynamics of cultural evolution. He is currently Co-Director of the Center for Partnership Studies in Pacific Grove, California.

We met with David and his wife, Riane on the Winter Solstice of 1988 at their beautiful home in Carmel, California. David offered us intriguing insights into the nature of morality and its relation to sexual distortion and denial. Pooling together his multi-disciplinary perspectives he spoke with passionate clarity on the subjects of cultural politics and the respective roles which the left and right sides of our brains have played in social evolution.

—RMN

DJB: Riane tell us, what was it that originally inspired you to write *The Chalice and the Blade*, a book described by Ashley Montagu as "the most important book since Darwin's *Origin of Species*," and what motivated you to complete the work?

RIANE: I think that what people choose to study is related to their life experiences. I was a refugee from Nazi Europe, and at a very early age I had to ask myself some very basic questions, the questions that I tried to answer in *The Chalice and The Blade*. And they certainly weren't just academic questions for me.

Because of my own life experiences, I was haunted by questions such as: Do we have to hunt and persecute each other? Do we have to live in ways that stunt our ability and willingness to be helpful and caring towards other people? Does there have to be war? And do we have to have the "war of the sexes"? One of the things my work shows is that there is an integral relationship, in systems terms, between war and the war of the sexes.

RMN: Just so that everyone is familiar with your cultural transformation theory, can you define the differences between what you have termed a partnership and dominator, or gylanic and androcratic society?

RIANE: I think the best way to answer this question is to begin with how I developed cultural transformation theory. About ten years ago I embarked on an intensive study, drawing from many fields, to re-examine our past, our present, and the possibilities for our future.

Most studies concerned with our global crises focus on modern times, on what's happening now, or on what happened in the last few hundred years. My database was much larger. As you know, it included the whole of our history, including our prehistory. And it also included the whole of humanity; in other words, both its female and male halves.

Perhaps fifty years from now, people will say, you mean that's not how it was always done? Because it's ludicrous, when you come right down to it, to just take one half of a species into account. Yet most books on history or sociology or anthropology, if there are six or seven mentions in the index about women, that's already terrific, right? It's a progressive book.

> *...it's ludicrous, when you come right down to it, to just take one half of a species into account.*

We all know that if we just look at part of a picture, we don't see the whole picture. What I started to see is what one can see if one uses a holistic or systems approach: recurring relationships or patterns that were not visible before. These patterns or configurations compose what I then called the dominator or androcratic and the partnership or gylanic models of society.

Each has a clear configuration. But we didn't see that configuration because we weren't looking at a very key component in it, which is the status of women and of so-called feminine values, such as caring, nonviolence, and compassion. In other words, at the relationship between the female and male halves of humanity, and with this, between stereotypes of "masculinity" and "femininity."

A lot of lip service is given to bemoaning that we don't have a social guidance system governed by these so-called "feminine" values that we now need for our survival. Only the talk about it is abstract.

If you look at the configurations of these two models, you see something very interesting, which is that the dominator system requires that values like caring and nonviolence and compassion (stereotypically associated with women) *not* be governant. You see that at the core of that system is the domination of men over women, of one half of humanity by the other. And that this domination is ultimately backed up by force or the threat of force.

Beginning with the ranking of one half of humanity over the other, the dominator system is also characterized by a generally hierarchic or authoritarian social structure and a high degree of institutionalized violence. Not only rape (a form of male terrorism against women), wife battering, incest, and other structural forms of violence designed to maintain men's domination over women; but also institutionalized violence designed to impose and/or maintain the domination of man over man, tribe over tribe, and nation over nation. That's of course what warfare is about.

RMN: Can you give us some examples of each model?

RIANE: If we look at human society using the templates of the partnership and dominator models, we begin to see that in all the seeming randomness around us there are actually patterns. Take for example, three very different societies: the Masai of Africa, Nazi Germany, and Khomeini's Iran —a tribal society, a highly technologically developed Western society, and a Middle Eastern theocracy.

Underneath all the surface differences, all three are rigidly male dominant societies. Moreover, they are all highly warlike. The Masai were the scourge of Africa —the most warlike of African societies. The violence of Hitler's Germany and Khomeini's Iran is well-known. But the institutionalized violence is not only in warfare, but many other areas—wife beating, genital mutilation of women among the Masai, the brutality directed against women not only in Iran but many other fundamentalist Muslim regimes. And in all three there was strong-man rule, be it in the family or in the state. And it was absolute, authoritarian rule. So in Iran the Mullahs will tell you that they have the only direct telephone line to God, and you had better listen to them—or else.

This dominator configuration of rigid male dominance, a high degree of institutionalized violence, and strong-man or authoritarian rule in both the family

> *...war is holy in the dominator model.*

and state is discernible in very different societies and groups. In the United States, you see the same kind of configuration in the rightist-fundamentalist alliance. "Get women back into their 'traditional' (a code word for subservient) place." And a lot of emphasis on "holy wars" and on strict obedience to "divinely ordained" commands.

But it isn't only that war is holy in the religious sense in the dominator model. The Nazis thought war was holy—because war is holy in the dominator model. That's why I chose the title *The Chalice and The Blade*—the blade becomes the highest power.

RMN: And the partnership model?

RIANE: As you move towards the partnership or gylanic model, you see the opposite configuration. You see power equated more with the chalice—with the power to give, rather than take, life. You also see a more equal partnership between the female and male halves of humanity. And you see a more democratic, more equitable system and a far lower degree of institutionalized violence. It isn't that there's no violence. But there's a very big difference, which is that in the partnership or gylanic model, male identity is not equated with domination and conquest—be it of women, other men, other nations, or nature. And violence and abuse are not institutionalized in parent-child relations and in other human relations.

One of the characteristics of the partnership model, as evidenced by prehistoric societies that we are now rediscovering, is that they had what we today would call an ecological consciousness—a real reverence for nature, which they venerated in the form of a Great Goddess. So the contemporary ecology movement is a very important partnership or gylanic trend with its growing understanding that we need to respect, rather than conquer, Mother Nature.

There are all over the world today many partnership trends. If you look at the Scandinavian nations, you find the strongest movement toward an integrated partnership configuration beginning to come together. In the first place, there is a more equal partnership between women and men. For example, in the Norwegian government, women constitute approximately forty percent of Parliament. (Compare this to the less than six percent in the United States Congress or none in rigid dominator regimes like Saudi Arabia.) Moreover, this goes along with a more equitable and democratic distribution of wealth—one that did not devolve into the Soviet Union's dominator form of socialism. There is also the fact that the Scandinavians boast the first peace academies and some of the groundbreaking work in human rights. And Scandinavian countries evidence more "feminine" values in their social governance—with a consequent emphasis not so much on technologies of destruction (weaponry) but on health, education, and welfare, as well as the environment (in other words on "women's" work such as caring and cleaning).

When you think about it, we're what's known as a dimorphic species, a species composed of two halves. It should therefore come as no surprise to anybody that the way that a society structures this fundamental relationship makes a tremendous difference.

DAVID L: An interesting thing to me is that when you confront a lot of social scientists with this idea that everything boils down to two models— they may not say this openly— but what's going on in the back of their heads, is that's just too simplistic. They tend to discount the idea on that ground. But I've looked at a broad range of phenomena in light of Riane's fundamental insight, and it *is* that simple. The term, incidently, partnership, is actually one I came up with. Riane was using the terms "androcratic" and "gylanic." It was pointed out by a friend of ours, the futurist writer Bob Jungk, that somewhat more accessible terms were needed for broad appeal.

DJB: Does your dominator-partnership model of human evolution require a revision in Darwin's theory of natural selection, which assumes that competitive and selfish reproductive success is the driving force in evolution, or do you think, perhaps, that symbiosis and cooperation could be viewed as a, or the, driving force in evolution?

RIANE: My book is very different in its basic assumptions and findings from Darwin's, and particularly from how Darwin has been popularly interpreted. It isn't like if species A survives, species B has to die. That's not how evolution works.

As a matter of fact, most of the world's ecosystem demonstrates a far more synergistic and symbiotic relationship between many species. And of course the great danger with that totally competitive dog-eat-dog approach, which is the dominator system approach, is that it is now, at our level of technology, not only threatening our species with extinction, but it's threatening all species.

> *It isn't like if species A survives, species B has to die. That's not how evolution works.*

Although I have to clarify here that there is also competition in the partnership system, just as there's also cooperation in the dominator system. But it's a different kind of competition and cooperation. For example, in the dominator model men cooperate to go to war, to better dominate or destroy. So the answer is not just cooperation. The issue is cooperation in the context of a partnership or dominator society. That extreme conquest-oriented dominator competition is truly not adaptive.

I am not a biologist, so I can only tell you that my work is more in line with new interpretations by biologists and evolutionary scholars, that the Darwinian model at best deals with only part of the picture. The biologist Humberto Maturana in Chile, for example, is very much involved in that kind of work.

DAVID L: Ashley Montagu characterizes the difference by saying that it isn't survival of the fittest, it's the survival of the fit. This has the implication that it isn't this dog-eat-dog battle for only one survivor out of many. It's the survival of the fit, and you can define the fit in many different ways, including the way that Riane is defining it.

RIANE: But I want to make a distinction here. Cultural transformation theory deals with cultural evolution. Also, we tend to think of evolution as a linear upward movement. But not even biological evolution is like that. And certainly not cultural evolution or technological evolution.

For example, if you look at technology, Minoan Crete (which was one of the last known prehistoric societies orienting largely to the partnership model) had very advanced technology, including indoor plumbing. This got lost until the Romans. Then it got lost again until very recent times. There may be a striving in our species towards ever higher cultural and technological development, but that striving will have to contend with the fact that there are other movements going on.

What cultural transformation theory posits, in a nutshell, is that the original thrust of our cultural evolution, the first civilizations, developed in areas where the earth was hospitable, fertile. As we began to develop agriculture, in the mainstream of our cultural evolution, we moved in a partnership direction.

But the evidence indicates that there was in our prehistory a period of tremendous system disequilibrium, when there was a fundamental shift in direction. We are now learning from non-linear and chaos theory that from the fringes of a system you can have a peripheral invader that comes in and changes the whole structure very quickly—what seems to be a small perturbation, in terms of Prigogine's language. These small perturbations become nucleations for a new system.

The same process seems to have occurred in our cultural evolution. There were peripheral invaders that during our prehistory came in from the barren steppes of the north and the arid deserts of the south—and we saw a shift toward the dominator model of society. And for five thousand years we've been on this course.

I think of it sometimes as a dominator detour. But the dominator model clearly is a choice for us as a species.

Now, as we approach the twenty-first century, we are in another period of tremendous systems disequilibrium. Nothing less than our survival as a species is now animating a very powerful partnership thrust.

> *Nothing less than our survival as a species is now animating a very powerful partnership thrust.*

Again it's from the fringes, from the periphery of the system, that so-called leading-edge thinkers, theorists, and researchers, the leaders in the so-called new consciousness, are emerging. But the dominator system is still very entrenched.

However, we wouldn't be talking here right now if there weren't already a lot of changed consciousness. We have an opportunity now, in this period of great system disequilibrium, for another shift. We're already on the road towards a partnership society. But the question is: can we complete that shift in time? One of my findings is that at a certain level of technological development the dominator system literally goes into self-destruct. The blade is the nuclear bomb. Even nature is rebelling against man's conquest of nature in acid rain, in air and water pollution. The message is clear: it is as if nature were saying to us, you either reconnect with your ancient partnership roots, or I'll find myself another species, perhaps another planet. Because we're doing so much intrinsic damage.

> *... it is as if nature were saying to us, you either reconnect with your ancient partnership roots, or I'll find myself another species...*

RMN: There's an ideology in current circulation that humanity is evolving toward a mutual expression of agape or fraternal, unconditional love, from eros, the kind of love associated with desire and sexuality, and that we are presently experiencing a transitional stage. What are your thoughts on this?

RIANE: Love has been one of the most abused and co-opted terms in dominator culture. It's interesting you use the word fraternal, as we are used to being so very male-centered. You know, fraternal is brotherhood. I think that even our language has conspired against us, because it's been a language that, to a very large extent, came out of a dominator or androcratic system. So I always make the point that what we're talking about is really sisterly *and* brotherly love.

RMN: I was thinking more in terms of like fraternal twins.

RIANE: It's very difficult. David and I deal with that in *The Partnership Way*, the new book we've written together in response to the many people who asked for tools to help accelerate the shift from a dominator to a partnership world. It's very hard, because we're all so used to dominator language. But part of our new consciousness for the twenty-first century is to free ourselves from the traps of that dominator language, so we don't, for example, continue to say "mankind" or "he," rather than "she or he." To get away from always the male in front, I have started to put "she" in front, rather than "he or she." Until we develop a gender inclusive pronoun.

DAVID L: Yes, that's a good example of what's going on in people's minds when they're captives of a dominator system. In other words, you have this false dichotomy between eros and agape. You have this idea that sex, eros, lust—all that is bad. And there is this more lofty, more saintly, more spiritual alternative, which is tied up with brotherhood and the love of humanity. This false dichotomy opens the way for pornography and many other bad things that keep us trapped. The hope for the twenty-first century is not to have a dichotomy between the two, but rather a good working relationship. In other words, an enjoyment of the fact that we have a body that has sexual identity, sexual capacities, a body and spirit that can relate to other people, either sexually, or in other forms of love, other forms of linking.

RMN: Right...well you've already anticipated the next question.

RIANE: I'd like to stay with that question a minute. When I was talking about the word fraternal, I was also going to make the point that when we think of brotherly love, fraternal love, which is the way agape has been conventionally defined, we say that's good. But that's love between men. That's the semantic implication of it. It implies that erotic love, the kind of love that is characteristic of the relationship between women and men, is inferior.

In line with what David is saying, I agree that that is a false dichotomy. If we go back and look at earlier partnership-oriented societies, we see that they do not make that spurious distinction that we have been taught to make between the spiritual and the natural, between spirit and nature.

In their iconography, nature is sacred. Now that's one of the biggest lessons for us, in terms of ecological consciousness. Because if we don't understand that the earth, the sky, the world, is sacred, that there is something askew about this myth of man and spirituality being above woman and nature, we're just going to keep destroying our planet. This is part of the dominator problem. I also believe that agape can in fact be a very important component in sexual love, in the sense of our bondedness, of our connectedness. So it isn't like here's one category, and there's another category.

I think some of the trends we're seeing today, where women and men are becoming loving friends to each other, as well as sexual partners, these are very important partnership trends. It used to be that, if you're a man, you have a wife who takes care of your household, you have a mistress with whom you have sex, and you have friends who are men. That whole schizophrenic thing is changing, so that there's truly friendship between women and men more as the norm. I see that as part of the movement toward integration, toward wholeness, towards healing and partnership.

RMN: Religion and sexuality have often been united in many pagan cultures— the Celts, Babylonians, the art of Tantra all combined religious and sexual ecstasy. Since then religions like Islam, Christianity, and Judaism have all attempted to separate the two—with often disastrous pathological effects. How do you see religion and sexuality co-evolving in the future?

RIANE: I believe that some of the things that you see in Tantra are rooted in this more partnership-oriented early spirituality, but they got very distorted. What I'm saying is that, again, I don't see a fundamental split between Eastern and Western. I see that most world religions today represent degrees of dominator overlay, covering and often distorting a partnership core. Of course, in the fundamentalist Christian and Moslem sects, it's horrendous. Whatever partnership core of spirituality was left is practically non-existent, because it's so encrusted, so crudded up by this dominator overlay.

Like the attitude that sex and woman are inherently evil and dangerous. That is a complete reversal of the earlier belief system, where woman and sexuality were central. What was celebrated in the earlier more partnership-oriented religion was the power to give life, to sustain life, to enhance life, to give pleasure, rather than pain. It was recognized that we all die, and the so-called "chtonic" or underground aspect of the Goddess was therefore also recognized, as these people believed that all of life came from the womb of the Goddess (the Earth), to then at death (like the cycles of vegetation) again return to her womb to be reborn. For example, in the Paleolithic, people worshipped in caves, which were symbols of the return to the womb, and there were I am sure important rites relating to this great mystery of birth, sex, death, and, in terms of their belief system, rebirth.

I should add that these people understood that it takes both the female and the male to give life—in other words that they understood and appreciated the role of sex as part of the life force. For example, in Catal Huyuk (the largest early agrarian or Neolithic site discovered to date) there is a sculpture of a woman and a man embracing, and right next to them, a woman with a child—the product of their union.

I mention this, because there are still people who believe that the moment that men discovered they also had life-giving powers, they were such brutes that they immediately enslaved women, and that this is how the shift to male dominant societies happened. (Of course that is really a dominator assumption about human nature, particularly male nature, that we are inherently evil.)

In relation to your question about religion and sexuality co-evolving in the future, I think that it is not coincidental that there is today so much interest in mystical religions. Because the way I look at mystical traditions is partly as remnants of the earlier more partnership-oriented religion, where sex and women were revered. But then a very sad thing happened. The original intent probably was forgotten, and, as in Tantric yoga (where female sexuality is still seen as the source of mystical illumination), these mystical religions also became very male centered—and thus distorted.

Now our job in developing a truly new consciousness, a new spirituality for the twenty-first century, is to clarify that, to understand that even the mystical traditions are out of balance, to restore that balance and get back to the hidden partnership core. And we now have the archeological data to help us do this, and that's tremendously exciting.

> *...it is a mistake to say, "The Eastern is terrific, and the Western is bad."*

I think that it is a mistake to say, "The Eastern is terrific, and the Western is bad." If we are going to have a partnership consciousness in the twenty-first century, we have to unravel and reweave just about everything.

DAVID L: A new book I'm working on deals with a crucial aspect of this consciousness, moral sensitivity. I believe it sheds light on this basic question about the separation of religion and sex, spirit and nature. I'm taking a new look at the founders of the scientific study of moral sensitivity—Immanuel Kant, Marx, Engels, Emile Durkheim, Sigmund Freud, Jean Piaget, moving into current times, including the key work of Carol Gilligan, Marija Gimbutas, and Riane bearing on moral sensitivity.

Out of this is emerging a new theory of moral sensitivity as an organic process. In other words, moral sensitivity has mainly been seen in terms of socialization, or conditioning—something imposed upon this lower organism. We are seen as animals who have to be stuffed with this moral sensitivity which comes from some higher mysticism. What I'm showing is that moral sensitivity arises out of the organism, developing through evolution. What I'm convinced will be part of the consciousness of the twenty-first century is this understanding that morality, that moral sensitivity, is not an "add-on." It develops out of nature. It also has sexual roots. Freud actually had this insight, but typically, as a captive of the dominator system, he and his insight were completely screwed up and distorted—the whole Oedipus complex thing, the primal hoard, killing of the father, and so on.

> *...moral sensitivity arises out of the organism...*

RIANE: I think that if we talk about sexuality, the Oedipus complex, we see that Freud very accurately described the dominator psyche—or rather, the male dominator psyche. Unfortunately he went around saying it's the human psyche, and people believed him.

> *...Freud very accurately described the dominator psyche...unfortunately he went around saying it's the human psyche...*

Now we're moving away from that. Maslow and a lot of feminist psychologists emphasize human growth needs, not so much what Maslow called defense needs. And believe me, in a dominator system defense needs are central. It's constructed so that there is constant war, even between the female and male halves of the human species. If you can't even trust the person you have the most intimate relationship with, how in the world are you ever going to have a harmonious relationship with people of a different color, or of a different belief system?

Sexuality has been distorted, beginning with this idea that woman is an object. Unfortunately, we see that in both Eastern and Western cultures. I can't stress this point enough in terms of twenty-first century spirituality, and it's hard for some people who have been very attracted by some of the Eastern disciplines, precisely because some of that old partnership core is, like a thread, still a little bit more visible. But look at Buddhism. Look at Hinduism. Look at how dominator-oriented those systems really are. Not all of the sects, of course, but, for example, this whole idea of the Zen master who beats his disciples to "enlighten" them—it really is a dominator approach. Not that there haven't been survivals of ancient partnership-oriented wisdoms in Eastern traditions. But superimposed on them are dominator religious teachings.

In Hinduism you have the caste system, and its justification of brutality by claiming that it's your karma to be of the lower despised caste and to suffer at the hands of the higher castes. If it's your karma, why change society? It's just a way of maintaining a dominator system. Like the Judeo-Christian idea that an inscrutable male God has decreed that we suffer in punishment for disobeying his orders and that all that matters is salvation in a far away heaven, rather than what happens here on earth. If you can't change misery, oppression, and exploitation because it's divinely ordained, why bother? That's how these religions have been used against us.

Getting back to sexuality, I think one of the great tasks for the twenty-first century is precisely the reclamation of our uniquely human sexuality, which is not only reproduction-oriented, it is also pleasure-oriented, ecstatically oriented, as in what we today call the pleasure bond.

It's very interesting that when you talk to women, they're often still hanging on to this earlier view of sexuality. It isn't this idea of conquest or scoring, as in the dominator male model of sex. It's the intimacy, the bonding, the sense of connectedness that they want. The ancients recognized that this intimacy, and this pleasure, were divine gifts, the gifts of the Goddess. To them sexuality was sacred.

Contrast that with the dominator view that equates sex with men's domination and humiliation and possession—and often brutalization and even killing—of women, with the dehumanized images of women and of women's bodies in pornography and advertising. Small wonder there is so much male violence against women! And this of course is *not* unrelated to the dominator religious teachings that women (and sex) are evil, that really "good" or saintly men do not have intimate sexual contact with women and the dominator ideal that "real" men only do so when they're clearly dominant, and thus won't be tainted by the inferior "feminine."

RMN: Do you feel that polytheism is more generally associated with the feminine principle, and monotheism with the masculine principle? How do you think this applies to the dominator/partnership model?

RIANE: I don't think that polytheism is necessarily more associated with the feminine principle. But let me try to untangle something about the feminine and the masculine principle first, may I? In my work I stress that the way we define masculinity and femininity is to a very large extent an artificial construct that has arisen primarily out of a dominator society.

We are just beginning to understand, for example, that this idea that the yin, the feminine, is passive and pallid is nonsense. One of the themes in earlier religion was the fire, the shamanistic fire of the priestesses, and the active creative sexuality of the Goddess. In fact some of the Hindu Tantric tradition has that in it still.

The idea that there is no contemplative element in the masculine, no caring element; that to be masculine is to be assertive, aggressive, and conquering is also a distortion.

So talking of the feminine and masculine principle is useful at this point because people make certain associations of clusters of human qualities with them. But I'm hoping that—as a new consciousness for the twenty-first century really develops—we will find other names for these qualities that are essentially gender-neutral qualities, like being active or passive, or being caring and non-violent or aggressive and violent.

> *Monotheism, as we have known it, has been basically, "My God's better than your God, and if you don't believe me I'll kill you."*

Monotheism, as we have known it, has been basically, "My God's better than your God, and if you don't believe me I'll kill you." That is very much associated with the dominator system. But I think it's a mistake to describe the earlier religion as a polytheistic religion, because it was more of what I would call—Campbell used the term—

synchronistic. I deal with this in *The Chalice and the Blade* in the chapter on the Legacy of the Goddess. Everybody had a different Goddess, and she had many manifestations, many aspects of the divine. She could be the Creatrix, the grandmother or crone. She could be the Mother Goddess. Or she could be the maiden. But there was also an underlying commonality.

Perhaps in Catal Huyuk the Goddess had her own name. In the Balkans, where UCLA archaeologist Marija Gimbutas has done her excavations, they also worshipped the Goddess and she had many of the same attributes, although they may have called her by different names. So I think that the whole distinction between polytheism and monotheism is again a construct of the dominator system. Because what we really have here is a basic recognition of certain universals, but also a recognition of, and respect for, diversity.

DAVID L: In terms of a twenty-first century consciousness, what I increasingly see is a recognition once again of the false dichotomy of this idea of monotheism versus polytheism. Generation after generation, we've been sold this idea that monotheism represented the great advance in religion. There were all those pagans worshipping all those gods and goddesses, and we were told how bad that was. There was this great advance that Moses and the Egyptian Pharaoh Akhenaton brought where one god prevailed.

Of course, one god—one male god—prevailed. If you were inventing a totalitarian society, that's exactly what you'd want. You'd say what we're going to sell all those dumb bunnies out there on is this idea there's going to be one god, and that god's going to be male—and of course we're going to control this god, he's ours, we the priests who get our money from the rulers. This then not only excludes all those people out there, all the masses, from any sense of direct access to the "higher power" it also excludes the possibility of anything approaching democracy at an early point in history. It condemns the mass of humanity to be in the hands of tyrannical structures century after century after century, by imposing this idea of a false monotheism.

The truth about the earlier situation is very difficult for most people to grasp, because—and this is again a function of a dominator system—our minds are firmly imbedded in the either/or mindset. It can't be both/and; it has to be either/or. Well, if you get out of this bind into the both/and perspective, and you look at the nature of the deity back there, you find both a unity *and* a plurality. You could have your own goddess for your particular locality, and call it A. And in the next country, people could call their goddess B, and others could have gods they called C or D. But they were all visualized as part of the same overriding deity. And when you had that kind of situation, you didn't feel compelled to go and beat up your neighbor, and rape all his women, and grab all his possessions, because that would be a breech of a sacred bond. You were all bound together as part of Gaia. This is the kind of peaceful attitude and respect for diversity that was shattered by this system we've been sold.

RIANE: But you would not think of women as "your neighbor's women." First of all, descent was matrilineal, it went through the mother, and women were not property. So that whole construction you've just used, your neighbor and his women, would not be part of that consciousness. Again, you see how the language, the way we're used to conceptualizing, has trapped us.

DJB: The values of a partnership society are obvious—peace, prosperity, creative expression, etc.—however, in viewing evolution from a holistic perspective, do you see the dominator type of society playing a beneficial role in the larger scheme of things?

RIANE: No. People seem to think that, if you look at evolution, just because something happened, it had to happen. That's in line with the deterministic, linear, nineteenth century, idea that everything moves in upward stages. Therefore, if we had this dominator phase, then there must have been some kind of great evolutionary design to it.

The most basic technologies on which all civilization is based, the fundamentals—agriculture, pottery, the social technologies of organized religion, of law-giving—are rooted in the earlier partnership societies. Now, you do get some real technological leaps when you go into the machine age, and now the electronic age. But I've always asked myself the question: what would the industrial revolution have been like in a society that oriented to a partnership model? Would we have built factories where people were cogs in machines? Obviously not.

So I think we need to make a distinction between the fact that we have this thrust towards higher technological complexity, and the accident that some of it happened in a time when we oriented very largely to the dominator model, and not try to always see causality here.

DAVID L: To me there are two aspects here, one logical, the other psychological. Logically we're asking was this a necessary step in evolution? Could we have gotten to where we are without it? And the tendency is to say, no, we couldn't have; it was just one of those awful necessary things we had to go through. But to me it's much more vivid if I look at it as a psychologist. The older I get, the more I'm horrified by the following picture of our development over a lifetime.

We're born as organisms into this world. We go through all this stress and strain of growing up. If we're a member of a fairly affluent Western family, for example, we escape from our primary family when we're in our early twenties.

Now in the *best* of cases, we spend the next twenty years, at least into our forties, in armchairs in the offices of psychologists and other counselors, trying to shed all the awful stuff that was loaded on us during our first twenty years. Then in our forties or fifties Jung's individuation and "maturity" takes over, and we begin to get just a little bit of freedom from all the distortions of our past, all the problems. We don't have to blame our parents any longer. We can begin to be maybe really creative, to think about other people. We begin to get the feeling for how to do this in our sixties, in our seventies, and so we reach this great stage where we can contribute something to the advancement of humanity—and we die!

There's been this whole life expended on trying to reach the healthy *beginning* point! And this is the story of humanity! Now what Riane's work has opened up is the vision of the alternative, both in personal human terms, and in historical terms. In personal human terms, just simply imagine what life could be like if you were born into a partnership-type society—that is, an advanced version of what we now know existed earlier, where you didn't have all the distortions, the imbalance, the degradation and the stunting of the dominator system to work through. Once you left the bosom of the family in your early twenties, why you just went automatically to work for the good things of the earth. You had anywhere from twenty to sixty years to enjoy life and add to the thrust of positive conscious evolution—rather than waste another lifetime adding nothing but the feeling of meaningless futility behind.

> *we reach this great stage where we can contribute something to the advancement of humanity—and we die!*

When we went to Crete we saw the remnants of the magnificent peak of that early culture, Minoan Crete. You look at these glorious ruins, and you realize that here was this very advanced state. They really knew what life was about, and what to do with it—the beauty, the ritual, the art, the trade, the economy, the greater sharing, rather than the hoarding of wealth. Then there's this great drop off, with the dominator takeover, and we're only now beginning to get back to the same place we were thousands of years ago. So I think the idea that the prehistoric shift from partnership to dominator systems was a necessary step in evolution is crazy.

DJB: Lynn Margulis and James Lovelock have together synthesized a theory which they have termed the Gaia hypothesis, to explain how the delicate chemical ratios in our planet's oceans and atmosphere are maintained such that life is possible. They claim that the planet earth operates much like a single living system—one huge organism. Does this theory, in your opinion, support the notion that our planet could, in a sense, be slowly transforming human existence into a global partnership community for its own survival and growth?

RIANE: They called it the Gaia hypothesis because Gaia was the ancient Greek Creatrix, she was the Mother Goddess. So I look at their Gaia hypothesis as a scientific update of the belief system of these earlier more partnership-oriented cultures who, as I said, did see the earth as alive.

RMN: Do you think that wars can be viewed as an intellectually organized attempt to externalize territorial/emotional conflict, and what do you think that men can learn from women about emotional navigation and expression?

RIANE: In the dominator system what happens is that we become a schizophrenic species. The women—the female half of humanity—in the androcratic, male-dominant version of this system are not supposed to have any say in social policy. This system negates the essentials. Caring, compassion, nonviolence, the things that make it possible for us to survive, and thrive, are relegated to women who have no say in decision-making. And male identity is equated with conquest.

So we start with this premise. But even if it were true—and the evidence isn't all in—that men are more predisposed to learn violent behaviors because of hormonal or whatever factors, because they don't give birth or some other factor, this would be all the more reason that we need to very rapidly leave behind a society which constantly and systematically teaches men these behaviors.

We hand the little boy a toy sword or a toy missile, and say go get them. We hand the little girl a doll and say be nice. But then we tell the girl, you have nothing to say in social policy. And we wonder why do we have a system where we don't honor caring, compassion, and nonviolence!

It's a crazy system. I think that yes, at this point, because we have for so long been in a dominator system, men have a great deal to learn from women. There's no question about it. But this is difficult, and it's not only difficult for men to learn from women, but it's difficult for women to learn from women, because of the whole idea that authority figures should be male. We've all been conditioned to think of God as a man. We have been conditioned to think of the person, the entity, that you learn from as masculine.

But this is not an issue of women against men, or men against women. We're dealing with a system, a dominator system, in which even the few women who make it to the top, like a Margaret Thatcher, have to keep proving every inch of the way when they're at the top of the male dominator system, that they're not too soft or "feminine." So, what's necessary is a mass entry of women into the public sphere. (Look at Norway for example, where they have a parliament that's about forty or more percent women and public policy reflects more of the "feminine" values.)

And it's also a question of the redefinition of what it means to be a man. The good news is that many men are now questioning the old models of masculinity, asking what does it really mean to be masculine or feminine?

And they're beginning to recognize that this whole conquest thing is not masculine. It's just plain brutal.

DAVID L: I see another aspect, from my current explorations into moral sensitivity. Without going into the reason for it, a fundamental contrast between the two models is that in that earlier state, toward which we may be moving if we're lucky now, moral sensitivity was the *norm*. In other words, spirituality was not a matter of an hour on Sunday. Spirituality was a twenty-four hour-a-day business, seven days a week, round the year, round the lifetime, and moral *in*sensitivity was *ab*normal. Now if you look at what has prevailed during the period of the rise of the world's so-called great religions—Christianity, Buddhism, Hinduism, Mohammedism—you see that under the dominator system, for a span of five thousand years we've endured a situation in which moral *in*sensitivity is the norm.

In other words, the average person is viewed as immoral, amoral, and the truly morally sensitive person is seen as *ab*normal, as the exception or as a freak. The people in leadership will say, Oh, I would love to abide by the golden rule and so on, but the world isn't set up that way. If I were to go act, they'd kill me. So, consequently, I am the president of the United States, but I must of course lie. Let's say I am Harry Truman, but I must drop the atom bomb on Hiroshima and Nagasaki—that's just the way the rotten world is. This relates to the fundamental question of why we have wars. In that earlier partnership-oriented system the question of war was almost unthinkable. In other words, it would be viewed as such a fundamental violation of the nature of one's relation to the universe that one would explore all kinds of alternatives short of war. There's no check, no limits, we'll go to war. We'll have this wonderful war because there just aren't the moral constraints.

RIANE: Just think of the term "nobleman." A very short time ago, the "nobleman" was the warrior. Talk about an immoral norm.

We've been gradually rejecting that. But organized killing or being a warrior was once the only "honorable" career for an upper-class male.

Back to the consciousness for the twenty-first century, if there's to be a twenty-first century, the whole issue now is leaving behind the dominator overlay. The partnership consciousness has always remained, but it's remained in the underground, if you will, either buried in mystical traditions, in religious rhetoric, or in the so-called women's world. It's been there because otherwise society couldn't have gone on. But now it's a question of breaking through, bringing it into social governance.

RMN: If males tend to demonstrate violence externally, do you think it's true that females are often more internally violent, and what do you feel that women can learn from men's tendency to intellectualize and thus objectify emotional states?

RIANE: People say that men aren't emotional, and that only women are emotional. But if you think about that, it's not true.

Men are socialized so that they're allowed one type of emotion: anger, contempt, rage. They're actually encouraged to be angry, and to express anger. It's a "masculine" thing to do—as it serves to maintain their dominance.

Women get all the rest of the emotions. Except anger. So naturally, if you can't ever express anger, what are you going to do? You internalize it.

So here we have this insane system again, crippling both women and men. Men certainly need other emotions, other feelings, "soft" feelings such as compassion and empathy. And women need to be able to assert themselves and to learn to express anger. And men need to learn to listen to women's anger.

I don't think it's an issue of women learning from men how to objectify. Education for women, which is what gives us the ability to better use our minds, is so recent that it's absolutely mind-boggling. Did you know that until the mid-nineteenth century there were no American universities that accepted women. Not one. The few women who had higher education got it through a tutorial system, where a father said, I want my daughter to also be educated. I think women have just as much of a capacity to be intellectual as men, or to be objective.

But I don't think that being objective is the answer. Because we now know that nobody can truly be objective, that we're all products of our cultures—and that often so-called objectivity is a way for men to detach themselves, to not feel anything when they are examining, for example, war. As in counting how many bombs were dropped, rather than dealing with the human suffering.

DJB: Richard Dawkin's theory of cultural evolution assumes the existence of what he calls memes— units of cultural information— that seek to replicate themselves by hopping from brain to brain, and like genes, are subject to the laws of natural selection. In this context, dominator and partnership models of society can be viewed as being composed of memes that are competing with one another for the occupation of human brains. Does this view add any further insight into your theory of cultural evolution?

RIANE: I prefer Vilmos Csanyi's and Humberto Maturana's views. Csanyi speaks of the replication of ideas, not only the replication of cells. And that's a very important component in cultural evolution, whether or not it happens, as Rupert Sheldrake proposes, through morphogenetic fields.

DAVID L: One reason for the popularity of gene theories is because it's hard for some people to visualize how all cultural transmission can be through reading books, and teaching, where it's a transmission of ideas from the printed page to the eyes, to the mind. They look at the evidence and think there's more going on there. Jung, for example, came up with the idea of the collective unconscious, that there is transmission through archetypes.

Sheldrake's idea of a giant invisible memory bank is that there is so much evidence of other forms of transmission. A huge amount of so-called psychic research into telepathy, clairvoyance, and that whole realm indicates there are other forms of transmission that enter the replication process which Vilmos Csanyi and Maturana articulate beautifully. I've also noticed that the gene-theorists tend to be more basically conservative and traditionalist. Here it may also be interesting to note that, in political psychology studies show a strong positive correlation between liberalism and empathy, and a negative correlation between empathy and conservativism.

RIANE: Let me put that into historical context, in the context of the tension between the partnership and the dominator models. The question of empathy is central here. Because one of the things that you have to do in the dominator system is to find some way to deaden empathy. For example, how in the world is a man supposed to do the kinds of things that he's supposed to do in war, and have empathy?

While we're on that subject, somebody was telling me of evidence suggesting that when we humans engage in helpful behavior, there is a release of a chemical bodily reward. We feel better for it. And yet in the dominator system that empathic impulse, that helpful impulse, is constantly being suppressed or distorted.

RMN: You have made use of Ralph Abraham's systems theory which explains the motions of cultural trends in terms of a response to chaotic or periodic attractors. What historical examples have you discovered which fit into this model of cultural evolution?

RIANE: Ralph speaks a great deal about attractors, and I have looked at the partnership and the dominator models as attractors. Using Ralph's terminology, if we look at prehistory as a basin, then the stable attractor there was the partnership model. I'm talking about the mainstream now, because obviously the attractor on the fringes was the dominator model.

Once we get into recorded history it becomes more complex. There are still elements of the partnership model, but they are coopted and exploited by the dominator system, like women's nurturing work in the family, which is given no monetary reward and little status.

Still, what you also see is what Ralph calls periodicity, periods when the partnership model becomes a stronger attractor. But it never quite makes it. You never see the change, the system's transformation, where it becomes the primary attractor, and in *The Chalice and the Blade*, I describe some of these periods. Such as early Christianity. But then the Church allies itself (under the leadership of the so-called church fathers) with the Roman emperor, Constantine. And what happens is that you begin to see again a very hierarchic, completely male dominant structure—no women allowed in the priesthood—and a very violent structure, as manifested in the Crusades and the Inquisition. In other words you've got the dominator model again.

Let's now jump to modern times, to the sixties, when women and men were beginning to definitely reject the sexual stereotypes. Women were rejecting their exclusion from leadership and from the so-called public sphere. And men and women were rejecting the equation of masculinity with warfare. Is it really heroic to be a warrior? Wait a minute, they said, no it isn't. But again you had a regression, the "new conservatism," the rightist-fundamentalist resurgence.

And today what we are continuing to see in the world is a mounting partnership resurgence. But it is against tremendous dominator resistance, as we can see all around us in what's happening, from the U.S. Supreme Court to the spread of Islamic fundamentalism. In fact, the stronger the partnership thrust, the greater resistance. Until there is a systems shift—which is where the new consciousness has a major role to play.

DAVID L: This is another reason for the force of Riane's book, because it puts the challenge of social change within the most forceful context I know of. Those of us who have worked at various stages for civil rights and other causes have certainly had the experience of this massive wall of resistance, the inertia within the system. Much of the evil force of the dominator system is just this inertia. In any kind of system the resistance against change is phenomenal.

So we've had this idea—and Darwinian theory helped lock it in - that all change has to come slowly. We've had the idea that it's going to take many generations. But ever since 1945 when the bombs went off, people have begun to realize we don't have time for slow social change. So to the activist, the great excitement about chaos theory is that it shows you can have a system going along, and a little blip appears within it that doesn't seem to amount to a hill of beans. It may appear and then disappear—but it may also spread with astounding rapidity, and become more and more prevalent until the whole system has changed. This is why the strange attractor phenomena is fascinating, not only to mathematicians such as Ralph Abraham, but to social theorists. Because they see here a model for hope that we may survive, that there may be enough of us creating what, in Prigoginian terms, is called a nucleation, which in dynamic terms is a strange attractor. And chaos theory shows that if there are enough of us, and if luck is with us, we can, in a relatively short amount of time, which is all the time we've got, transform the whole system.

Ilya Prigogine can show this happening in chemical solutions. Ralph

Abraham can show it happening with computer projections. What is exciting about Riane's book is that she shows this happening on a global scale in prehistory. For these were the dynamics of the Kurgan invasions. The Kurgan invaders acted in effect as a strange attractor. You see the strange attractor at work, coming, going, until within a relatively short period of time the whole system has been taken over by the dominator culture acting as a "peripheral invader," to use Eldridge and Gould's term.

Because we now at last have the pre-historical data that shows us how this shift happened in a negative and anti-human direction back there, we can now understand how the same kind of rapid shift can happen today—but this time in a pro-human direction. Another implication of chaos theory is extremely important. Just going by the mathematics, or chemistry of chaos theory, one might think that when we move over from natural to social science this remains a random process, and we have to just sit by and hope that we're part of a strange attractor. But other systems theorists—Ervin Laszlo, for example, who heads the General Evolution Research Group, which Riane and I helped forum—are showing the effect of human change agents. We don't have to just sit back and wait for this mystic scientific process to maybe work in our advantage. We can show that human intervention, through change agents, can definitely make a difference.

DJB: Do you think that there is a relationship between the two types of human civilization that you define, and the over-specialization of specific hemispheres in the brain?

RIANE: I think that that's a very complex question, and David probably could answer it better. But I think that it's a fallacy that people seem to think that this earlier archaic prehistoric period was all right brain.

If you look at Crete, if you look at the technology, they obviously did some very logical, linear so-called left brain thinking. If you look at Stonehenge, at these massive ritual centers, they had to have had some left brain capacity to do this. And look at all the inventions that we owe to these people!

Clearly prehistory wasn't all right brain. I think it was more balanced, and I think in that sense you're right about an over-specialization of the left brain in dominator societies. But of course you know it's not that clear that they're that localized either, these faculties. And David can tell you more about that. I think that when we're talking about a partnership society, we are talking about an integration of what we now think of as right and left brain, about more of a system view, a holographic view.

DAVID L: Certainly, the earlier culture was more right brain oriented than our culture tends to be, but there is all this evidence indicating that it was a much more balanced holistic functioning, where you're able to draw upon both halves of the brain with some facility. As Riane pointed out in the example of Stonehenge, there are indications of a high mathematical capacity in early partnership-oriented cultures. But at the same time there is a correlation between left brain dominance and the dominator system. We speak of right brain dominance, left brain dominance, and the reason we do is that brain research shows that one or the other can dominate and suppress the other modes.

The prototypical situation for somebody today, particularly a male in the male dominant culture that has prevailed for five thousand years now, intensified by the so-called Age of Reason —is that you sop up a little bit of insight from the right brain half, but then you immediately suppress that original source of information. You shift wholly into the mathematics, or an elaborate left-brained rationality process. You develop the logic but suppress and shove under the whole feeling side of life, the whole realm of affectivity, which tends to be handled more by the right brain half. So there is a correspondence there, but it's not this simplistic notion the earlier culture was just blindly right brained. Julian Jaynes popularized the idea the earlier culture was right brained, and the later dominator culture was left brained, and this later culture not only represented true civilization but also the first appearance in human evolution of consciousness!

DJB: Could you make use of Rupert Sheldrake's recently refined theory of morphogenetic fields— that is, non-material regions of organic influence—to shed any more light on the evolution of dominator and partnership societies?

DAVID L: I recently finished writing an introduction to a new book by Ervin Laszlo in which he provides substantiation for Sheldrake and other morphogenetic field theorists from many different scientific fields. I think the easiest way to see the possible relation between Sheldrake's theory and the shift to a dominator or a partnership system is what people have picked up on in the one hundredth monkey story.

In other words, Sheldrake's theory suggests that if you go back into the early partnership culture, there was a certain point at which the numbers of dominator-system-oriented nomads along the periphery, all carrying the same killer ethos, reached a critical point in imprinting this ethos on the morphogenetic field, or the "cosmic schmaz," or whatever you want to call it, and it began to crowd out the other. I think in our time the same process is going on, only in reverse. And so it's extremely important for those of us who have regained this partnership ethos to both increase in numbers and feel intensively about this to re-imprint this ethos with greater effect, greater force on the "cosmic schmaz." I think there's something there, and I think it relates to the dynamics, but of course we're still a long way off from fully understanding it.

RMN: The gylanic principle flourished during the sixteenth century Renaissance with a partial marriage of art and science. What other historical examples have you observed where the symbiotic union of the subjective and objective realms are indicative of a gylanic society, and do you see the current interest in fractals, brain machines, and the poetic musings of quantum physics as being examples of a reunion between these two areas of human experience?

RIANE: I think that these may be manifestations of emerging gylanic conscious ness. But I also think that a lot of the so-called leading edge thinking today continues to be the male intellectual game.

Now certainly one of the very interesting things that's happening with fractals, for example, is that it's an image that's very much like a mandala. If you look at some of the art of the Neolithic, the meanders, the serpentine lines, you see a lot of mandala-like images. These were epiphanies of the divine, of the Goddess. So I see a relationship, but I also see that without the partnership mythos, we are always back to the same thing. Without the integrative story, and without the understanding that a truly new science requires not only integrating the "feminine," but real live people called women, we are just going to keep dancing around the problem and neither science nor art nor society is going to fundamentally change.

DAVID L: Yes. This is something about which I feel intensely as a male who has actively worked within male-dominated scientific contexts to try to inject the feminist perspective, to get more women involved. Take fractals, take chaos theory, this whole fascinating computer generated mathematical excitement without what Riane is talking about, without this larger balanced masculine/feminine or feminine/masculine ethos, and all this "new science" will become merely another male head trip. That is, it will be reduced to merely another entertainment for primarily male academics who gather in symposia, which in one way or another are in the end sponsored by the military industrial complex, which all too often still pays the bulk of their salaries.

This is the horrible alternative we face with every one of these great discoveries reconnecting with the past. There is this danger they will be coopted, degraded and defused by the present system, unless the people who are leading the revolution in "new science" understand this larger picture and ethos. The man who wrote the enormously popular book *Chaos*, James Gleick, for example, has no understanding of this larger context that I can see. He's done a beautiful job of providing information, but typically this can all go to simply serve the purposes of entertainment and the military industrial complex.

DJB: How do you envision civilization and human consciousness to be one hundred years from now?

RIANE: That depends on whether we take the dominator or the partnership route. But I'm convinced that if we take the dominator route, there won't be much in the way of any kind of human consciousness in a hundred years, because chances are that we won't be here.

If we do take the partnership route, I see a tremendous growth of empathy in both women and men. Even in women in the dominator model it's very selective. We've been permitted empathy for those around us, but we're not permitted any action to follow that empathy. So what good does it do?

I see a society where doing good will not be an insult, as it is now, as in the pejorative "do gooder" or "bleeding-heart." I see a world where the most highly valued work will have the consciousness of caring.

Marx spoke of the alienation of labor. I speak of the alienation of caring labor, which is the work that's traditionally been relegated to women and to volunteers, and has not been paid or has been paid very poorly. So I think we'll become much more conscious of what's really valuable.

I think that our consciousness will not make the artificial distinction between spirituality and nature, with the male being associated with the spirit and woman being associated with nature. We will also have gotten over our ridiculous love affair with technologies of destruction, which is inherent in the dominator system, because here the technological emphasis has to be on technologies that make it possible to more efficiently dominate—be it the new technologies of mind control, be it weaponry, or be it exploitative technologies.

I think we'll become conscious that women's issues are not secondary or peripheral, but rather the most critical issues. Take population, for example. That's a women's issue, an issue of reproductive freedom, of access to birth control technologies. Even more important, it's an issue of life choices for women other than breeders of sons for men.

If you look at the most overpopulated, poorest, and most violent regions in the world today, the Middle East, Latin America, or parts of Africa and Asia, you see there the dominator configuration.

So with a new partnership consciousness we will be able to see reality far more clearly. I think that we'll be much saner.

RMN: Do you see man/woman teams presiding in future governments? Can you give us a historical perspective on this? What effects do you think this would have on areas such as ecology, nationalism, and the distribution of wealth, for example?

RIANE: I love your question, and I could spend a day on it. I think that one thing that we're beginning to see is that we've been taught to think of leadership as power over. And now we're beginning to understand, even in the corporate sector, that a really good leader is a person who inspires people, who can get from them their highest productivity, their highest creativity.

Women have been used to doing this, because that's part of the training we get for child rearing. So I think that the role of women in leadership is indispensable. And I think that it will affect everything!

Take for example ecology. Men are socialized in the dominator system not to clean up after themselves. So that's exactly what they've done with nuclear waste, they've just put it out there with no notion of what in the world to do with it. Women would never do this because, you see, a man is brought up in the dominator system to think there's always going to be someone to clean up after him—namely a woman.

DJB: How have your personal relationships, particularly your marriage, inspired your theories of global evolution?

RIANE: I really want to honor David here. Without his partnership, I couldn't have done it. It's just that simple. He has been my friend, my mentor, my sounding board. He has sometimes critiqued me, made me worry about what I was doing, and he always gave me tremendous amounts of information. Above all, he gave me tremendous amounts of support.

DAVID L: From my point of view, it's been extremely important to me to interact with a woman who is able to love me as I'm able to love her on some basis of equality. Rather than have the old superior-inferior relationship, which many men and women have. It takes up so much of a lifetime, so many marriages, and so many affairs these days to work through all these difficulties of the dominator-dominated patterning that's built into us. It's just wonderful to me to reach a stage in life where all that, at least, is in the past. But of most importance to me is the intellectual advantage. I often think I was tremendously fortunate to happen to link up with a woman so important in making this breakthrough we've been talking about. Women are making this breakthrough and they've begun to see out beyond this cage that every male is still encased in, almost without exception.

I feel fortunate in that I happened to link up with a woman at the forefront in her time in getting outside that cage and seeing it for what it was and is.

You see, Riane took these insights, added to them, and built them into this forceful new theoretical framework. It hangs together as a theory of cultural evolution, of historical development, and as a weltanschauung or world-view; once you've grasped it, you can actually re-evaluate the whole of your intellectual experience. You can turn your head clear around and for the first time see life and it's possibilities in a balanced perspective.

In my own intellectual development, five systems of thought have been important to my mental growth. The first was the Christian mythos. The second was the Freudian. The third was the Marxian. The fourth was the field theoretical perspective of Kurt Lewin and the fifth has been systems science. Each reoriented my whole intellectual universe. But the sixth was Riane's perspective, and I now find it by far the most useful because it embraces more than any other, more questions, and corrects the imbalances of these perspectives. I feel it's very much a weltanschauung for the twenty-first century.

Don Harris

Robert Trivers

"...will we do away with whole areas of the earth, then face what it's like to have ten to twelve billion people on this planet?"

Replicating Genes
with Robert Trivers

Are social behaviors genetically inheritable? Do they evolve through time like physical characteristics? The science of sociobiology has developed in order to study these questions. In the controversial field of sociobiology, there is no one as controversial as Robert Trivers, for he has certainly been the most daring in applying the "selfish gene" theory of sociobiology to human behavior and psychology. Recognized as one of the world's most eminent sociobiologists, Robert Trivers was born in 1943 in Washington D.C. to a Foreign Service Officer and a poet, as the second of seven children. His early academic interests ("after the Bible," he clarifies) included astronomy and mathematics. He earned his B.A. from Harvard in U.S. History in 1965. Then he wrote and illustrated children's books for two years before returning to Harvard, where he studied biology, and received his Ph.D. in 1972. He taught at Harvard until 1978, and after that at the UC Santa Cruz, where he continues to teach to this day. In May 1979 he joined the Black Panther Party, and has been referred to by his colleague Burney Le Boeuf as "the blackest white man I know."

Dr. Trivers is perhaps most famous for his theory of reciprocal altruism, which is a model for explaining and predicting altruism in animals precisely based on return-effect or chances of reciprocity. He has also written papers on parental investment and sexual selection, sex ratio theory, parent-offspring conflict, and the social behavior of lizards and insects. He is the author of Social Evolution, *a fascinating sociobiological textbook which was published in 1985 by Benjamin-Cummings of Menlo Park. He spends a good deal of time in Jamaica with his children, and has described himself as "Jamaican in my soul or spirit." He is currently working on the evolution of "selfish genes" and resulting intra-genomic conflict, the effects of blood parasites on sexual selection in* Anolis *lizards, and deceit and self-deception. We met Bob on the evening of January 18th, 1989 at the Woodshed, a country bar in Felton, California. Bob spoke to us about his theory of reciprocal altruism, selfish genes, the evolution of sex, and muses with us on how and why consciousness evolved. There is a wild unpredictable quality to Bob's personality. He seems untamed and street-wise in a rather charming sort of way.*
—DJB

DJB: Bob, what was it that originally spawned your interest in biology and the evolution of social behavior?

ROBERT: When I graduated from college I was offered a job writing, and later illustrating children's books for part of a curriculum. The curriculum was called "Man: A Course of Study," and was meant to be the new social science, analogous to the new math, and the new physics. Since I didn't know anything about humans, they asked me to work on some animal material that they wanted to include in the course. I also didn't know anything about animals but they cared less about getting that stuff accurate.

So my first exposure to animal behavior came through this job, and I was impressed with two things. One, by watching movies of baboons, I was impressed by how psychologically similar they seemed to ourselves, and that any explanation therefore of our own psyche would have to include arguments that could apply to baboons as well. And the second thing was I learned about the concept of evolution through natural selection. So within about six months of graduating from college, I had had my life turned around. I had never had biology before, never had chemistry, and I became convinced that the basis for a scientific theory of psychology lay in animal behavior and evolutionary theory. So I threw myself into it.

DJB: Can you briefly describe your theory of reciprocal altruism?

ROBERT: Reciprocal altruism is very, very simple and encompassed in the folk saying, "You scratch my back, I'll scratch yours." It simply posits that organisms, besides humans, or in addition to humans, are capable of trading altruistic acts over a period of time, in which each individual is sensitive to the tendency of the other individual to be reciprocal, or perhaps not to be reciprocal, or as I put it, to cheat on the relationship. So the theory of reciprocal altruism applied to humans says that traits like friendship did not evolve before reciprocal altruism as a prerequisite, but evolved after reciprocal altruism as a way of motivating and shaping our reciprocal relationships.

> *Reciprocal altruism is...encompassed in the folk saying, "You scratch my back, I'll scratch yours."*

RMN: According to the theory of natural selection, species evolve to adapt to the local environment to align with the forces of the external world. For example, the spots on the heads of gull chicks will co-evolve with the parental ability to recognize them. Have you considered the possibility that this process may operate *both* ways; i.e., that the environment may also adapt to conform with the needs of the organism it is nurturing—and does natural selection support the idea of evolution as a co-creative transaction between the organism and the environment?

ROBERT: I have considerable difficulty with that notion, except in the sense that you probably don't mean it: that the environment consists of other living creatures, and so the environment and the species we're considering both evolve. The species we're thinking about imagining is selected by the environment it lives in, but the environment it lives in is itself made up of living organisms which are being selected by reference to their environments, which include the species we're imagining. But, if you ask can I see how the environment would evolve to nurture the species, I'm dubious.

DJB: What percentage of human behavior do you think is genetically hard-wired and what percentage of human behavior do you think is due to environmental learning, and what evidence can you call upon to support your viewpoint?

ROBERT: I don't think your question really permits any kind of precise answer. I think it's inherently impossible to assign a percentage to environment and a percentage to genetic influences. The only way you could do that would be to specify the full range of environmental contingencies, and the full range of genetic contingencies, and that seems like a hopeless way to operate. For example, traits like two legs and five toes on each leg are "hard-wired" genetically, but we can always produce an intervention in early embryology which will interrupt the natural train of events, and result in someone with no limbs, or with an unusual number of digits. So, if we include that environmental range, then the percentage of genetic determination drops below a hundred percent. I don't see any way to state how much of human behavior is genetically hard-wired, whatever that precisely means, or how much is environmentally determined.

DJB: Bob, you wrote the introduction to Richard Dawkins' book *The Selfish Gene*, the first place I ever heard of the concept of memes—that is, non-genetic clusters of information that replicate themselves from brain to brain much as genes do from body to body, and appear to evolve through a process akin to natural selection. In light of this theory, can you explain why some people forfeit opportunities for genetic reproduction in order to propagate memes—many artists and scientists, for example, never have children—and do you think it's possible that the goal of evolution is not really genetic replication, but rather information replication?

ROBERT: Once again, I just have to express myself as being dubious. I was dubious of the attention that Dawkins gave to the concept of memes in his original book, and I don't see ideas replicating themselves between people, and being selected in a process analogous to natural selection. I see each of us trying to influence others via our ideas, and each of us being selective regarding the ideas we accept and the ideas we reject, and the way in which we decide to modify ideas that we do accept.

A general term like information transfer, or information maximization, might work better. I just don't know how to relate to it within the one system of thought that I'm comfortable with, which is evolutionary theory. Regarding the notion that many artists and scientists have few or no children, I don't know what the evidence for that is. If it were true, I suppose I would fall back on some hunter-gatherer imaginary scene in which the shaman or the artist made a disproportionate contribution to the welfare of his or her local group, and this made up for any deficiency in personal reproduction.

RMN: You say that natural selection is described as *disruptive* when it favors extremes to create a polarity and you cite human sexual dimorphism as an example. What do you mean by this?

ROBERT: Well, you'd have to go a ways back in our own lineage, but if you go back in any species that has two sexes, you'd reach a species where there's only one sex, an original hermaphroditic form, which gave rise to the species with two sexes. Now, once you have two separate sexes, if selection operates against intermediates, then it'll tend to push the two sexes further apart.

So to use a crude compelling example, men with breasts or women with masculine characteristics may be less well off than firmly belonging to one sex or another. So to that degree selection operates against the intermediates, and we have to imagine, whenever we see dimorphism in nature—and sexual dimorphism is just one example—that somewhere along the line selection was disrupted, acting against the middle, and in favor of two different positions, not extremes, but two different forms or morphs.

RMN: So, by disrupted you mean it's moving away from the middle?

ROBERT: Yeah, I think so. The only other image of disrupted that I can think of is that if you have a normal distribution to begin with— a single uniform distribution— and you disrupt it, you'll end up producing two distributions instead of one.

RMN: The term "disruptive" sounds a little pejorative.

ROBERT: Well, if you'll pardon me, I wouldn't attach too much significance to the term disruptive as in disruptive selection. I see your objection and did when you were asking your earlier question, but it's just a term like normalizing selection and directional selection, just for describing a kind of selection. Now, getting back to the union of opposites—sure, in some cases, as in the sexes in producing offspring.

But, I guess answering your question I realize that I came out of a world twenty years ago in which differences between the sexes or within species tended to be minimized and conflict tended to be minimized, and there was always some claim of a higher purpose, benefits for the group or the species, and insufficient attention was paid to conflict, even within relationships that have a cooperative goal. So regarding the sexes, yes, especially in species with male parental investment, especially in cases of monogamy, you can have a large overlap of self-interest between a male and a female, so they're involved in a higher goal, a common goal of, let us say raising offspring together.

RMN: Which is what life is all about, right?

ROBERT: Eventually. But that still should not obscure the fact that they have conflicting self-interest, and that their self-interest may not be maximized in the same way.

DJB: James Lovelock and Lynn Margulis have proposed a theory, which they have termed the Gaia hypothesis, to explain how and why life forms on our planet work in such a cooperative fashion together to achieve the delicate chemical ratios in our oceans and atmospheres, which are maintained in such perfect balance that life is made possible and sustained. They claim that the whole earth seems to function much in the way a single organism operates. Do you have any thoughts on this, and how does the "selfish gene" theory that you subscribe to explain this extraordinary phenomenon?

ROBERT: Well, I'm really not familiar with this area. From my bias, I've always imagined, in so far as I've thought about it at all, that the organisms are just busy concerning themselves with what's good for each other, and the result is some kind of steady state that is beneficial, more broadly put. Some organisms consume oxygen, others generate oxygen. There's going to be a balance struck between those two sets of organisms, some kind of density-dependent laws that come into effect.

I think that it would be a mistake to imagine that the organisms are attempting to set up something in the biosphere itself, or to create a biosphere, but I may be a little bit old-fashioned in that approach, and I know that geologists, and people that study the earth as a whole, do often imagine that it's like an organism, and maybe it is. I just don't know. Nothing in my line of work would suggest so, that I know of.

RMN: You refer a number of times in your book *Social Evolution* to the "apparent coincidences" of natural selection. When literally translated this term coincidence means simply the coordination of incidents. Would you venture further and postulate as to the directing force that is coordinating these incidents? Do you see any kind of teleology in nature or do you view all events as the product of mere chance? Does Natural Selection play dice with the universe, and is the only meaning to life in your view, really, more life?

ROBERT: I don't see any teleology in nature. The teleology was beaten out of me in my training. It was an important aspect of paleontology, for example, to learn there were no trends, inevitable trends, of groups tending to always get larger, or always go in one direction or another.

RMN: What are your views on genetic engineering and the possibility, which to some scientists is a very real one, that we will soon have the ability to control our evolution by programming our future genetic forms?

> *I have not been frightened by genetic engineering...I...do not believe it will create monsters that will run rampant.*

ROBERT: I have not been frightened by genetic engineering. I do not believe it will create monsters that will run rampant. I've always believed that natural selection would still be acting, and acting very strongly.

RMN: On the scientists that create the genetic mutations?

ROBERT: Well, I was thinking on the genetic mutants themselves. In other words, when the, say, anti-frost bacteria were first sprayed on plants here in California experimentally, people said, well Jesus what happens if you got a monster bacterium that's going to cut loose and cause all sorts of havoc, and run amok. I just didn't imagine that it would happen because monsters are being produced, probably daily, in this world, through mutation and recombination, and are being selected against, and I didn't see, and don't see any reason why artificial forms created in the lab wouldn't be subject to strong selection too. As for genetic engineering in the human species, I imagine it's inevitable, and probably in a hundred or two hundred years we'll scarcely be able to imagine the genetic manipulations that'll be possible.

RMN: In your book *Social Evolution* you state that the primary function of sex is to generate genetic novelty in the offspring, which can better adapt to the changing environmental conditions. You also say that natural selection favors individuals who maximize the number of offspring. Two factors are being described here—that of quality and that of quantity. How do you see these factors operating in evolution?

ROBERT: The simple answer is that quality can always be converted into quantity for the purposes of evolutionary theory. So, one pair of parents can produce four offspring of low quality, where quality is measured as their ability to survive and reproduce, and another pair of parents can produce two offspring of high quality, were quality is again defined the same way. In that case, after awhile, the high quality offspring win out, are more numerous. That's just a tautological system, in which quality refers to eventual ability to survive and reproduce, and therefore converts into quantity.

RMN: Do you see these influences as being equally potent— fifty-fifty?

ROBERT: Yes.

DJB: Approximately 22,000 Americans commit suicide annually. Clearly suicidal behavior is non-adaptive, and it appears to be related to sexual development— that is, the behavior seems to emerge during adolescence, and is often triggered by the loss of a lover. How do you explain it evolutionarily?

ROBERT: I don't necessarily explain it evolutionarily. Twenty-two thousand out of two hundred million is still a relatively low frequency. Evolutionary arguments have to start being evoked where you get up to one percent of the population, or something like that, as in schizophrenia. Your statement that suicide is clearly non-adaptive, I think, has to be viewed with a little bit of suspicion. I'm not saying that it is adaptive, but I'm saying one can imagine circumstances under which suicide is adaptive.

You can start with the old Eskimo story of the elders who walked out into the cold to die, to save their children energy and effort. A certain amount of suicide of the elderly has that form. It is also possible for suicide to be adaptive when the alternative is murder of close relatives, or some other behavior that's going to bring genetic consequences. I think there might be a recent paper, that I've not read, on an adaptive approach to suicide, but I don't see any obvious adaptive sense to it.

RMN: Neophobia, the fear of novel stimuli, can be viewed in some situations as enhancing reproductive success, and in other situations as inhibiting it. If one species evolves to be fearful of novelty, and one species evolves to embrace novelty, how do you think those two species will fare?

ROBERT: I think put in that extreme form one would tend to place one's bet with the species that embraced novelty, just because novelty is intrinsic to the living world. Evolutionary novelty is occurring in all species, and other species are part of our environment. So even leaving aside geological and climatic changes, which are themselves occurring, there's novelty always being generated. So it's hard to imagine a long-term strategy successfully based on extreme neophobia. On the other hand, a lot of creatures, speaking strictly off the top of my head, seem to show some sort of balance between extreme neophobia and just rampant embrace of everything new. I could think of different species, different examples, where the young are, like I say, somewhere in between.

DJB: Do you believe that life may have evolved on other planets and star systems, and if so, what possible courses of evolution do you think they might have taken that would be different from our own?

ROBERT: I do believe that life has almost certainly evolved elsewhere. Our best understanding of astronomy and of the origin of life on this planet suggests that there are plenty of stars that are appropriate, plenty of planets presumed around those stars that are appropriate.

DJB: Several years ago, Nobel prize winner Francis Crick, the co-discoverer of the structure of the DNA molecule, wrote a book entitled *Life Itself*, in which he proposes the idea that life may have been seeded on our planet by a species of higher intelligence than our own, through the use of genetically engineered spores that are blown through space by radiation pressures. In the light of our own species' progress with genetic engineering, do you think this is a possible explanation for how life originated on our planet, and if so, do you think it is possible that evolution may, in some sense, be developing according to a particular plan?

ROBERT: I think it's possible. I don't quite see the gain to the other organism in doing this process. The seeding of the earth, according to our understanding, would have then occurred about four billion years ago, and it took four billion years to produce

> *...it took four billion years to produce creatures as humble as ourselves.*

creatures as humble as ourselves. We can't do yet what Crick is saying the other creature can do. So after four billion years they still ain't got nothing that matches themselves. I don't quite know what the function of this would be.

RMN: There is much concern these days about the problems of over-population. It seems that the survival of the human species, and possibly the planet, may now depend upon our ability to limit reproduction. As natural selection theory depends upon the idea of reproductive success being the main goal of evolution, what are your views on this?

ROBERT: I think that, next to nuclear warfare, it's probably the best candidate for driving us to extinction, perhaps in conjunction with nuclear warfare, of any of the possible candidates. I think a lot will depend on how far we deplete resources before we reverse the population explosion, assuming we finally reach a stage where we do. Certainly at some point we have to limit reproduction to a ZPG, zero population growth, or steady-state. We know that from elementary considerations.

> *...next to nuclear warfare (the population explosion is) probably the best candidate for driving us to extinction*

When I think about the future in that regard, which I do very rarely, I imagine the next hundred years will be crucial in determining what we have to bring ourselves back from. In other words, do we all go the road of India before realizing that there are unfortunate consequences of depleting your natural resources. In India you can go to these beautiful geological strata, four thousand feet up, the mountains and hills near Bombay for example. You see the complete deforestation of these areas, which leads to the alternate cycle of floods, where hundreds and thousands die in floods, and then tremendous periods of drought.

> *...the next hundred years will be crucial in determining what we have to bring ourselves back from.*

I remember coming back down from this place, going towards Bombay, and there are these Mangrove-like trees that send out roots from their lowest limbs, and goats were reaching up on their hind legs, and nibbling the growing tips of these roots, that far from the ground, and they weren't going to reach the ground, because there was always going to be enough goats to keep them from reaching the ground. So the trees weren't going to grow anymore, and it just seemed like ecological chaos. So anyway, when I think about the future at all, I imagine will we do away with the Brazilian forest? Will we do away with whole areas of the earth, and then face what it's like to have ten to twelve billion people on this planet? Or will things get under control before then?

DJB: Bob, do you think it's possible that the introduction of psycho-active plants into the food chain of early primates had any influence on our evolutionary development? Terence McKenna thinks that psilocybin mushrooms catalyzed the enlargement of the neocortex and the development of language. Roland Fisher has shown that low doses of psilocybin increase visual acuity.

ROBERT: I don't imagine it's had any, or much of an evolutionary effect.

RMN: Do you have a theory about why the brain size of Homo sapiens increased so rapidly over such a short period of time?

ROBERT: I don't have any particular theory, no. It seems to me obvious that it must have been bound up primarily with language. Which is another great unique development in our own lineage. We know now of animal languages, and in primates we know that various species do use some sounds symbolically. But these are very, very rudimentary compared to our language. So, I think it must have gone hand in hand with language. I think reciprocal altruism was bound up in it, because I don't think you get selection for much language, unless you have a back and forth kind of relationship, where each benefits from the interaction. Even then I think of language initially as starting in families, and spreading among close relatives, and being beneficial that way.

RMN: What possibilities do you see for our future evolution, of humans or other species?

ROBERT: I haven't thought much about future evolution. Again, it's contingent in our own species' case with getting the population growth under control, and what form that's going to take— whether it's natural disasters and non-nuclear war, and that kind of thing, that's going to keep populations under control, or whether it's some kind of voluntary restraint, it's hard to guess. It's hard for me to visualize what system of reproductive competition will exist in the species, after we get the population growth under control.

DJB: How do you think consciousness evolved, and how do you see it evolving into the next century?

ROBERT: Well, I'm not sure what consciousness is. I think insects are conscious to a limited degree. I don't think they're highly conscious or acutely self-conscious, but I think there's a little light turned on in insects that I've played with, and they're conscious of what's going on. How do you see it evolving in the future, Dave?

DJB: Well, I see brain capacity, and information processing abilities increasing, for one thing.

ROBERT: Increasing? So, that assumes now that bigger-brained people are leaving more surviving offspring?

DJB: Well, what I'm looking at is the overall 4.5 billion years of evolution, and brain capacity has increased, intelligence has increased.

ROBERT: Yeah. Right.

DJB: So, I see the pattern continuing on into the future.

ROBERT: But do you disagree with my statement? In other words, you see bigger-brained people leaving more surviving offspring.

DJB: Well, actually, I think I see exactly the opposite. I don't know about the size of people's brains, but I see those who are less educated reproducing more quickly than the more educated, unfortunately. I wonder why this is?

ROBERT: Well, you see this is the conflict between a teleological or orthogenetic view of evolution, and one that always insists that natural selection be behind it. You can't extrapolate from past patterns, unless you imagine there is some momentum, or force, carrying you through to the future. If you believe in evolution through natural selection, then you believe in the changes, which have been general, but not universal towards greater brain size. If you look at the vertebrates, there's been increase in brain size, in mammals over the last 150 million years. Been no increase in fish in 400 million years. No increase in amphibians, so far as I know. Increase in birds. Even in human lineage, I think there's no evidence of any increase in the last 100 thousand years. I'm not so sure about that statement. I know cro-magnan man was sort of a large-bodied form, but it had...

DJB: A larger cranium.

RMN: I heard that at some point they had brain capacities larger than we have now.

ROBERT: I've heard that too.

DJB: Why do you think consciousness evolved in the first place? How is it even adaptive?

ROBERT: Well, again, it depends on what we mean by consciousness.

DJB: Awareness, the opposite of being unconscious.

RMN: Or the ability to receive and transmit information.

ROBERT: Yeah, to me, it's just some kind of a heightened mental faculty, allowing heightened learning, and quicker responses to on-going events, which, however, is costly. I always use the analogy of an electric light being switched on, or not being switched on, partly because we're so visual, and our images of consciousness are so visual. And a light bulb is expensive, so we sleep, or we have periods of unconsciousness to rest what is a very expensive kind of ability.

DJB: Can you explain your theory of self-deception?

ROBERT: I tend to imagine that in social species, especially where there's been selection for deception, and spotting deception, then there's been selection for self-deception. This is a new kind of unconsciousness, where you systematically hide the truth from yourself. I tend to think that self-deception has been as important in human history as mental acuity itself is.

> *I tend to think that self-deception has been as important in human history as mental acuity itself is.*

I'd rather have a leader that was minimally self-deceived, and not quite as quick with his brain, than someone who was quicker, but practiced a lot of self-deception. So when you talk about the future of consciousness, my mind goes around, and I think about self-deception, and how selection is operating with regard to that, and it's just so hard to speculate when we're talking about things on a time-scale of a few thousand years, at the least, to get some natural selection going that's going to show up with something.

While at the same time, we know that in the next couple of hundred years we're going to see radical changes, I think, in our environment, including our medical environment, including this bio-engineering business. Because bio-engineering starts to get into conflict with natural selection if we start talking about changing our genome, the genome that's in our gonads. A small amount initially would create only a small effect, so we're going to go in, and we're going to get rid of my bad eye genes, and a few other bad genes. That's very minimal.

More extensive revision of yourself is like almost interfering with personal genetic reproduction, and I think those forces are going to be large and looming before regular old natural selection has had time to produce a human that's much different than ourselves. An issue that I cut myself off from has to do with social cost. Normalizing selection chops off the extremes all the time, and keeps the species close together.

Right now there's three percent mortality in our society between age zero and age twenty-five. That's very very small. Next to no variance can be generated by that small a

> *Normalizing selection chops off the extremes all the time, and keeps the species close together.*

selection. So then let's assume ninety-five percent of individuals couple up, or marry, and it isn't too far off from that right now. And let's assume everyone has two children, and let's assume you're supposed to have two, and you're not supposed to have any more than two, and if you lose one, you replace it.

Well, an intriguing argument that was published a few years back said after awhile the species will start coming apart, because you'll no longer have normalizing selection. So, in the extreme case, after fifty generations of this or something, your baby will require a certain kind of pills to keep it from having trembling spasms, and my baby will require that it keep it's left leg in warm water for a half an hour at night, and all of us will grow up with these environmental demands that are necessary to compliment what normally would just have been taken care of genetically.

So the social costs begin to go up, but right now we already have so many social costs from related biological things that don't have to do with natural selection. I'm thinking of matters like the elder generation and the result of medical advances. Now we have people who can live miserably between eighty and ninety, just dreadfully. I don't know if you all have been into any of these nursing homes. My wife worked in them and I used to pick her up. I couldn't take it. I'd wait outside. There were people screaming all night long. You know, they've been in there for six years screaming, and they'll be in there for five more screaming, and that's it. They're looking forward to death, because the screaming is all they're doing.

> *Now we have people who can live miserably between eighty and ninety...*

So, there is a case where suicide, I think, can be adaptive in several senses of the word. It certainly makes some sense if there was a dignified, good way to do it. I'd just say well, Dave is eighty-three now, and he's not taking care of himself, and he's going to have this farewell party, and we're going to say good-bye.

RMN: It'll be a happy occasion.

ROBERT: Yeah, something like that—a happy occasion. His relatives and friends gathered around.

Khola Shou Herbert

Nick Herbert

"I think that mind is as fundamental to nature as
light or electricity."

Faster than faster than light
with Nick Herbert

Nick Herbert holds a Ph.D. in experimental physics from Stanford University. He was senior scientist at Memorex, Santa Clara, and other Bay Area hardware companies specializing in magnetic, electrostatic, optical, and thermal methods of information processing and storage. He has taught science at all levels from graduate school to kindergarten including the development, with his wife Betsy, of a hands-on home-schooling science curriculum. Nick was the coordinator (along with Saul-Paul Sirag) of Esalen Institute's physics and consciousness program and has led many workshops on the quantum mechanics of everyday life. He is the author of Quantum Reality: Beyond the New Physics, Faster Than Light *(published in Japan under the title* Time Machine Construction Manual*),* Elemental Mind: Human Consciousness and the New Physics, *and he devised the shortest proof of Bell's interconnectedness theorem to date.*

He has written on faster-than-light and quantum theory for such journals as the American Journal of Physics *and* New Scientist, *and is Fringe Science columnist for* Mondo 2000. *We interviewed Nick April 23, 1989, on a hill overlooking Santa Cruz, California. Nick spoke with us about the implications of Bell's Theorem, superluminal loopholes in physics, and the secret technologies behind time travel and contacting the dead, including step-by-step instructions on how to build your very own time machine. Nick is an ardent disciple of quantum theory's left-hand path, and his abilty to humanize science and his imaginative speculations on time travel make him both fascinating and fun. He has a way of making even the most complex concepts of quantum physics easily understandable. He is very warm, has a contagious sense of humor, and has an uncanny talent for making the mundane seem mysterious.*

—DJB

DJB: What was it that originally inspired your interest in physics?

NICK: I started out in a Catholic prep school. I took religion and Latin there, and the idea was to become a Catholic priest. That was my goal, and somewhere through that I got derailed. I decided that wasn't the ultimate thing. I changed my mind, and decided science was probably the place where all the hot stuff was. The hottest part of science was physics, so I went to Ohio State and majored in physics. I think it's kind of a quest for what's the hottest thing going in this culture. At one time I thought it was God, but now I think, at least for me, it's science.

DJB: Kind of a quest for the ultimate nature of reality?

NICK: Yes. My patron saint is Saint Christopher. You might know about him as the guy in automobiles, the patron saint of travelers. But actually he's the patron saint of people who are seeking to serve the ultimate power. He was the strongest man in the kingdom, and he went around offering his services to kings and princes. He wanted to give this power that he had to the highest service. He always found that the kings had feet of clay, and they weren't really worth serving. He'd quit one king and serve another, but it would be just the same. So then, after giving up on kings and princes, he decided, well one thing I could do is I could take people across this river. That was what he did with his life. He took people across this river that didn't have a bridge.

Finally this one little kid came along and he said, "Can you take me across?" "No problem," he says, and Christopher starts taking him across. The kid got heavier and heavier and heavier. Finally he could barely hold this guy. He stumbled across to the other side, and said, "Whew, what was that?" The kid says, "You were carrying Christ, who holds the whole world on his shoulders." So he finally found the person to serve. That's why he's called Christopher—the Christ bearer. I like that story, and I'm still trying to find some ultimate master to serve. Right now it's some kind of science. So that's the physics. I'm looking for the ultimate problems, and trying to do my best, whether it be religion, science, or little things on the fringes of science.

RMN: Could you explain to us the essence of Bell's Theorem, and the ideas about the nature of reality which those experiments have inspired in you?

NICK: Okay, that's a good way of putting it, the nature of reality. I make the distinction that philosophers often make, between Appearance, Reality and Theory. Appearance is what you see, and everything around is Appearance. Reality is the hypothetical essence behind things, the secret behind things. Theories are stories that we make up about these events, Appearance and Reality. What Bell's Theorem—a proof derived from physics—says is that the Appearances, certain

Appearances in physics, certain experiments cannot be explained unless we assume something about Reality. What we have to assume about Reality is that when two systems come together, then separate, and aren't interacting any more, they're still connected in some way by a voodoo-like connection, that instantly links the two systems. This is faster than light, can't be shielded, and doesn't diminish with distance. It's a very mysterious connection.

However this connection is on the level of Reality, not on the level of Appearance. It's an underground connection, but it's as certain as two plus two is four that this connection exists. The question is what do you do with it, since it only appears on the level of Reality, not on the level of Appearance? So that's the essence of Bell's theorem: there is an underground connection that we can prove, but not see. I wrote a little song called "Bell's Theorem Blues," and the jist of it is, if we're really connected baby, how come I feel so all alone?

DJB: Do you see Bell's Theorem, and our understanding from astrophysics that all particles in the universe were together at the moment of the Big Bang, as being a possible explanation for mysterious phenomenon such as telepathy and synchronicity?

NICK: Yeah, I do. But I think that it would be too easy to say that because we're all connected we have telepathy. Because, again, why do we feel so all alone?

DJB: Doesn't it have something to do with the recency of the connection?

NICK: Yeah. If you make a connection, separate, and then make any other connections, those later connections will dilute the first connection. It's just as strong, but now you have another connection that's speeding into you. So it's a little bit like what's been called the coefficient of consanguinity, which measures how close people are linked genetically. Your mother is the closest to you, then your grandmother, and so forth on down. You're all linked by connections, but the more recent connections are the strongest. But even then, even when you've just met somebody, and separated, the telepathy between you is not really readily apparent. It would be be something, wouldn't it, if we lived in a society where the last person you met you had a telepathic contact with, until you met somebody else. That doesn't seem to happen, though, at least on the level we're aware of.

So the real question is why is telepathy so dilute? I would expect a proper science to explain that fact. Then, of course, once we had that explanation, we could increase it, make it greater, or overcome the diluteness if you didn't want to have telepathic contact with certain people. So that to me is the biggest mystery. Bell's Theorem

> *Bell's Theorem could explain telepathy, but what explains the lack of telepathy?*

could explain telepathy, but what explains the lack of telepathy? That's something I don't think anyone has really addressed. There are a few people who have addressed this fact on the level of psychology, but not physics, as to why we don't have telepathy. The most convincing answer that I know about is that it would be just too terrible to look into the hearts of people, because there's so much pain around that it would be excruciating to tap into that.

RMN: Also, it seems that a lot of people don't want to be that open about themselves, maybe they don't want people seeing into them.

NICK: There's that too—I don't want people to look into me. But suppose you want to look into other people? A reason not to do that would be that it would be very painful.

RMN: There seems to be an idea among physicists that by persistent analysis, they will eventually discover the fundamental particle, the stuff from which all matter is formed, and yet they continue to discover smaller and smaller versions of this particle. What are your thoughts on this?

NICK: Oh, ultimate particles, huh? I'd be perfectly content if physics came to an end—that quarks and leptons were actually the world's fundamental particles. Some people think this, that physics is coming to an end, as far as the direction of finding fundamental particles goes. It's okay with me. I don't think that's the most interesting way to go, looking for fundamental particles. You know my real notion is that consciousness is the toughest problem, and that physics has basically taken off on the easy problems, and may even solve them. We may find all the forces and all the particles of nature—that's physic's quest—but then what? Then we have to really tackle some of these harder problems—the nature of mind, the nature of God, and bigger problems that we don't even know how to ask yet. So, actually I'm not too interested in the problem of finding fundamental particles, but my guess is, from what we know now, that we're very close to that situation.

DJB: So you really do think that there is a fundamental particle?

NICK: Yeah, I do; it might be a quark or a lepton.

DJB: You don't think that quarks are made up of even smaller, more fundamental things, and that it goes on and on and on?

NICK: Naw, I don't think so. That's just my guess.

RMN: Could you describe what is meant by a "measurement"?

NICK: By a measurement? No, I can't. There's something in quantum physics called the measurement problem, and I could describe that. The main problem in quantum physics is that it describes the world differently when you measure it, than when you don't. When you don't measure it, when you don't look at the world, it's described as waves of vibrating possibilities, buzzing opportunities, promises and potentia. In some ways it's not quite real, and it's all vibrating. It sounds a little bit like drugs doesn't it? All these oscillating possibilities. Then when you look, it's perfectly normal. The possibilities change into actualities, and these actualities are point-like. They're called quanta, quantum jumps, like little dots on the TV screen, or on a color photograph in a magazine. So, to make it brief, the world changes from possibility waves to actual particles, from possibility to actuality, from waves to particles. And the door through which this happens is called a measurement. When you make a measurement, that's what happens, but quantum physics doesn't tell us what a measurement is. What's a measurement? No one knows. It's not in the theory. There are lots of guesses about what a measurement might be. Some extreme guesses are that consciousness has to be involved—only when some entity becomes aware, do the vibratory possibilities change into actualities. That's one guess.

> *The main problem in quantum physics is that it describes the world differently when you measure it, than when you don't.*

Another guess is that whenever a record is made, whenever something becomes irreversible, not take-backable, as long as you procrastinate your measurement, and refrain from making a real decision, then the world remains in a state of possibility. But as soon as it becomes irrevocable, then it's happened, and it's actual. So you look into nature for irrevocable acts, and that's where measurements happen. But, there are problems with both of these guesses. Physicists don't really have a really good model of what a measurement is. As I say, it's called the measurement problem in quantum physics, and it's the main philosophical problem. But fortunately, or unfortunately, physicists never have to confront this problem directly, because we know how to make measurements. We do it all the time. Even ordinary people know how to make measurements. So no one ever sees this quantum world directly, the vibratory possibilities, because we have ways of making measurements.

DJB: We have ways of making the universe unambiguous.

NICK: Yes, we have ways of making the universe unambiguous. They're called the senses. Now, it's my feeling that when we look inside we actually experience some of this quantum ambiguity. Looking inside is not actually making a measurement all the time. We can actually dwell in this, on the other side, the other side meaning the vibratory possibilities. Some of our mind is there all the time, and part of mental life is taking this vibratory possibility and transforming it into actualities. Not all of mental life, but with some of our mental life, that's what we do. So we're aware of both sides in our mental life, but not in this external life.

DJB: How has your study of quantum physics influenced your understanding of what consciousness is?

NICK: Yeah, we're already getting into that. I feel that quantum physics is one side of consciousness, it's the material manifestation of consciousness. Quantum physicists are basically describing something that's conscious, and the inside of quantum physics is what we experience as awareness. I mean, this notion of potentia becoming actual, doesn't that sound like what goes on in your mind?

DJB: From out of the realm of all things that are possible, we pick out a few things and make them actualities.

NICK: Yes. Exactly. Yeah, doesn't that sound like something mental beings do, making decisions?

DJB: Yeah, it does. So then do you think it's possible for consciousness to exist without a physical container, so to speak?

NICK: Yes, in a sense. But I don't think it's possible for our type of consciousness to exist without matter around. But it needn't be this kind of matter in your brain. Different minds, different highs. The kind of practice we humans know about is taking possibilities and making them actual. You've got to have a universe to make them actual in. So we probably need matter then. It seems that our kind of consciousness and matter are inseparable. So that when I die, probably most of my consciousness dies with me, because it's an interaction between the big mind, the big possibilities, and the small range of possibilities alloted to human bodies. But I may change my mind. I've been reading Ian Stevenson's book *Twenty Cases Suggestive of Reincarnation*, where little kids, when they begin to talk, say, "You're not my mother and dad. My parents live in this other town about four miles away." Then they begin giving details about who their brothers and sisters are. It's very spooky stuff.

DJB: But there are other explanations besides reincarnation. They could be tapping into some kind of field or genetic memory, for example.

NICK: Oh, yes, definitely. But it certainly stretches your idea of what the mind is capable of, no matter what explanation you have. So I may have to revise my ideas. I would not believe in that ordinarily. I was perfectly willing to say that my individuality dies with my body. There might be a large mind that goes on, but this small mind probably dies with the body—the memories and that sort of thing. That's what I would have said before reading this book. I had always dismissed reincarnation as wrong. But Stevenson's book is very persuasive. He describes just twenty cases, but he has six hundred cases of more or less validity. And, of course, if any one of those cases is true, it would invalidate the notion that consciousness dies with the body.

RMN: You have described quantum theory as a theory of possibilities, and have emphasized that it constrains not just Appearances, but Reality itself. With this in mind, in which ways do you feel that the understanding of the quantum world can affect the barriers and structures in human experience, which act to limit the enjoyment of these possibilities?

NICK: Oh! The Pleasure Dome Project. Yeah, I would sum up my feelings in that area this way. It's to take the metaphor of inner space seriously—that there is an inner space, and that for some reason, some accident of biology and evolution, each of us is restricted to this tiny little cave in inner space. But there's this vast area that we could explore, including telepathic union with other caves, and even going into other non-human areas of mind. To me, quantum physics suggests this—that there is this potentia out there which we could basically surf. We do play with a little bit of it each day, but we could probably expand the area of possibility further. It's like we're living in a little tiny bay, and we could go out into the ocean. That's the possibility, I think, that quantum physics suggests to me. That someday we'll be able to go outside our own little bays, and go out into the great ocean of mind.

...someday we'll be able to go outside our own little bays, and go out into the great ocean of mind.

RMN: And voyage the quantum uncertainty, that sounds nice.

NICK: Yes, surfing in the quantum sea. There is something in quantum theory called the Fermi sea, which is the area of possibilities for electrons, all the possible spaces, the momentum and position spaces, that electrons can occupy. A metal's Fermi sea has a free surface. But an insulator has a lid on its surface so its Fermi sea of possibilities is completely full—all the way to the top. Since all possibilities are spoken for, the insulator has no new options. It just sits there, inert, and does not conduct electricity. But metals have lots of live possibilities open to them—all sorts of wave motion can occur on the surface of a metal's Fermi sea. So the reason that copper conducts electricity and polyethylene does not is related to this quantum picture of matter being made up of vibratory possibilities.

Metals conduct because their electrons possess lots of open possibilities. Insulators can be made to conduct by "doping" them—Yes that's what it's called—introducing certain impurities into the insulator which widen the realm of electron possibility. Now, if consciousness is somehow also a consequence of quantum possibility then that's one way I see of going—the literal expansion of consciousness, of getting out of our little caves. And somehow I think that quantum physics ought to help us do that. If we really did find a connection between mind and matter, and this was a quantum connection, then we'd find some way to get out of our caves, and hop into the ocean.

DJB: Nick, you do a column for *Mondo 2000* on "Fringe Science." Can you explain why you think this subject is important.

NICK: I worked awhile in Silicon Valley doing research, and we had a lot of talks there about what real research was. How could we build an environment that would encourage research? What they really wanted there was an environment that would encourage short-term, profit-making research. They didn't want a real environment for research. What I think a research environment should do is protect people for a while from practical life, from the day-to-day worries of making a living. It should also allow people to be wrong, so, you see, you're protected from the consequences of your thoughts too, and you don't have to worry. You can play around. A real playground, that's it, a giant playground, for a while.

Universities and industrial research labs should ideally provide this. They should provide playgrounds where people can mess around, without suffering the consequences of their messing around. But they don't do this in general. In general they're very timid places. People will follow fashion and profits. The industrial labs don't follow fashion so much as universities, but you gotta publish all the time. You gotta keep something going. So you're looking around and seeing what's hot, what the guys next door are doing. So fringe science is people who aren't bound by university and industrial constraints. They're just people who are out there, for their own reasons, and these people may really be a key to our next evolutionary jump. The people who are just out there possessed by, for whatever reason, some quirky notions of their own.

To my mind one of the quintessinal fringe scientists is a guy named Jim Culbertson in San Luis Obispo. He was a professor at Cal Poly for many years, and he worked at Rand Corporation for a while, so he worked for both the government and the educational establishment. But his real goal has been to work out a theory of consciousness. He wrote a book in the sixties called *The*

Minds of Robots, and he wonders how one could make robots that would have inner experience, just like us. He has this elaborate theory based on special relativity, and he's obviously been working on this for years and years and years, not listening to anybody, just off on his own little obsession. It's a beautiful kind of work—just totally out there, not connected with anything. And it may be partially right. We need more of these people, like Culbertson, off on their own trip. I would like to consider myself a fringe scientist, but I think even I'm too much affected by fashion, and by what my colleagues are doing. Although I try, I'm contaminated by the opinions of my peers, by the prevailing fashions of the avant garde.

DJB: Well, there's something to be said for networking with other people though—cross-fertilizing and sharing ideas.

NICK: Yes, it's important to have colleagues, but you have to somehow keep your independence. There's this balance between contact and independence that you have to keep. One of the ways that I currently manage to do this is by living out in the woods, and by not being connected with any institutions, except these private ones that we set up. We've had something going called the Consciousness Theory Group, which Saul Paul-Sirag and a few others started in the early seventies to ruthlessly track down the roots of consciousness. We would go anywhere, talk to anybody, or do anything to find out more about this elusive problem.

RMN: Einstein spent his life searching for a unified field theory, and many scientists are working towards the same thing. Do you think it's just a matter of time before it is discovered, and how do you think that the understanding of the unified field will effect human consciousness?

NICK: As I mentioned before, I think we're close to that. It wouldn't surprise me if the unified field were discovered in the next couple of years. Somehow this might just succeed. It would mean that we have a picture of the world that was more compact. It wouldn't take so much talk to describe what the world was made of. You could simplify it. Right now there are four different kinds of forces, and there are a hundred and some different elementary particles. However, they still come in two classes. The classes themselves are quarks and leptons basically, and the force particles. What we would be able to say then is that there is just one kind of entity, and everything follows from that. So, it would be a definite economy of description. But what else? I don't know any practical applications of this, but it'd be definitely easy to describe the world. You could just say it's just made of this one kind of stuff, and that's all—everything else is just various manifestations of this one kind of stuff.

DJB: Would it make any new technologies possible?

NICK: Probably not right away. This is all very impractical. It would still leave consciousness out in the cold. It's funny that back in the Medieval days people doing alchemy and ceremonial magic—thought of as the predecesors of science—felt that the mind was connected with what they did. They thought that one had to be in the right state of mind—you had to say prayers and incantations—or the reaction wouldn't work. It sort of mixed up the notion that chemistry, physics, and mental stuff were all together in their mind. So at some point in the development of science, scientists said, "Let's do science as though the mind didn't matter. Let's see how much science we could do that's independent of how you think. Let's forget about the mind, and let's see what we could do with this hypothesis." And, amazingly enough, with all physics—from the elementary particles all the way up to the cosmos—it doesn't seem to matter. There seems to be a lot you can do without bringing the mind into it. Seemingly.

> *...at some point in the development of science, scientists said, "Let's do science as though the mind didn't matter.*

Now, my fantasy is that we've missed most of the world. That all the stuff that physicists can explain is just a tiny amount of the real world, because there is a real world that physics is a minute part of. But, because of a certain illusion that we have, it looks as though there's an awful lot of matter around here, and not much mind. Mind is confined to little tiny elements in certain mammalian heads. But there's a lot of matter, there's galaxies and quarks, and everything all around, but not much mind. One of my guesses is that's totally wrong. There's a lot of mind, at least as much as there is matter, and we just aren't aware of it. I suspect that physics is just a very tiny part of that world.

DJB: This really ties in with the next question. Do you see the physical universe as being alive, evolving, and conscious, and if so, does this perspective, in your opinion, have any influence on how physicists approach the natural world?

NICK: It does fit right in. Up to now physics has, I think as a kind of exercise, asked how much can we explain about the world without ever bringing consciousness into it? Surprisingly, the answer is a lot! Suppose there were chemical reactions that needed to be prayed over before they worked, then physics would have to say we can't explain these reactions, because that involves the mind. Anything that involves intention, where intention is important for its outcome, is outside of physics, by definition. So, we have to call that something else. Either that, or expand the notion of what physics is—once the mind begins becoming involved with the world. What I'd like to see are hybrid types of experiments.

Experiments where the mind is necessary, and where matter is also necessary, kind of a mixing of physics and psychology. But I don't know of any such experiments, except maybe psychokinesis experiments, and those are very unreliable. It's hard to get data.

RMN: The mind is a very unreliable thing. That's probably why physicists have nothing to do with the mind.

NICK: Yeah, unreliable, that's one way of looking at it.

DJB: What possibilities for faster-than-light and time travel do you feel offer the greatest potential for actualization, and how do you feel this will effect human consciousness in the future?

NICK: Well, I think that there are about half a dozen options for faster-than-light travel, but the two I would bet on are the space-warp, and the quantum connection. The former is based upon the ability to warp Einsteinian space-time. You can make short cuts in space-time, and essentially travel faster than light. We don't know how to do this yet, but the equations of general relativity allow it. So, it's not forbidden by physics. We may have to use black holes or something like tongs made out of black holes. It would take that kind of thing. Interestingly, when my book *Faster Than Light* came out in November of 1988, the same week it came out, there was a paper by three guys from CalTech in the journal *Physical Review Letters*. The article was about a way to make a time machine, using warped space-time.

It was actual instructions on how to do it. We can't do it yet—but here's, in principle, how to do it. There are these quantum worm holes coming out of the quantum vacuum. They're little connections between distant places in space-time. They're not so distant actually, as the distances involved are smaller than atomic dimensions. So you have to find out how to expand these worm holes, to make them connect larger more distant parts of space and time. But that's a detail. These worm holes are continually coming out of the quantum vacuum, popping back in again, and they're unstable. Even if you could go into one of these, it would close up before you could transverse it, unless you could go faster than light.

So, the argument was about how to stabilize quantum worm holes. The way you do that is you have to have some energy that's less than nothing, some negative energy, which is less than the vacuum. In classical physics that would be impossible—energy that's less than nothing. Every time you do something you always have positive energy. But there's something called the Casimer force in quantum physics, which is an example of negative energy. So you thread these worm holes with this negative energy, and it props them open. So then you can use these things as time tunnels.

This article was prompted by Carl Sagan's book *Contact*. Sagan got in touch with these physicists, who were experts on gravity, and asked if there was anything that he needed to know, because in his book *Contact* there were tunnels that go to the star Vega, I believe. You sit in this chair, you go through this time tunnel, and a few seconds later you're in Vega. That's definitely faster than light, as Vega is some tens of light years away. So these aliens have mastered this time tunnel technology. Carl Sagan asked these guys if this was possible, and they said "Well, we'll think about it." So they came up with this actual scientific paper on how one might really build a time tunnel, like Carl Sagan's. So here's a situation where science fiction inspired science.

DJB: Isn't that the case a lot, actually?

NICK: Ah, not really. I guess there are some things. Of course Jules Verne wrote about trips to the moon long before before we went.

RMN: Maybe a lot of people become scientists, after reading science fiction.

DJB: I would just imagine that many scientists had read science fiction when they were young.

NICK: I certainly did. I read a lot of science fiction when I was young. I loved it. Still do. But I don't know about specific inventions coming from science fiction—where someone reads a science fiction book, and then goes out and works on that particular idea. I think the influence is more general. But this is one example where a specific science fiction story—Carl Sagan's *Contact*—influenced, at least in principal, a time machine. The other possibility for faster than light-travel, aside from using space warps, would be to somehow use this Bell connection. I don't think we can send anything concrete this way, but maybe information or mental influences could go between minds faster- than-light. But, unlike these three CalTech people, there's no demonstration of how one could do that. I spent about three or four years trying to use Bell's connection to send signals faster than light, using thought experiments and such, and every one of them has failed. It looks as though this Bell connection is something that nature uses to further her nefarious ends, but people can't use the Bell connection.

RMN: How would you test the results of a time travel experiment?

NICK: Wouldn't that be easy? If you wanted to send something back in time... Ah... I guess, you're right, it would have already happened, wouldn't it? Well, a lot of these time travel experiments depend on what your opinion of the past is. Is the past always the same, or is it changeable? Are there alternate universes? It's a good question. That really depends on your model of the past. If the past is not changeable, then you can't go back in time, or you already have, and you're the results of it. One of my best guesses is that the past is partially changeable—there are things there that are frozen, that you can't change, and there are other things that are up for grabs, that are still in the quantum potentia, and those things you could change. So, when you went back there you could have some funny restrictions on your activities, and basically you could only make changes that were consistent with what we already know to have happened here. We have this present. There's a lot that we know has happened. There's lots of things we didn't care about, and nobody knows whether they happened or not. Those things you could change. But you couldn't change something that some human being knew had happened already.

DJB: As long as it's an ambiguity, and hasn't become a actuality.

NICK: Yes, as long as it hasn't become an actuality you could change it.

DJB: Why do you think it is that time appears to flow in one direction only?

NICK: God, who knows? That's a good question. It's a psychological reason I think. Einstein said something about how the past and the future are illusions. Physics makes no distinction between past and future. The present doesn't have any special status in physics. In four-dimensional space-time, it's all just a huge block universe that's eternal. So, the fact that time seems to flow is a kind of illusion that our kind of existence gives rise to. It's an illusion of consciousness rather than anything in physics. It's funny that if we didn't know any better, if we just took the equations of physics as truth, we wouldn't even know about this flow of time, this illusion. The universe would seem to be a kind of eternal, ever-present process.

> *Physics makes no distinction between past and future.*

RMN: You have asked, "Why does nature need to deploy a faster than light subatomic reality to keep up merely light speed macroscopic appearances." Could you venture an answer to your own question?

NICK: That's the idea that, although Bell's theorem says of Reality that once some things are together they are always connected faster than light, Appearance is not. You don't ever see anything like this. Why does nature bother to go to so much trouble? Underground connecting everything, and yet above ground it's not connected. Why bother? Sounds a little bit like God, doesn't it? This omniscient entity lying behind the phenomena that keeps its kind of divine providence, so that nothing gets lost. I don't know. That's still a puzzle to me, why that is. I would not like to believe in an omniscient divine providence, because it seems such an easy solution.

I've been spoiled by learning about quantum physics. One of the things that philosophers try and do, is they guess what all the possibilities are for human thought. Try and second guess all thinkable things. Philosophers worry about different categories of mind, monism and dualism, and varieties of that, all the possible ways something could be. People have been doing that for a long time, but they never came up with something as weird as quantum theory. Physicists didn't like quantum theory at first either. We were forced into this strange way of thinking about the universe by the facts, into a way that had not been anticipated by the philosophers. Quantum theory is a strange mixture of waveness and particleness that no one had ever anticipated, and that we still do not completely comprehend.

DJB: Isn't it similar to what Eastern philosophies have to say about the world?

NICK: Oh, in some sense, but not in particulars. There's a vague similarity to Eastern philosophy, more than to Western philosophy, that's true. But this notion of probabilistic waves changing into actual particles has never been present in any Eastern philosophy. Eastern philosophy talks about connectedness, everything being connected. It talks about the Tao, that's unspeakable, wholeness that envelops everything, and the flavor of that is like quantum theory. There's no doubt about that. More so than a mechanistic clock-work universe. But the details—

...quantum mechanics was just a kindergarten lesson for how we're going to have to change our minds to make the next step.

no one ever anticipated that kind of universe. So, my guess is that, when we get a fuller picture of the world, it will be equally unguessable. It would not have been anticipated, and quantum mechanics was just a kindergarten lesson for how we're going to have to change our minds to make the next step.

DJB: It wouldn't be fun without surprises.

NICK: Well, yeah, not only surprises, but that all our guesses have got to be, and are always going to be, too timid. Nature is going to overwhelm us, and surprise us with the next step. Nothing we could imagine will be as amazing as what's actually there. So whenever someone comes up with a simple solution like there's a divine providence underneath it all, it's too simple. Try and imagine something more complex and marvelous than that, please.

DJB: Nick, one of my favorite ideas in your book *Faster Than Light* was the notion that time travel may only be possible into the future and back into the past, only so far as to the development of the first time machine. If we were to take a leap of faith, and imagine this scenario to actualize itself, how do you envision that monumental day to occur, when the first time machine is invented, and everyone from the far future comes back to visit the historic day?

NICK: Big party. Sure, that's what it would be like. It would be very crowded that particular day. From that point on, life would be very confusing, when all of space-time is open to our view.

DJB: What would that do to human consciousness? How would the progression of events occur? How could people keep track of things?

NICK: I don't know. I think it would be very confusing. Much more confusing than it is now. We'd learn to live with it, though. What it would be like, partly, is that time would just be another kind of space, if you can imagine that. We don't think that traveling back and forth in space is so strange. We have this prejudice that we shouldn't be able to do that in time. So if time becomes another kind of space, what are the consequences of that? I don't know. It's really hard to think about. I have to pass on that one. Another problem related to that is when you go faster than light, time and space, in the equations, they reverse. The roles of time and space reverse when you go faster than light. I don't know what that means. This reversal happens in the math but what would happen in the world? This same time/space reversal happens, by the way, in the vicinity of black holes.

RMN: What about time travel paradoxes? Like the case of being able to travel backwards through time to kill your grandmother. The parallel universe theory seems to resolve this, but what are your views on this?

NICK: Yes, the easiest way to resolve that would be to have a parallel universe, where you kill your grandmother, but she's not your grandmother, she's the grandmother of somebody else, who would have looked very much like you, who doesn't get born in that parallel universe. Another way of resolving that paradox, is this notion I mentioned before about there being fixed things and soft things in the past, and you can only change the soft things. So that things that are fixed like your grandmother's existence, you'd find that you couldn't change. My guess is that when you went back in time, it would be like in a dream, where there were certain things you could do. If you tried to do something that would change the past, you couldn't move that way. You

> *My guess is that when you went back in time, it would be like in a dream...*

could only make certain moves. It would be like being in molasses. In certain ways you'd find it very easy to move, and others you just couldn't do, because it would be that that had already been definitively done.

RMN: It had been filled up.

NICK: Yes, it would be filled up. That had already been done. So there are islands of reality in the past, but they float in a sea of possibility. As far as I know, that's original with me, that solution to time travel paradoxes. The place to look is in science fiction, for solutions to time travel paradoxes. There are a number of very original solutions to that.

DJB: What are some of the best ones?

NICK: Well, the most popular is with alternative universes. Science fiction's full of them. Another is that you can visit the past, but can't change it. You can only change the future through your time machine. You just become a disembodied viewpoint in the past, and you can't act at all. There's nothing you can do to change all that, it's like watching a movie. But if you go to the future, you can change the future. That's a pretty good one I think, but I wouldn't bet on it.

DJB: What do you think lies in the center of a black hole?

NICK: Well, there's supposed to be the dreaded singularity there, where space and time are infinitely warped. Talk about warped—everything is infinitely warped there, and nothing, not even light, escapes. All physics stops. Matter as we know it would be crushed to a mathematical point. It's bad news. The center of a black hole is a bad trip. Some physicists claim that quantum mechanics would intervene before that happens, but they haven't proved that. It looks as though everything is just crushed to this infinite density, including time itself. Time and space itself are just crushed out of existence. Physics ends at the center of a black hole. No one knows what goes on.

RMN: You say that quantum tantra could revolutionize human relations. What do you mean by this?

NICK: Well, it's related to us getting out of our little caves, and into the open ocean. I envision it as a way of exploiting and enjoying Bell's Theorem, of actually bringing the Bell connection into being. Bell's Theorem talks about this voodoo-like connection, and one of the preoccupations of voodoo is love charms—to make other people love you, and to break up a couple where you'd like to love one of the members of the pair. So, these making and breaking spells are what I envision quantum tantra to be—love charms that work because of physics. Some kind of thing you could do, object you could exchange, or medium you could plunge into, that would either connect you, correlate you, unconnect you, or anti-correlate you. There are Bell connections where you have opposite correlations. They make you unlike, rather than alike. There are these Bell correlations and Bell anti-correlations flickering in the world of particle physics. They eternally hold the world together, which is the basis of all chemical bonds. So one could imagine these occuring at the level of human beings. So, that's what I imagine quantum tantra to be, a way of exploiting the Bell connection on the human level. But I don't have the slightest idea how one would go about doing that. Just guesses.

DJB: Could you tell us about your plans for a "Pleasure Dome" project, and how do you see the future science of pleasure advancing? What new forms of pleasure do you forsee for our future?

NICK: Well, of course, some would find quantum tantra pleasurable—the union with another human being, at the quantum-mental level of existence—although others would find it horrible. So it would be both. The Pleasure Dome Project is an idea to use fundamental physics to increase pleasure for the pursuit of happiness—to put the pursuit of pleasure on a firm scientific basis, rather than in the amateur ways we've pursued it so far as individuals. Amplification and enhancement of the senses is probably the easiest way to do it. Find out how our senses work, and just increase that process.

> *The Pleasure Dome Project is an idea to use fundamental physics...for the pursuit of happiness.*

I was talking with Greg Keith about the pleasure dome project as we were walking down here along the San Lorenzo River, and noticed that there's a pleasure research facility here on the beach—the Santa Cruz Beach Boardwalk. Places like that offer clues to the nature of pleasure. What happens here at the Beach Boardwalk? People get scared out of their life in safe environments. So, this must partly be what pleasure is. To be scared, but to really be safe. To be frightened, but secure. So we have to look about for new ways of doing that—scaring the hell out of people, but making them secure at the same time. So there'll be some scary rides at The Pleasure Dome, I think, but ultimately safe.

RMN: Could you tell us a little bit about telesensation?

NICK: Oh, that's one of my favorites. Telesensation is the idea of achieving a new body image by building robots of various kinds, and linking with them—through radio or optics—and taking on their body image. Taking on the body image of a human robot, or a robot that's shaped like a fish, an eagle, or a bat, and just being that entity for awhile—taking on their trip, and sensing with their senses, with an ant or an eagle's sense.

RMN: It'd be great for ecology.

NICK: Great for ecology yes!

DJB: Are you familiar with Jaron Lanier's work, building Virtual Reality simulators at VPL Research up in Palo Alto?

NICK: Oh, no, I don't know about this. I've heard rumors of this kind of research, but I don't know anyone who's actually doing it. There have been some science fiction stories about telesensation, where it's used to develop or do work on the surface of planets like Jupiter. In one story I recall the man is actually in orbit around Jupiter, but he feels as though he's on the surface of Jupiter, in a gravity of 30 Gs, or something like that, and doing mining work.

DJB: The Japanese have actually already developed something like that.

NICK: Is that right?

DJB: Yeah, it's written up in Grant Fjermedal's *The Tomorrow Makers*. Grant talks about the out-of-body experience he had using one of these machines, while looking at his body from a convincing three-dimensional perspective outside of it.

NICK: Well, one of the things I wonder about is this—if consciousness really is separate from the body, how come there are cases of multiple personalities—where many personalities inhabit one body—but there's never the case of one personality inhabiting two bodies—where you look out of somebody else's eyes, or out of two people's eyes at the same time? If consciousness were really distinct from the body, you might think that would be at least a possibility.

DJB: Some people claim that, though.

NICK: They've looked out of other people's eyes?

DJB: Some people claim that they've formed a unification between their consciousness and that of another person.

RMN: Usually a couple.

NICK: Well, if I couldn't see something, but because I was in this state, then I could. If that actually happened, then I'd be impressed. I would think that quantum tantra would allow us to do this. That would be one of the tests of quantum tantra, the ability to watch TV facing away from it. Not a very impressive ability, is it? There might be other, more interesting things to do with this, than watching TV with your back to the television. You can do that with a mirror I guess, without the threat to your integrity.

RMN: The penultimate question. I hear you've been working with technology with which to contact the dead. Can you tell us about your ideas and experiences concerning this?

NICK: This is a notion that quantum processes are somehow connected with consciousness, that some quantum processes are unspoken for, and can be taken over by discarnate spirits. So what we do is, we get these quantum processes, and link them to communicating devices. Then we encourage spirits to inhabit the processes and speak to us through quantum mechanical mediums. If the dead can occupy brains, why can't they occupy these machines? So in the seventies we tried to make machines that discarnate spirits could inhabit. These involved radioactive sources connected with computers, and they were connected with typewriters or with speech synthesizers. So, when we turned the machine on, it would rapidly type pseudo-English, or make sounds which one observer said sounded like a Hungarian reading *Finnigan's Wake*. I don't think our devices were complicated enough to be occupied by spirits.

RMN: Complicated enough?

NICK: Complicated. Like they were maybe the brain of an ant, something like that, or maybe even smaller.

RMN: It was just too basic.

NICK: Yes, it was just too basic a system. What we would want is a more complicated quantum system.

RMN: But you were getting something.

NICK: Oh, we got some funny prankish things that occured. The most exciting thing happened at a Houdini seance, when we spent all day trying to get Houdini to come back from the dead through our typewriter. This was on the hundredth anniversary of his birth, and it was in San Francisco. We had Houdini posters up on the walls. We held seances in the dark, joined hands, and lit candles, the typewriter chatting away all the time—a metaphase typewriter this was called. A couple of people dropped acid for the event. We went through the text and couldn't find any real printing, any real message, but the one thing that we did find that happened for sure, was right at the beginning—the typewriter jammed. It didn't print straight, so there were these lines of type going all over the place, and they made a little frame, a little oval, that wasn't typed in. There was one line in the oval, and it said, "In an infinite time." All with no spaces—"inaninfinitetime"— something like that. Now that message could be taken many ways. A million monkeys typing on a typewriter could type anything in an infinite time. An infinite time could be meaning to talk to us, a busy signal, that kind of thing. The ultimate busy signal.

In any case, it convinced me that the universe has a sense of humor. It's really about the funniest thing that could have been said in a few words. But nothing else seemed to occur that particular day. We had pounds of stuff to go through. Actually, this page was lost. Afterwards, we'd all saw it, but people had taken some of the pages for souvenirs, and I guess somebody got that one, and we never found out where that page ended up. So it's another one of those experiments that doesn't have any data. We don't have that sheet anymore. So it depends on the memory of all of us. Thomas Edison apparently worked

> *...the universe has a sense of humor.*

on experiments to contact the dead, and there is a videotape about some of his exploits. I guess someone had a movie camera around, and had caught this for posterity. There's a videotape, it's something about collected weirdness, and it's just full of like *Mondo Cane*, or something like that. One of the scenes in this videotape, which I read about, was Edison, and his early model of something to talk to the dead with. But it never worked, he never got it to the point where it actually worked.

DJB: Edison would be a good person to try to contact probably, because he had an interest in it.

NICK: Well, there actually were some people who tried that. Yeah, Gilbert Wright, the inventor of Silly Putty, and some friends of his tried to build a machine to contact Edison. They claimed to get Edison through mediums, and Edison actually, through these trance mediums, gave them instructions for building a machine, through which he would try and talk. It involved batteries and radio-like devices, but Edison wasn't able to use that machine. It didn't work.

DJB: Could you tell us about any projects that you're presently working on?

NICK: Well, my next project is going to be a book on the mind called *Elemental Mind*. It's a book on a long-shot model of mind. All the smart money these days, for a model of consciousness, seems to be put on either of two models—a computer or a biological model. The computer model assumes that the mind is some kind of software in the hardware of the brain, some kind of exquisite software that involves a self-image—it's a self-image program, a little "I." I was talking to a friend of mine—his slogan is "We're the guys that put the I in IBM." You could have conscious computers that would have these little software programs, with self-awareness built into them.

RMN: Little egos.

NICK: Little egos, yes. That's one guess, that the mind is the software in the hardware of the brain. The other guess is that mind is somehow an emergent feature of certain complex biological systems—that it will arise whenever the biology gets complicated enough. Self-awareness is just an unsuspected evolutionary possibility of living meat. *Elemental Mind* explores the hypothesis that none of that is true. It's a long-shot—that mind is as fundamental to nature as light or electricity. It's all around in one form or another, and our minds are just specific examples of it, specific ways that the Universal Mind has manifested. So I'm looking for evidence for this sort of thing, and ways of making *Elemental Mind* more plausible. By the way, I tried to think of a word for the other kind of mind, and the best I could come up with is molecular mind. Molecular mind versus elemental mind. Molecular mind is where you put stuff together and make a mind, and elemental mind is where mind is already fundamental. So you don't have to make it, it's already there. All you have to do is have systems that will manifest it. So my latest project is to work on that, and make that make sense.

> *...elemental mind is where mind is already fundamental.*

Paul Schraub

Ralph Abraham

"Chaos is very much the same as the steady state;
it's not scary at all."

Chaos and Erodynamics
with Ralph Abraham

Ralph Abraham is renowned for bringing a fresh perspective to mathematical thought. His study of dynamical systems as the building blocks of reality, has led him to extrapolate fundamental mathematical principles into his philosophical outlook. A Professor of Mathematics at the University of California, Santa Cruz, he received his Ph.D. at the University of Michigan in 1960. He taught at UC Berkeley, Columbia and Princeton before moving to Santa Cruz in 1968 and has held visiting positions in such various locations as Amsterdam, Paris, Warwick, Barcelona, Basel, Florence and Siena.

He is the author of numerous mathematical books. Linear and Multi-Linear Algebra, Foundations of Mechanics *was written with J.E Marsden and* Transversal Mappings and Flows *with J.Robbin. He wrote* Manifolds,Tensor Analysis and Applications *with J.E Marsden and T. Ratiu, and the highly successful four-volume* Dynamics, the Geometry of Behaviour *with C.D Shaw. His latest book entitled,* Trialogues on the Edge of the West *is a group of discussions with Terence McKenna and Rupert Sheldrake on the relationship between science, philosophy and religion.*

Travelling through Europe in his twenties, living in a cave in northern India and working as a professional gambler in Las Vegas were all experiences which helped to shape Ralph's philosophical outlook. He has been active on the research frontier of dynamics in mathematics since 1960, and in applications and experiments, since 1973. In 1975 he founded the Visual Mathematics Project at the University of California, Santa Cruz to explore the use of interactive computer graphics in teaching mathematics. He is the founding editor of Eagle Mathematics *and* Applied Global Analysis.

We talked with Ralph on March 4th 1989, in the cozy living room of our dear and mutual friend Nina Graboi, who has often worked as his editor. We found him to be a soft-spoken, intensely thoughtful and down-to-earth character, with the gentle tone of a person who has become philosophically resigned to seeing further than others.

—RMN

DJB: Ralph, you're recognized as one of the leaders in the mathematical study of chaos. Can you tell us what it was that originally inspired your interest in mathematics and the mathematics of vibrations and dynamical systems?

RALPH: Well, I didn't get interested in dynamics and decide that's what I was going to study. It was just left foot, right foot, or some series of miracles. It happened like this.

I was an engineer and worked in a physics project, so I became a student of physics. Then one day a physics professor said in class that if you want to understand physics you have to study mathematics. So I changed to mathematics at that point. And I found a mentor, somebody who took care of me and helped me out, a wonderful man, Nate Coburn. I started studying what he was doing because he was my only contact in mathematics. One reason I responded to his program was that it had to do with general relativity. Einstein had been a household word when I was growing up. My father respected Einstein very much. It was said that only eight people in the world could understand Einstein. My teacher apparently could and was writing in that field.

I had taken very few math courses during that period. I remember two or three very influential courses. One of them was a differential geometry course taught by Raoul Bott who became a very famous mathematician. Some concepts were included in that course that I later found useful in dynamics, So I had some math background, but not the kind of background I would have had if I'd done a Ph.D. under a famous professor of dynamics.

Then I was looking for a job. I had one offer for some place where I didn't want to go and at the last minute, before the school year began, I got a letter from Berkeley offering me a job. In 1960 there wasn't any big mathematical center there, but of course I took it.

After I got to Berkeley I was engaged in rewriting my thesis for publication. One day I discovered that they were having tea in some little room in the back of the building, and I had already been there for two or three months and hadn't met anyone. So I went to the tearoom to meet some people and to find out what was going on. And in this way I discovered a couple of people who later became my best friends in mathematics. They happened to be there in September of 1960, along with a lot of other people that I met. Everybody had just arrived. Overnight, Berkeley had become one of the most important mathematical centers in the world—and I just happened to be there, apparently because of a clerical error.

One of the people I met that day at tea was Steve Smale. I was done rewriting and was looking for something new to do. So I said, "What do you do?" and he said, "Well, stop by the office and I'll show you." The next day I stopped by his office and we started working together. Later I found out that he was a really famous mathematician. He won the Fields Medal which is the mathematical equivalent of the Nobel Prize for doing the very work that he was showing me.

So I found myself on the research frontier in mathematics, working with some really wonderful people who all thought I was fine, because in this group there was no insecurity. It was just, "This is what we do and if you fit in, fine." So we worked together and had great fun. We had fantastic parties where we played music and danced and got drunk and we did a lot of creative work in what became a new branch of mathematics called "global analysis." And all this happened in just one or two years. Part of this program was "non-linear dynamics" as practiced by mathematicians on the research frontier at that time, using tools called "differential topology." It's a far cry from what people are doing now under the name of chaos, non-linear dynamics, and so on, that you read about in stories like Jim Gleick's book *Chaos*.

All that I did in those early days was mathematical. It could be explained to a lay person without some very hairy preparation, and I've tried to make that explanation possible in my four picture books called *Dynamics: The Geometry of Behavior*. The third of these four books is devoted to "tangles." In 1960, Steve Smale and I would take turns at the board drawing these tangles and trying to make some sense out of them and figure out what was going on. Tangles are like the skeleton of a beast. If you go into the Museum of Natural History and there's a skeleton of a dinosaur hanging from the ceiling, you can walk around it and from the skeleton you can imagine the whole thing. But if you saw the whole thing you couldn't see the skeleton inside without an x-ray machine. It's just like a blob. These tangles are the skeletons of chaos. We didn't discover them; they were known to Poincare in 1882 or so.

> *Tangles are like the skeleton of a beast... These tangles are the skeletons of chaos.*

In 1960 we were just trying to figure out these skeletons and relate them to the eventual behavior of all dynamical systems, which includes practically everything in the world: that's all kinds of processes, including the human process and the process of history itself. All these are dynamical systems, their skeletons are these tangles, and the tangles have aspects known under these words: fractal, chaotic, and so on. But they are much more: they are highly regular, they're dynamic, they're symbolic, they're mythical and they're beautiful. In fact, they're mathematical.

DJB: Just so that everyone is familiar with the extraordinary work you do, can you briefly explain what chaos theory is about and what role you are playing in this exciting new field of research?

RALPH: Chaos theory is a small branch of dynamics which is a very important region of the intellectual frontier. It overlaps mathematics, the sciences, and computer science, but it's not any of those things. It's not a branch of physics or of mathematics—it's dynamics! So we have a really unusual area which is not mathematics and it's not science, it's not a department of the university and there are no dynamicists with titles of "professor of dynamics."

But in spite of the fact that it hasn't been acknowledged, it is a really central human activity and really important to our adventure of understanding the world around us. I would say that its position is mid-way between mathematics and science. Mathematics is not science—science has all these branches, and mathematics is not one of them. Mathematics is completely separate in its philosophical outlook and in the personality of the people who pursue it, who are somehow diametrically opposite to scientists. Scientists are bottom-up in their style of understanding and believing, while mathematicians are sort of top-down. Dynamics is a huge area in between, which comprises the encyclopedia of mechanical models used to understand processes.

Since we have to understand processes in science, dynamics is very important. I do not think that chaos theory is quite so important. The chaos revolution is the biggest thing since the wheel, but I don't think it's fundamentally important. Dynamics is providing us with process models which are much more important than chaos.

The chaos revolution is primarily important because chaos is everywhere. For some reason there was an historical accident, and for six thousand years people repressed chaos to the unconscious. So there has been a totally unnecessary gap where there should have been chaos theory. And the filling of this gap is really a big thing only because the gap was there. But after it's filled, it is perfectly normal to have chaos models, and wheel models, and static models. It was very bizarre that among

> *...for six thousand years people repressed chaos to the unconscious.*

all these models there was such a huge gap. But now it's filled, now we're back to: "No big deal, aha, fine, so it's chaotic."

But dynamics is offering more. It's offering bifurcation diagrams, catastrophe models. It's offering fantastically good models for processes. And few of these models would actually be there on the shelf for our use in trying to understand the world around us if we denied the existence of chaos—because chaos is ubiquitous in process. You can't model process very well if you're in denial about the existence of chaos. You're certainly not able to model any process which is full of chaos, and that's practically all of them, most especially those involved with life, love and creativity. So we do have something important in dynamics, and chaos has an important role in a sort of double-negative sense. That's what's going on with dynamics.

As far as my work in it is concerned, I think it doesn't matter very much. Some people think I shouldn't waste my time at a computer terminal doing research on specific problems because my role is to go around saying what I just said.

DJB: What are some of the problems that you see with the present state of American mathematical education and how do you think improvements could be made?

RALPH: Well, I would say a good thing to do with mathematical education in the United States or in the world today would be just to cancel it and start over again from scratch, two or three generations later. The whole thing is in a really dangerous plight. And I've been saying this for years and so have other people, but only recently has the problem risen to a scale of national prominence where even the president and the governor and everybody's saying, "Well hey! our Gross national product might be threatened, because our people are no good at mathematics."

So we have a serious situation. First of all, mathematics is akin to walking as a human experience; it's just really easy. I mean it shouldn't be easy, how can you tell somebody how to walk, you know? But people do find it easy and they naturally learn how to do it. They just watch, and by imitation they can do it. It's the same with mathematics! It's part of our heritage, all of us, to be genius at mathematics. It is a completely human activity. It involves the resonance between prototypical objects in the morphogenetic field and specific examples of similar forms in the field of nature, as they're experienced by human beings through the doors of perception. And as life forms a resonant channel between these two fields, it's just as natural as understanding anything, including walking, playing tennis, and so on. Mathematical knowledge is part of our human heritage.

> *It's part of our heritage, all of us, to be genius at mathematics.*

Furthermore it's essential to evolution. Where there's no mathematical knowledge there can be no evolution, because evolution to a stable life form requires a kind of mathematical, sacred guidance. This can be understood in many different images, the least controversial one being that there would be a harmonious resonance between all of the components, parts, sub-systems and so on involved in the life process. Where there is an disharmonious resonance, or dissonance, there would be some kind of illness whether the organism is a snail, a human, a society, or the all and everything that we know by the name history. So for the harmonious resonance to be maintained during the process of our own growth, or social evolution, evolution requires mathematical understanding. You see the dissonance of the lack of mathematical understanding through the gross national product, or the number of wars, or the spread of AIDS, for example.

> *Where there's no mathematical knowledge there can be no evolution...*

Another importance of chaos theory is in correcting a problem in mathematical education that has consisted, in part, of denial. People have been taught the non-existence of some of the essential mathematical forms, namely, chaotic forms. This kind of denial produces an educated adult somewhat less capable than an uneducated adult. So that education which functions in this way is not the same as no education. It's worse, because it destroys intelligence, it destroys functionality, it destroys harmony with the resonance of the all and everything which is necessary for health. Our educational system, in short, is producing sickness and contributing to the global ecological problems on the planet by destroying the native intelligence that children have, the capability they have to understand the world around them in its complexity, in its chaos, in its resonance and harmony and love, destroying it through the inculcation of false concepts and through the production of avoidance mechanisms connected with certain mathematical ideas.

It's a very serious problem. One possible response would be to revise mathematical education so that, within the same system, one would try to provide teachers who are more highly trained. That could only make matters worse, you see, since the teachers are already highly mistrained. Many have already been taught to hate mathematics and so they can only teach hatred for mathematics. They don't really have any idea what mathematics is. For them, it's a knee-jerk response of this dark emotion, so retraining them more wouldn't help. Rather than revision of the schools—which are full of false ideas and bad habits built into the field on a deep level—the most efficacious, practical solution would be the construction of a new educational system outside the usual channels of the school system This is not too radical, as we have all been brought up to think of our real education as going on outside the school system. In school, for example we do have music classes, yet if parents want their children really to know music, they provide a separate teacher outside the school. We also have religious instruction and dance instruction outside the school—anything that you really want to learn is studied outside of the school. And so also it may be with mathematics.

I think that one practical solution to this challenge to create a school outside of school would be a new breed of learning machines based on computers, educational software, and digital video. Even programs like Hypercard on the Macintosh, for example, could provide alternative education that could be approached by individuals without teachers. So far, however, the creation of educational software has proved to be a very unrewarding activity for authors. And in spite of all different kinds of alternative funding agencies, nobody has seen this as a very important problem although the National Science Foundation, the American Mathematical Society and like organizations have convened conferences to discuss possible solutions of the crisis in mathematical education. The most promising alternative solution at this time has not been funded. And so there are very few existing alternatives for children now. Maybe after another generation or two there will be.

RMN: The principles of chaos theory and other mathematical ideas appear to echo in the myths and philosophies of some ancient cultures; the Greeks had a Goddess of Chaos, for example, and the *I Ching* is full of references to such ideas. What level of understanding do you think earlier civilizations had of these concepts and how was this expressed?

RALPH: Well, the repression of chaos began with the patriarchal takeover six thousand years ago. So to look at an example of a high culture accepting chaos as part of their mythological pantheon and in their arts and behavior, one has to go back before that takeover. And the most common example of such a culture is Minoan Crete. This culture was excavated by Sir Arthur Evans, and his recon-struction of the temples and religion, etc., have since been seriously questioned by archeologists. In short, there was a controversy as to what were their arts, their social patterns and so on.

A lot of things are known through mythology that are traced back to Crete. One thing that's known from paintings is the dance with bulls. There were the Bacchic mysteries, derived from the Orphic, the Dionysian and so on. Following this backwards, like tracing roots or Ariadne's thread, you come to a certain mythic kernel which would be associated with Minoan Crete. I wouldn't say these are expressions of chaos. They might be, but there are so many differences between our culture and the Cretan culture. We know something about Dionysian ritual: the importance of music in ritual, the dichotomy of religious ritual into two types, outdoors on the open plain and indoors in a cave. The mystic revelation that came with Gaia sees the planet as an organism, and the plain as its surface. Gaia is very chaotic, so if you reject chaos, you reject Gaia. It goes together: the orphic trinity of Chaos, Gaia, and Eros.

That's what I suggest to you to think about: Gaia as the Earth, the love of the planet, the integrity of life-forms; Chaos as the essence of life: more chaos is healthier; Eros as human behavior in resonance with Chaos and Gaia. It's rumored that the Minoans had a very high degree of bisexual activity, licentious behavior and wild parties. This may be the quality of the genders in a partnership society as described by Riane Eisler.

RMN: Why do you think it was that later Western Culture tended to view chaos as an undesirable quality in nature?

RALPH: Well, that's a very big question, and speculation can't be taken too seriously, but I think that this has to do primarily with the patriarchal takeover. The repression of Chaos, Gaia and Eros is characteristic of the patriarchal paradigm, which turned out to be the dominant one in our recent history. And it could be that sexual repression is somehow its key.

Human society is an evolving system—including its psyche, its mythology, its cultural structure. This evolution is punctuated by bifurcations, mutations caused by the planetary equivalent of lightning: comets. Comets were probably very important in the history of consciousness; they still are. There are some mutations where changes are made in the memes, the cultural genetic structure. Then there's a kind of natural selection which goes on when two societies are in conflict over a common goal, due to seasonal inundations and so on, and in this conflict one would be selected not just by military strength, but perhaps through the stability of its social structure.

And in the long run, in evolutionary history, there are dead ends. A lot of species become extinct without the necessity of a comet or of global catastrophe, but just because they're the wrong idea to begin with. It seems likely that the human species is the wrong idea to begin with and may not succeed in having a stable long-lived civilization on this planet. We know that Egyptian society lasted for three thousand years and that's a fine record for a society. Since the Renaissance we're up to one thousand years now, and we'll see how long this goes on. I'm not placing any bets. It may turn out that there are some structural flaws that are endangering the future of human habitation on this planet. The planet is in symbiosis with the human infection. This could be a very good symbiosis; it could mediate some sort of divine plan on a cosmic scale with the actual material of planet Earth, and that includes the consciousness of the human species. There is a certain promise there, I don't deny it.

> *It may turn out that there are some structural flaws that are endangering the future of human habitation on this planet.*

However, archaeologists coming from another star system in the future may say that a structural flaw in our society resulted in the advantage of patriarchy over the partnership model. It could be that the basis for the stability of our violent society is the nuclear family, so that the repression of Eros, Gaia and Chaos—the repression of the Bacchic, the Orphic, the Dionysian—by the patriarchy was chosen by people who had grown up in a nuclear family. And when two civilizations came into contact, the one that had the nuclear family won. This is just one possibility among many, in answer to your question why chaos was rejected.

The chaos societies had moon festivals such as we had in the sixties. This is no coincidence, because the sixties, the Italian Renaissance, the Renaissance of the troubadours in the twelfth century, the early Christianity, the Pythagorean Academy in Croton—all these have the common aspect of temporary resurgence of Orphic ideals, followed by massive and violent repression by the conservative society. All these have been foci in history for burning people at the stake. Of all the forms of terrorism, burning people at the stake seemed to be the most appropriate for the patriarchal society, in repressing revivals of the preceding form involving the Goddess. In the sixties, which was one of these Orphic revivals, we got to experience what life was like in Minoan Crete, in the Garden of Eden. We had moon festivals, and people abandoned themselves to their feelings, to Chaos, to Gaia, to Eros. Many of these groups, which experienced the Garden of Eden, eventually broke up. The sixties came to an end. A number of breakups were caused by patriarchal, sexual jealousy.

RMN: The trend of science towards reductionism led quantum physicists to the realization that the whole does not equal the sum of its parts. Now chaos theory seems to clarify this statement by saying that this is because we cannot know the sum of all the parts. What do you think are the implications of this idea in how we may arrange and organize information in the future?

RALPH: This is exactly the reason why I said that chaos theory isn't very important, except as a kind of double negative, while on the other hand, dynamical systems theory does offer something very important. We need to understand whole systems, and whole systems cannot be understood by reduction. The terrific gains in understanding made by the reductionist scientist will, I'm sure, be used in the future to understand whole systems by means of some process of synthesis. The reduced understanding of the biochemistry of the adrenal cortex, for example, will be synthesized into models of whole systems, such as the stress response and the immune system. The technology for modeling whole systems is on the frontier of science at the moment; it is the crucial frontier for the solution of our global, planetary problems.

> *The technology for modeling whole systems…is the crucial frontier for the solution of our global, planetary problems.*

Dynamical systems theory, specifically the branch called complex dynamics offers a strategy for the re-synthesis of fractionalized scientific knowledge, and an understanding of complex whole systems. Complex systems theory has replaced chaos theory on the fashion pages of the science newspapers of our day. And I think the fascination of intellectuals with complex systems theory is not going to be a short-lived flash in the pan. This is somehow the real thing. Our challenge now is the reintegration of the sciences after their dissolution in the Renaissance into an understanding of whole systems, particularly planetary systems, that is to say the hydrosphere, the lithosphere, the atmosphere, the biosphere and the noosphere.

> *…complex systems theory is not going to be a short-lived flash in the pan.*

Within the lower spheres, a new direction called global modeling is already under way. Global modeling tries to put together reductionist models people have made for the oceans, for atmospheric phenomena, and for solar radiation. Individual models made by reductionist scientists of these different areas—the oceanographers, the atmospheric chemists, the solar physicist—are being synthesized into one global model. This global synthesis requires two things. First of all it needs models for the separate components or organs of the planetary system to be made in a common strategy so that they can relate to each other. Secondly, it requires a wiring diagram to put them together. In the field of global modeling a tremendous synthesis is now taking place, including conferences on the wiring diagram, which will provide a global model of the geosphere.

For the sociosphere, we must start from scratch. We don't yet have many specialists producing mathematical models for society, although there are a few outstanding pioneering first steps. There are for example the archaeologists and anthropologists worrying about the demise of the Mayan civilization in Central America in the fifteenth and sixteenth centuries, because it was so complex and there are so many hypotheses, and it was such a controversial question, they tried to resolve it by building mathematical models. There are now a number of competing complex dynamical models for the Mayan society, taking into account the food chain, the weather, the population, and the distance between ceremonial centers.

All these factors are built into different competing models. Then they run them and try to see which one wins the best relationship to the archaeological data. And thus a model system can be created, because Mayan civilization was relatively small. This pioneering first step might lead to similar models for larger societies—for ancient Greece, for example, or for the downfall of Rome, where many more factors and more people were involved. Navigation, naval trade, the effect of inventions like better clocks for navigating: all these things might be included in the model.

So in the future then, as global planet models become more successful, global social modeling will begin. Then individual components have to be modeled, such as the political and economic systems of individual nations, their interactions, and so on. They have to be made into a common strategy, so they can be connected together. And then one has to extrapolate from the Mayan models and gain wiring diagrams for these different component parts, including psychological and medical factors. In the reductionist physical sciences, we will only have to connect existing components together, following a diagram, to get global models. For the social sciences we'll have to start from scratch.

We're going to have to make models for the organs, do experiments in simulation with various wiring diagrams, compare with data, improve the component models, the global models, the data, and so on. After many circuits of this hermeneutical circle we might create a global social model. Then the global planet model and the global social model have to be connected together. There's also the mythological and the spiritual dimension and the understanding of the world of the unconscious. In other words, the whole thing has to take place once again in the noosphere, and then that has to be connected up. Eventually, we hope to get some kind of model for understanding what—if any—are the effects of choices we could make upon our long-range future. This may never happen, but if it did, mathematics would be of use to Gaia in creating the future, through the direct, conscious interaction with the evolutionary process. This seems to be our challenge.

DJB: Could you tell us how your travels in India and the experiences you had in a cave there have influenced your outlook on life and mathematics?

RALPH: What I had done that was respected by mathematicians in the way of frontier research work was ancient history by the time I went to India and lived in a cave. So, to answer your question, I should first of all identify what I've done since then that could be regarded as mathematical. I would say that the computer revolution has presented enormous opportunities to mathematics, to the profession and to the individual mathematicians, which have not yet been seized. Many mathematicians have rejected the significance of computers, so far. But if we could say that experiments with computers represent mathematical research, you could see the evidence of my stay in India in the cave on my outlook on mathematics.

My computer experiments involve the concepts of vibration, harmony, resonance and mathematical models for these phenomena. We would like to understand how a person is in morphic resonance with a field, if these metaphors have any function from a perspective of pattern modeling, which is what I think mathematics is all about. The processes where this kind of metaphor is proposed—whether in the Indian Samkya philosophy or in Rupert Sheldrake's theory—are always in a living, biological, mental sphere. So the data, if there are any data, would necessarily be chaotic.

So first of all we would have to extend or map the notion of resonance from the circular sphere where the concepts first evolved in the context of chaos. When you have two strings of a guitar, you pluck one and the other one vibrates by so-called sympathetic vibration. This vibration is understood as a non-chaotic phenomenon; it is just oscillation. Each point on the string vibrates, left, right, left, right, left, right. So from this, which I'll call the circular or periodic domain, the concepts have to be extended to the chaotic. If the two strings were chaotic instead of periodic, which means they would sound raspy and noisy instead of harmonious and sweet, then could there still be a sympathetic vibration of one caused by the nearby chaotic vibration of the other?

I came back from India in January 1973. By January 1974 I was already involved in experiments with chaotic resonance, and this has dominated my research to the present day. For example, one discovery we made is that the Rossler attractor, which is one of the simplest of chaotic forms, does have sympathetic vibration as one of its characteristics. So after India I concentrated more on vibration and resonance, whereas before, we were involved with the general, skeletal structures of chaos. And they're related in that the theory of chaotic resonance is based upon an understanding of the skeleton, the so-called homoclinic tangles, as I've tried to explain in my picture books.

RMN: Could you tell us about your experience with John Lilly's dolphins?

RALPH: Well, I think that people who live in cities are not much in tune with animals. Actual communication with an animal is a rare experience for most of us. And some people are more sensitive to animals than others. They have a favorite pet, or they just really like animals. In my case, I grew up on the edge of town in Vermont, where they have, as it is said, two seasons: winter and July. Winter is very long, and a lot of times I was outside playing in the snow, usually alone. I used to go on long treks after school and on weekends on my skis, communing with animals and trying to figure out where they had been by the study of their tracks. And to this day I have a special love for animals, which is one of the reasons that I'm a vegetarian. I'm not only a vegetarian, but vegetarianism has a very great importance for me. It's a big thing, not just another habit.

Anyway, I like animals, and so I was very keen to swim with the dolphins. I had bought it, like most hippies, that dolphins are more intelligent than people. They had had the brilliance to flee to the sea a long time ago, and there they have lived in peace ever since, except for a few tuna fishermen. So I had a sort of double setup to have a good experience with these dolphins, and I had read a little bit about other people's experiences swimming with them. I knew that they have a very strong connection to the Orphic trinity of Chaos, Gaia and Eros. They're connected to Chaos most directly through the experience of hydro-dynamical turbulence, that is, white water.

Now white water is the most perfect chaotic thing we have: you hear it, you see it, you feel it—it's chaos personified. Dolphins know Chaos. They also know Gaia. They can find their way over great distances in the sea, their playground is thousands of miles across, they explore it all, they know their

Dolphins...are connected to Chaos...through the experience of hydro-dynamical turbulence, that is, white water.

way around. They can sing and speak to each other over tremendous distances. Through their sonar communication apparatus they have a global sense which transcends our own. And then as far as Eros is concerned it's rumored that they're loose, they're sexy and they like to get it on in the water.

So that's the background. I went to John Lilly's place in Redwood City for a routine swim with Rosie and Joe and had a fantastic experience with them. They were very violently playful. I had communicated nothing, I was just there, and I wasn't adequately prepared for what they actually do. They like to take your hand into their mouth and press, but not too hard. You have to have some sort of faith that they're not going to bite you, because they have very strong jaws and sharp teeth. So I was kind of scared of this mouthing game. And then they had the flying body game. They would go down to the bottom of the tank, which was pretty deep, turn around, get ready and let go with their maximum accelera-tion and velocity, heading straight toward you, turning aside only at the last minute to brush gently against your side. It was kind of heavy; they were very heavy with me.

I was trying to figure out what to do. Should I grab on and go for a ride? I tried that; they slowed down and became more gentle. If I played with one, the other one appeared to be jealous, but it was all a game. There were a lot of interesting things, very much like playing with people, or at least children. But I was a little scared because I'm not that great a swimmer and they were very good swimmers. My faith had flaws that day, I suppose.

Then I decided to try a mental experiment. We know they're mental—they have memory and intelligence and language and so on. So I proposed an experiment in telepathy. I swam out of the tank into a little nook or cranny to regroup. I had this fantasy of lying still in the water, and they would both lie still as well, and one of them would face me in the water so that we were co-linear, head to head on a straight line, and then we would just exchange thought without any further ado. They were thrashing around in the water. So keeping this picture in my mind I swam out again, and they both became totally still, just as I had visualized.

I believe it was Rosie who got into position: on a line, still, head to head and so on. And then I thought, "Okay, let's exchange a thought." Booom! Loud and clear came a thought. She said, "Do you think it's nice in this tank? Would you like to live in this tank? It's too small; it's ugly; it's dirty. We want out!" So I said, "Wow, yeah, I can understand that; I'm certainly going to get out pretty soon and I wish you could too." Then we played a little bit more and I got out. I wrote in the log book about this experience just as I told you. Later there was a revolt of John Lilly's crew over the question of conditions in the tank.

DJB: Have your experiences with psychedelics had any influence on your mathematical perspective and research?

RALPH: Yes. I guess my experiences with psychedelics influenced everything. When I described the impact of India and the cave on my mathematics I could have mentioned that. There was a period of six or seven years which included psychedelics, traveling in Europe sleeping in the street, my travels in India and the cave and so on. These were all part of the walkabout between my first mathematical period and all that has followed in the past fifteen years. This was my hippie period, this spectacular experience of the gylanic revival (G.R. wave), —after Riane Eisler—of the sixties.

I think my emphasis on vibrations and resonance is one thing that changed after my walkabout. Another thing that changed, which had more to do with psychedelics than with India, was that I became more concerned with the application of mathematics to the important problems of the human world. I felt, and continue to feel, that this planet is really sick; there are serious problems that need to be faced, and if mathematics doesn't have anything to do with these problems then perhaps it isn't worth doing. One should do something else. So I thought vigorously after that period about something I had not even thought about before: the relationship of the research to the problems of the world. That became an obsession, I would say.

DJB: Why do you think it is that the infinitely receding, geometrically organized visual patterns seen by people under the influence of psychedelics resemble computer generated fractal images so much?

RALPH: I don't know if they do, really. You know there's a theory of the geometric forms of psychedelic hallucinations based on mathematics by Jack Cowen and Bard Ermentrout. It has to do with patterns of biochemical activity in the visual cortex which is governed by a certain model having to do with neural nets. This model has geometric patterns in space-time, dynamical patterns, which are patterns that any structure of that kind would have. So these two mathematicians see psychedelic hallucinations as mathematical forms inherent in the structure of the physical brain. Now I'm not very convinced by that, but I think it's kind of an unassailable position. One cannot just argue it away on the basis of one's personal experience.

What I think about psychedelic visuals is not so different, except that I would not locate them in the physical brain. I think that we perceive, through some kind of resonance phenomenon, patterns from another sphere of existence, also governed by a certain mathematical structure that gives it the form that we see. I can't speak for everyone, but in my experience, this form moves. Now the historic pictures that they show us don't move. And the mathematicians of fractal geometry have made movies and they don't move right. So I think that the resemblance between fractals and visuals is very superficial.

I do have a general idea about the mathematics of these patterns. I call them space-time patterns, and they're fractal perhaps as space-time patterns. But the incredible symmetries, the perfect regularities, I think, are based on some other kind of mathematics. It is called Liegroup actions. And there are reasons why this kind of mathematical structure is associated with the brain. But even if you believed in the internal origin of these patterns in the physical brain and in the Liegroup action approach, some kind of mathematical source could be expected for these visions because they look so mathematical. They have regularity and perfection. How can an image of something perfect appear in the brain? It just doesn't make sense. So I suspect these visuals are actual perceptions.

RMN: Dynamical systems are arranged by organizing agents called attractors. Could you explain how these abstract entities function and how they can be used in understanding trends in biological, geographical and astronomical systems?

RALPH: Well, attractors are organizing centers in dynamical systems only in terms of long-term behavior. They're useful as models for processes only when your perspective happens to be that of long-term behavior. Short-term effects are not modeled by attractors but by a dynamical picture called a phase portrait. Its main features are the attractors, the basins and the separatrix which separates basins. Each attractor has a basin, and different basins are separated by the separatrix. It is said that mathematicians study the separatrix and physicists study the attractors, but the overall picture has these complementary things that have to be understood. The separatrix gives more information about short-term behavior, while the attractors determine the long-term behavior. What is most amazing about them is that there aren't very many. And that's kind of surprising because there's so much variety in the world. I would have expected more variety in the mathematical models for the long-run dynamical behavior, but most of them look alike.

RMN: When an attractor disappears due to sudden catastrophic change, the system becomes structureless and experiences a term of "transient chaos" before another attractor is found. How have you applied this idea to cultural transformations?

RALPH: Well, that's actually a commonly expressed idea which might turn out to be unfounded. People—including me—want to use this aspect of dynamical systems theory called bifurcation theory to model bifurcations in history. History is a dynamical process and it has bifurcations. And here we have a mathematical theory of bifurcations, so let's try it. That makes sense. But the bifurcations that are known to the theory, as universal models of sudden change in a process, are not usually characterized by this transformation from one equilibrium stage to another through a period of transient chaos. That's very exceptional in the theory, and I don't know if natural systems show this characteristic either.

Let's say you could collect data about a civil war where you had maybe monarchy before and democracy afterwards, and the monarchy was very steady with institutions that you can depend upon, and so was the democracy, and in the middle you were constantly overrun by the troops of one side or the other, or by guerillas. If this whole history were reduced to data and then you applied the rigorous criteria of dynamical systems theory to these data, and measured the degree to which it's chaotic, you might find that the monarchy had a chaotic attractor as the model for its data, in the democracy there is also a chaotic attractor of a completely different shape, and in between you don't have chaos at all; the transient is not transient chaos but is transient something else, or it's transient chaos but it's much less chaotic.

You know that heart physiology shows more chaos in the healthy heart and less chaos in the sick heart. I think it's dangerous to take the casual aspects and implications of these ideas of chaotic theory and start wildly trying to fit them into some preconceived perception of external reality. A better idea is to get some data and try to construct a model. There's no lack of numerical data about social and historical process. For example, the total weight of mail sent in mail bags from the American Embassy in Russia to Washington, D.C. is known for over a century. Political scientists have an enormous amount of data. I think the serious applications of mathematical modeling to the political and social process will proceed in the numerical realm. The result might not fit someone's preconception based on an intuitive understanding of these chaos concepts. So I don't know if social change is going to be characterised by chaos or not. I guess it might, according to some measures and observations, and might not, according to others.

> *...heart physiology shows more chaos in the healthy heart and less chaos in the sick heart.*

DJB: Do you see the process of evolution as following a chaotic attractor, and if so does that mean there is a hidden order, so to speak, to evolution? May what has appeared to evolutionary biologists as chance and randomness actually be a higher form or order?

RALPH: No. I think that the understanding of dynamical systems theory presented in popular books is extremely limited and a lot of physicists for example have studied attractors exclusively while as I said the mathematicians have been studying the separatrices. Attractors are very important in modeling physical processes in some circumstances, and that is very fine, but when you're speaking about evolution, if you want to make models for an evolutionary process, then probably the best modeling paraphernalia that mathematics has to offer you are the response diagrams of bifurcation theory. Bifurcations have to do with the ways in which attractors appear out of the blue, or disappear, and the way in which one kind of attractor or size of attractor changes into another.

These transformations appear in scientific data and in mathematical models in a much smaller variety of transformation types than you would suspect. And dynamical systems theory, at the moment, is trying to accumulate a complete encyclopedia of these transformation types called bifurcation events. Bifurcation events assembled in some kind of diagram would provide a dynamical model for an evolutionary process. Therefore, the actual attractors involved are almost of no interest. From the bifurcation point of view it doesn't matter if the process is static, periodic or chaotic. What's important is whether the attractor appears or disappears. And here there is plenty of room for chance and randomness.

And so as bifurcation theory becomes better known, I think the style of making models of process will undergo a radical and very exciting revision. The main point of my books, *Dynamics: The Geometry of Behaviour*, is to present the beginning of the bifurcation encyclopedia as far as it is known to date. There are about twenty-two different events there.

DJB: Do you think it's possible to form, or have you already formed, a mathematical theory to explain the phenomenon of how consciousness interacts with the material world?

RALPH: No. There are models, specific mathematical models, for different perceptual functions of human mammalian physiology which represent the frontier of neurobiology today. One example is Walter Freeman's model of the olfactory bulb. These models are mathematical objects known as cellular dynamical systems, which include neural-nets and excitable media as special cases. These mathematical models for perception pertain to the question of how consciousness interacts with the natural world. And they comprise a conceptual frontier today. In that context, what would an idea be?

In the context of the olfactory bulb, what is a smell? So it turns out that from the perspective of reductionist science, along with its mathematical models, a smell is a certain space-time pattern on the olfactory cortex, a pattern of excitation. The cortex consists of a sheet of oscillators side by side vibrating. A certain pattern in their frequency, phase relationship, and amplitude, is a smell. There is a certain picture, where inside a region there is a larger oscillation, and outside, a smaller one. This picture is recognized as a smell.

This kind of modeling does provide the possibility of making a simple model for the natural world, a simple model for consciousness, and a simple model for the interaction between the two. The interaction model, in this cellular dynamics context, is based on resonance. A lot of my work has to do with vibration and resonance phenomena in this context and has provided a specific mechanism for the transfer of a space-time pattern from one such medium to another. However, these mechanical models may be too simple to provide intuition as to such things as how your mythology, your perceptual filter, function so as to limit your perception of the natural world to a certain paradigm in your consciousness? Such models, which I think is the essence of your question, would have to do with a more linguistic or symbolic approach rather than at the mechanical model level.

DJB: Could you define beauty in a mathematical way?

RALPH: People do say mathematics is beautiful, and some mathematical objects are certainly beautiful. Whatever beauty is, if you could define it in some way, it would include mathematics within it somehow. If you define it, for example, in terms of cognitive resonance, then mathematics provides the ultimate opportunity for cognitive resonance because the bare bones of cognition itself are represented by these mathematical objects. The strongest resonance of forms takes place in certain special areas, precious little rings of human experience. One is mathematics, another is music, and then of course, mysticism—the three M's, three crown jewels of beauty. But I wouldn't know what the experience of beauty really is, and I certainly wouldn't think a mathematical definition would be appropriate.

DJB: From chaos theory we know that small errors in calculation can grow exponentially in time, making long-term prediction difficult. With this in mind do you think it's possible to foresee what life for humanity will be like in the twenty-first century?

RALPH: This idea of the exponential divergence, the so-called sensitive dependence on initial conditions, is very much misunderstood. When a process follows a trajectory on a chaotic attractor, and you start two armchair experiments, two processes, from fairly close initial conditions, then indeed they diverge for a while. But as a matter of fact what is happening is that both of the trajectories go round and round. You can think of yarn being wound on a skein. So they diverge for a while, but pretty soon they reach the edge of the skein, and then they fold into the middle again. They always come back close together again.

They have a certain maximum separation—it might be four inches or something—and that's it. That's not very scary. They do not diverge indefinitely and go off into infinity. That's exactly what doesn't happen with chaotic attractors and that's why chaotic

> *...chaotic attractors might be very reassuring to people who would otherwise have anxiety about chaos.*

attractors might be very reassuring to people who would otherwise have anxiety about chaos. Because the chaos in a chaotic attractor is very bounded and the degree to which things go haywire is extremely limited. So that's the good news, and after you know the process for a while, you know it forever. Chaos is very much the same as the steady state; it's not scary at all.

Now if our evolutionary track, this species on planet Earth going into the twenty-first century, for example, were modeled by a chaotic attractor, then we can answer the question where will we be in the twenty-first century. Because it would be pretty much the same mess as now. But it's not modeled very well by a chaotic attractor. A better kind of mathematical object for modeling an evolutionary process is a bifurcation diagram. In this context, a chaotic attractor is changing in time. There may be bifurcations, for example, a catastrophe, a comet or something. Who knows? And it may be that some bifurcations occur under the action of parameters controlled by us, such as how much energy we use, how much waste we make. And that's why bifurcation diagrams are more interesting than chaotic attractors for modeling our own process. Under this more general kind of model we cannot say where we will be in the twenty-first century. Or if we'll be.

RMN: Why do you think that the understanding of chaos theory is vital to our future?

RALPH: This fantasy of the importance of mathematics has to do with the idea that we might have a future, that we might have something to do with it, and that conscious interaction with our evolutionary process is possible and desirable. And in this case, things will go better if we understand our process better.

The importance of chaos theory to our future is that it provides us with a better understanding of such processes, the behavior of complex systems such as the one we live in. This is due to the fact that chaotic behavior is characteristic of complex systems. The more complex the system, the more chaotic its behavior. And if we don't understand chaotic behaviour, then we can't understand the complex system that we live in well enough to give it guidance, make informed decisions, and participate in the creation of our future.

DJB: Would you tell us about any current research projects that you're working on?

RALPH: I have an ongoing project with visual music which is just one of a family of related projects having to do with chaotic resonance in cellular dynamical systems. If you had a cellular dynamical system such as a two-dimensional spatial array of three-dimensional dynamical systems, and the state of each of the dynamical systems in the two-dimensional array were visible as a color, then you'd see the simultaneous state of this complex system as a colored picture, and the evolution of this system as a movie of colored pictures. This is experimental dynamics and graphic art, all at once.

Complex dynamical systems have very high dimension, they are really hard to see. The conventional methods of scientific visualization, an important field in computer research today, only work for low dimensional systems, for simple systems. But we want to understand very complex systems. So we have to develop a technology to visualize complex systems. And I believe that this kind of development will take place not only in the physical sciences, but more in the biological sciences, even more in the social sciences, and much more in the domain of the visual arts. So my current research is on the frontier of cellular dynamical systems, chaotic resonance, and the visual arts.

Arlen Wilson

Robert Anton Wilson

"…information is the source of all wealth."

Firing the Cosmic Trigger
with Robert Anton Wilson

Robert Anton Wilson earned his doctorate in psychology from Hawthorn University. From 1966-1971 he was Associate Editor of Playboy, *and since then he has written over 26 popular books. He is perhaps best known for* Illuminatus! *a classic science fiction trilogy which he co-authored with Robert Shea. His* Schroedinger's Cat *trilogy was called "the most scientific of all science-fiction novels" by* New Scientist, *and has been reprinted in many languages. In the area of social philosophy Bob wrote such books as* Cosmic Trigger, Prometheus Rising, *and* The New Inquisition. *He also wrote the introduction to my first book* Brainchild. *Bob has appeared as a stand-up comic at many clubs around the world, and regularly teaches seminars at New Age centers such as the Esalen Institute. Bob's poetry has been widely published and in 1986 he was a guest of the Norwegian government at the Oslo International Poetry Festivel.*

Bob has also starred in collaboration with the Golden Horde on a Punk Rock record entitled The Chocolate Biscuit Conspiracy, *and a comedy record called* Secrets of Power. *Bob's play* Wilhelm Reich in Hell *was performed at the Edmund Burke Theatre in Dublin in 1986, and many other theatres. He presently lives in Santa Cruz, where he continues to write, and co-edit the futurist journal* Trajectories *with his wife Arlen. We interviewed Bob on the evening of June 18th, 1989, at his previous home in West Los Angeles. A sharp-witted imp with a Brooklyn accent and a twinkle in his eye, Bob never fails to have a joke up his sleeve. He is a jolly prankster with an alchemical talent for blending cultural mythos. Bob spoke with us about the Illuminati conspiracy, brain machines, synchronicity, mysticism and science, nanotechnology, ecology, extraterrestrials, and the mysterious mythic connection between Satan and Santa Claus.*

—DJB

RMN: What was it that first sparked your interest in consciousness enhancement?

ROBERT: Korzybski's *Science and Sanity*. I was in engineering school and I picked up the book in the Brooklyn Public Library. He talked about different levels of organization in the brain-animal circuits, human circuits and so on. And he talked a lot about getting back to the non-verbal level and being able to perceive without talking to yourself while you're perceiving.

It was 1957. I was very interested in jazz at that time, and I told a black friend about some of Korzybski's exercises to get to the non-verbal level, and he said, "Oh, I do that every time I smoke pot." I got interested. I said, "Could I buy one of these marijuana cigarettes from you?" He said, "Oh hell, I'll give it to you free." And so I smoked it.

I found myself looking at a quarter I found in my pocket and realizing I hadn't looked at a quarter in twenty years or so, the way a child looks at a quarter. So I decided marijuana was doing pretty much the same thing Korzybski was trying to do with his training devices. Then shortly after that I heard a lecture by Alan Watts, and I realized that Zen, marijuana and Korzybski were all relating the same transformations of consciousness. That was the beginning.

DJB: Many of your books deal with a secret society called the Illuminati. How did your fascination with this organization begin?

ROBERT: It was Greg Hill and Kerry Thornley who founded the Discordian Society, which is based on the worship of Eris, the Goddess of Chaos, discord, confusion, bureaucracy and international relations. They have no dogmas, but one catma. The catma is that *everything in the universe relates to the number 5*, one way or another, given enough ingenuity on the part of the interpreter. I found the Discordian Society to be the most satisfactory religion I had ever encountered up until that point, so I became a Discordian Pope. This is done by excommunicating all the Discordian Popes you can find and setting up your own Discordian Church. This is based on Greg's teaching that we Discordians must stick apart.

Anyway, in 1968 Jim Garrison, the D.A. of New Orleans—the jolly green Frankenstein monster, as Kerry later called him—accused Kerry at a press conference of being one of the conspirators in the Kennedy assassination. Garrison never indicted him—he didn't have enough evidence for an indictment—so Kerry never stood trial, but he brooded over it for years. Then he entered an altered state of consciousness. I'm trying to be objective about this. Kerry, who served in the same platoon as Oswald, became convinced that he *was* involved in the assassination and that when he was in the Marine Corps, Naval Intelligence had brainwashed him.

Kerry decided Naval Intelligence had also brainwashed Oswald and several others, and had been manipulating them for years, like the Manchurian Candidate.

He couldn't remember what had happened, but he had a lot of suspicions. Then he became convinced that I was a CIA baby-sitter and we sort of lost touch with each other. It's hard to communicate with somebody when he thinks you're a diabolical mind-control agent and you're convinced that he's a little bit paranoid.

Somewhere along the line, Kerry decided to confuse Garrison by sending out all sorts of announcements that he was an agent of the Bavarian Illuminati. That got me interested in the Illuminati, and the more I read about it, the more interested I got. So eventually we incorporated the Illuminati into the Discordian Society. Since the Discordian Society is devoted to promoting chaos, we decided that the Illuminati is devoted to imposing totalitarianism. After all, a Discordian Society, to be truly discordant, should have it's own totalitarian branch that's working against the rest of the Society.

Pope John XXIV threw out six hundred saints on the grounds that they never existed. They threw out Santa Claus and a whole bunch of these Irish saints. The Discordian Society accepted them on the grounds that we don't care whether these saints are real or not. If we like them, we'll accept them. And since these saints were without a home, being thrown out of the Catholic church, we accepted them. In the same way we accepted the Illuminati, too, since nobody else wants them.

Then, I appointed myself the head of the Illuminati, which led to a lot of interesting correspondences with other heads of the Illuminati in various parts of the world. One of them threatened to sue me. I told him to resubmit his letter in FORTRAN, because my computer wouldn't accept it in English and I never heard from him again. I think that confused him.

RMN: Who do you think the Illuminati really were—or are?

ROBERT: The Illuminati has been the label used by many groups throughout history. The Illuminati that is believed in by right-wing paranoids is a hypothesis that leading intellectuals of the eighteenth century were all members of the Bavarian Illuminati which was working to overthrow Christianity. I don't think that's quite accurate; I think there's a lot of exaggeration in that view. I don't think that Jefferson was a member of the Illuminati; he just had similar goals. Beethoven was probably a member, but Mozart probably wasn't. Voltaire probably wasn't, although he was a Freemason. Anyway, to the extent that the Illuminati conspired to overthrow Christianity and to establish democracy, I'm in favor of it.

DJB: What were the Illuminati out to achieve?

ROBERT: The historical Illuminati of the eighteenth century, as distinguished from all other Illuminati of previous centuries, had as it's main goals, overthrowing the Vatican, overthrowing monarchies, establishing democratic republics and giving a scientific education to every boy and girl. Most of these goals have more or less begun to be achieved. Compared to what things were like in the eighteenth century they've largely succeeded, and I think that's all to the good.

RMN: Many formerly held secrets known only to a select group of initiates, perhaps like the Bavarian Illuminati, are now available at the local metaphysical bookstore. What do you think are the sociological implications of such information exchange?

ROBERT: Oh, I think it's wonderful. I believe very much that secrecy is the main cause of most social evils. I think information is the most precious commodity in the world. As a matter of fact, I think that *information is the source of all wealth.* The classical economic theory is that wealth is created by land, labor and capital. But if you have a piece of land, and you've got capital, and you hire labor, and you drill for oil, and there's no oil there—you won't get rich. What makes somebody rich is drilling for oil where there is oil, and that's based on having correct information. I'm just paraphrasing Buckminster Fuller here. All wealth is information. So therefore, all attempts to impede the transfer, the rapid transmission of information, are making us all poorer.

DJB: Why do you think it is then, that it took so long for occult knowledge to come out of secrecy and into the open?

ROBERT: Well, that's largely because of the Catholic church. Anybody who spoke too frankly for many centuries was burned at the stake. So the alchemists, hermeticists, Illuminati and other groups learned to speak in codes.

DJB: So you think it was the fear of persecution, rather than a feeling that most people weren't "ready" for the information quite yet?

ROBERT: Well, I think that's a rationalization. You can't find out who's ready, except by distributing the information. Then you find out who's ready.

RMN: The wars in the Middle East and the rising fundamentalism in the West have been seen by some as the death screams of organized religion. Both Islam and Christianity, however, have survived many "Holy Wars." What do you think the fate of organized religion will be?

ROBERT: I would like to think that organized religion is on it's way out, but I've been doing a lot of research on the eighteenth century for my historical novels. Voltaire thought that the Catholic church would be gone in twenty years, and it's hung around for two hundred years since then. When the Pope disbanded the Jesuits, Voltaire said that's the end, the Catholic church is falling apart. Well, a few years later they reorganized the Jesuits. The Knights of Malta are running the CIA apparently, and the Catholic church just refuses to die. Fundamentalism has staged a comeback. It's fantastic.

I'm a big fan of H.L. Menken. He was a very funny social critic of the 1920's. His books went out of print for a while, because the things he was making fun of didn't exist anymore. Now his books are coming back into print because all those things exist again. He was making fun of the same type of thing that Jerry Falwell, Jim Bakker, and that whole crowd stand for. It's astonishing the way that this seemingly dead historical institution came back, like the Frankenstein monster. Every time you think it's dead, it rises up again to afflict us. The Ayatollah. The Grey Wolves. The Grey Wolves are the biggest heroin dealers in the Mid-East because they believe Allah wants them to kill Jews and they can't get enough money to buy guns without selling heroin. That makes about as much sense as most of the Christian theology I've heard.

I'm a mystical agnostic, or an agnostic mystic. That phrase was coined by Olaf Stapledon, my favorite science fiction writer. When I first read it, it didn't mean anything to me, but over the years I've gradually realized that "agnostic mystic" describes me better than any words I have found anywhere else.

> *...“agnostic mystic” describes me better than any words I have found anywhere else.*

DJB: How about "transcendental agnostic"?

ROBERT: Yeah. The word agnostic has gained the association of somebody who's just denying, but what I mean is something more like the ancient Greek concept of the zetetic. I find the universe so staggering that I just don't have any faith in my ability to grasp it. I don't think the human stomach can eat everything, and I'm not quite sure my mind can understand everything, so I don't pretend that it can.

RMN: In Riane Eisler's *The Chalice and the Blade,* she proposes that there has been a cultural transformation from a cooperation between the sexes to the dominion of male over female. She says that we're now at a stage when men should be learning from women. What do you think about this?

ROBERT: Curiously, I was an early advocate of the theory of the primordial matriarchy. I got turned onto that by Robert Graves when I was in high school. I read *The White Goddess,* and then I happened to read a little-known book by a

Scottish psychiatrist named Ian Suttie called *The Origin of Love and Hate,* in which he used the model of history evolving from matriarchy to patriarchy and back to matriarchy. Some of these ideas have been around my head for about forty years.

Currently I tend to agree with Eisler. There's no evidence of a matriarchy at all. There's evidence of a partnership society. It's been coming back for the last two hundred years. Arlen calls it "stone-age feedback." As European civilization conquered and exploited the Third World, ideas from these places came drifting back to Europe. Diderot, Voltaire, Rousseau, the whole enlightenment was influenced by the ideas of these "primitives" having a more natural and happier way of life than we do. Democracy, socialism, anarchism, and all the radical ideas of the last two hundred years were inspired by studying stone-age cultures from the first proto-anthropological reports.

I've been an advocate for a partnership society for years, before Eisler used that term. The term I used was "voluntary association" which comes out of the American Anarchist tradition. This was a school of philosophical anarchists in New England in the nineteenth century who are very little known. I got fascinated by them in the sixties and read most of their books. The idea of voluntary association migrated to Europe and became syndicalism, only the syndicalists added to it the idea of overthrowing the existing system by violence, so the whole idea developed a bad reputation. I think the basic idea of voluntary association, or partnership, is the one towards which we should aspire. It's the most human, just, fair, decent and intelligent form of society.

RMN: Do you have hope that we can achieve it?

ROBERT: Yes, I do, in spite of the evidence we see on all sides of stupidity, ignorance, bigotry and the seemingly inexhaustible lust of the masses to be trampled on by Fuhrer figures and father figures. I see the last two hundred years as a staggering, groping, fumbling toward a partnership society.

RMN: Riane Eisler doesn't address the masculinity of the Devil—the fact that in this society, the dark side as well as the light side of spiritual power is depicted as male. Do you have any ideas about that?

ROBERT: They do have some shadowy feminine counterparts. There's the Lilith, the female Devil, and buried in Judaism there's the Shekinah, the female aspect of God. I'm more interested in the way that the Devil infiltrated Christianity disguised as Santa Claus. Very few people realize that

Satan is the caricature that the Christian church created, but the fertility god came back as Santa...

the archetypes are the same. It's the old pagan fertility god. Satan is the caricature that the Christian church created, but the fertility god came back as Santa, and he wears the same red suit as the Devil. The name Satan and Santa are made up of the same letters; you just move one and you've changed Santa into Satan.

RMN: That's interesting. The Devil and sexuality are correlated in many people's minds. Religious and political authorities have consistently attempted to control human sexuality and nip individual freedom in the bud. How do you see the role of sexuality evolving into the future?

ROBERT: I was just reading Jean Shinoda Bolen's book *Gods in Everyman* yesterday, and I found some of myself in Hades, though that's the younger me back in my adolescence and early twenties. I also see parts of myself in Hermes, but I see a great deal of Dionysus. My mystical feelings and my sexual feelings are so close together that I find it hard to understand how Western society ever separated them. But that just goes to show that I'm a Dionysian type. Our society is run by Zeus types and Apollo types to whom the separation is perfectly natural.

RMN: Do you think society is evolving towards a more Dionysian character?

ROBERT: Yeah. We have been since the sixties. Woodstock was a Dionysian festival—it was the rebirth of Dionysus—and right away the lid came down. My God Dionysus is loose! King Pentheus immediately called out the cops. The Dionysian religion had entered his kingdom and he tried to crush it, but he was torn apart by his own mother. That's a warning of what happens when you try to suppress Dionysus; it's one of the classic Greek myths. Look what happened to Nixon—he got torn apart. The only president to be forced to resign. Reagan escaped unscathed but I still have an intuition that he's going to be repudiated. I think the people are going to be as disgusted with Reagan as they were with Nixon—eventually. I even had high hopes that George Bush was going to be impeached. Of course, he picked Quayle as impeachment insurance, but I just have a strong suspicion, based on Confucius, that the general decline of morals and manners in this country, the general increase in the sleaze factor in American life and the general corruption and crookedness, are all due to the fact that people like Nixon and Agnew get away scot-free. They had television pictures of DeLorean peddling cocaine. When I heard about this I said, "A man with that much money isn't going to be convicted, even if they have him on television." And he wasn't.

Once everybody becomes aware that the rich can commit any crime in the book and get away with it, then the general attitude is, "Well, why don't we do the same?" The whole sociobiology of Confucius is when the ruling class are decent, honorable, gentlemen scholars, the people will be well disposed; when the government is a bunch of thieving rascals, the people will become thieving rascals.

We've seen so much of that, and the only hope I can see is that some of the malfactors in high places get punished so that a sense of justice and order is reestab-

lished in this country. I'm not a vengeful person and I have a great deal of compassion, even for Nixon and Reagan, but I think some of those people have to go to jail to restore the idea that there is justice in the universe.

RMN: The whirlwind ecstasies of the sixties have, for many, settled down into a gentle breeze. What do you feel were the fleeting and lasting effects of this cultural phenomena, and how have your attitudes developed since that time?

ROBERT: Well, we were just talking about that this morning. What survives of the sixties? What survives in different forms? I think Bucky Fuller hit the nail on the head. He said that around 1972, the brighter people realized that there are more effective ways of challenging the system than going out in the streets and running their heads against policemen's clubs. So they got more subtle. People are working on different levels and in different ways, and it's become less confrontational, but I do believe there are still a lot of people working for the ideals of the sixties.

DJB: You mean like in the movie industry?

ROBERT: Yeah, and in television, in computers, in banking, all over the place.

DJB: Really, in banking?

ROBERT: Yeah. I've met a couple of bankers who are really very hip people.

DJB: Timothy Leary and Aleister Crowley both played similar roles in history and both had a significant influence on your evolving belief systems. Tell us about the effect these two people have had on your understanding of consciousness.

ROBERT: Well Crowley was such a complicated individual that everybody who reads Crowley has a different Crowley in his head. There's a million Aleister Crowleys depending on what part of him people are able to understand and integrate. Crowley, as the leader of the Illuminati and the Argentum Astrum, the Ordo Templi Orientis (OTO), was continuing the project of overthrowing Christianity and added his own twist of reviving Paganism (which goes back to Giordano Bruno who wanted to do the same thing). Crowley is an interesting figure and has had a bigger historical impact than most people realize. The Neo-Pagan movement is bigger than anybody knows, except the Fundamentalists, who think it's a Satanic movement—which from their point of view, I guess it is.

> *The Neo-Pagan movement is bigger than anybody knows, except the Fundamentalists, who think it's a Satanic movement...*

The Crowley who interests me is the scientific Crowley. He travelled all over the world, got initiated into every secret society he could, studied every occult system, studied Sufism in North Africa, Taoism in China, Buddhism in Ceylon and he tried to understand them all in terms of organic chemistry and physiology. He laid the groundwork for the scientific study of mysticism and altered consciousness. That's the Crowley I'm fascinated by—Crowley the scientist, who co-existed with Crowley the mystic, Crowley the poet, Crowley the adventurer and Crowley the Great Beast.

RMN: The Golden Dawn from which Crowley got much of his inspiration was a mystical school which is still lively today. Have you found this system able to remain flexible enough to adapt to the cultural and psychological revisions that have occurred since the Order was first established?

ROBERT: There are several Golden Dawns around, like there are several OTO's and several Illuminatis and so on. All of these things are fractionated, and of course, everybody with a power drive involved in these things claims to be the leader of the real and authentic Secret Chiefs. The Golden Dawn which I find most interesting is the one of which Christopher Hyatt is the Outer Head. He's a fully qualified clinical psychologist with a good background in Jungian and Reichian therapy and a great deal of theoretical knowledge of general psychology.

He was trained in the Golden Dawn system by Israel Regardie who was also a psychologist as well as a mystic. I think Hyatt knows what he's doing; I think he's got his head on right. He doesn't have delusions of grandeur. He's not a prima donna and he's free of most of the deviant and aberrant behavior that's chronic in the occult world. What are the goals of the Golden Dawn? Unleashing the full positive potential of human beings.

RMN: What are the methods involved?

ROBERT: The original Golden Dawn in the 1880's used Kabbalistic magic. Crowley revised it to include Kabbalistic magic and yoga and a bit of Sufism. Regardie revised it to include a great deal of Reichian bodywork, and an insistence that anybody who enters the Order should go through psychotherapy first. He became aware that people who get into Kabbalistic-type work, especially in the

Golden Dawn tradition, who haven't had psychotherapy, are likely to flip out or scare themselves silly. Regardie also insisted that they should know General Semantics, which is interesting since it was General Semantics which got me interested in the study of alternative consciousness.

RMN: Why did Regardie want this to be included?

ROBERT: General Semantics is a system that is very useful in clarifying your thinking. If you understand the rules of General Semantics, you're more or less immune to most of the errors that are chronic at this stage of civilization. One of the rules of General Semantics is *avoid the is of identity,* which is a rule I just broke when I said "General Semantics is..." It's very hard to avoid the *is* of identity in speech. We all use it all the time. I'm getting pretty good at avoiding it in my writing. Whenever you're trying to figure out what the hell is wrong with my thinking? Why can't I get to the bottom of this? Why am I confused about this problem? Write it down and take out every "is" and reformulate it in some other way. You'll find that your thinking has been tremendously clarified.

It's like the celebrated problem in quantum physics in the 1920's The electron is a wave. The electron is a particle. Those two things contradict each other totally, which led to a lot of physicists saying that the universe doesn't make sense, the universe is irrational and so on. If you reformulate it without the "is" of identity, there's no paradox at all. The electron appears as a wave when we measure it in certain ways. The electron appears as a particle when we measure it in other ways. There's no contradiction. There are a lot of other ideas in general semantics that are equally useful in clarifying thought.

DJB: That's one of the claims of the recent technology of brain machines. What experiences have you had with them, which ones do you find the most promising and what kind of potential do you think they hold for the future?

ROBERT: The most outstanding experience I've had with a brain machine was with the first one, the Pulstar. I had an out-of-body experience which registered as flat brain waves on the EEG, and that fascinated me. That was the first objective sign I had ever seen that something was going on in out-of-body experiences besides heightened imagination. I don't see much difference between a lot of the brain machines around. Some are demonstrably inferior, and out of charity I won't mention their names. Some claim to be very superior to all the others, but as far as I can see, most of them function pretty much the same.

At present, I'm more interested in the light and sound machines than I am in the electro-magnetic machines, because there is some legitimate cause for concern that sending electro-magnetism into your brain too often may not be good for you. The whole field is growing very fast. There's a bunch of tapes put out by Acoustic Brain Research in North Carolina. They use only sound, but they combine it with subliminals and Ericksonian hypnosis in a way that I find very effective. They're using sound at the same frequencies that you find in the electro-magnetic machines, or the light and sound machines.

The Graham Potentializer does seem a little more powerful than any of the other machines, but I wouldn't guarantee it because I haven't had enough experience with it yet. What I want to see is more controlled, double-blind studies of these machines, because everybody has their own anecdotal impressions, but we don't really know yet which are the best. Which wave forms are the best? We don't know that yet. Why do some people respond better to one than to others? We don't know why. There's a lot more to be learned and I'm very eager to see more research.

RMN: Do you think that the use of brain machines requires an accompanying discipline?

ROBERT: I suspect so. One manufacturer told me that the return rate is about fifteen percent. I think these machines are much easier than the biofeedback machines, but they still require some discipline. I think they require some previous experience with Yoga, or Zen, or some consciousness-altering work. You need some kind of previous experience or you just won't know how to use the machine. I don't think the machine really works as an entrainer unless you practice between sessions, trying to revive the state without the machine. A lot of people can't do that, they just assume that the machine will do all the work for them, which is kind of like thinking that you just get in the car and it'll take you where you want to go.

DJB: The potential of nanotechnology seems far more vast. How do you think it's development will affect human consciousness in the future?

ROBERT: I haven't thought much about that. That's an interesting question. It's going to change everything. Nanotechnology is a much bigger jump than anything else on the horizon. It's bigger than space colonization, bigger than longevity. It's a million times bigger than the industrial revolution. It's going to change things so much that I can't begin to conceive how much; but everything's going to get dirt cheap. The ozone layer will get repaired rapidly. We could create redwoods as fast and as many as we want, and then there's star-flight. I don't know; it's just a whole new ballgame, and it leads directly into immortalism.

> *Nanotechnology is a much bigger jump than anything else on the horizon.*

DJB: How about new ways to alter the brain?

ROBERT: Oh, of course. Eric Drexler, in his book on the subject, talks about constructing micro-replicators that, if you let them loose in the body, they run all over the place, inspecting every cell. If it's not functioning properly they go back, get information from the main computer and repair it. You can obviously do the same thing with brain circuits. It'll probably replace psychiatry. Nanotechnology is so staggering, we can't think about it without hyperbole, and it's coming along rapidly. The Japanese are spending fantastic amounts on that kind of research.

RMN: What do you think about the idea than many inventions are actually rediscoveries of technologies that have already existed in the past?

ROBERT: That's always seemed very implausible to me. There are some cases—the steam engine was discovered in Greece and forgotten until Watt rediscovered it—but I doubt that there are many. Most things weren't discovered until they *could* be discovered, until there was the time-binding heritage, or until the information accumulation had reached the necessary level. This is why you have so many cases of parallel discovery in science, where in five years three people patent the same thing in different countries. As Charles Fort said, "It's steam engines when it comes steam engine time."

RMN: What if there were times when the information had accumulated but not the political or social climate necessary to appreciate it? Libraries have been burned and knowledge chased underground by authoritarian forces.

ROBERT: Well, "Whereof one cannot speak, thereof one should remain silent."

RMN: A lot of people feel that technology is at odds with their ecological thinking. What do you think is the evolving role of the science of Ecology.

ROBERT: The first book I ever read on ecology was way back in the forties. It was called *The Road to Survival.* I've always been fascinated by ecology because I'm fascinated by whole systems. That's why Bucky Fuller fascinates me. He always starts with the biggest whole system and works his way down. I've written a lot of satirical things about pop ecology because I think a lot of people have got on the ecology bandwagon who don't know their ass from their elbow about science, and it's turned into a kind of late Christian heresy like Marxism. It's become a new blame game, where people go

> *Guilt is very fashionable in Western civilization.*

around laying guilt trips on other people. Guilt is very fashionable in Western civilization.

Albert Ellis said the most popular game in Western civilization is finding and denouncing no-good shits. I found that so impressive I've incorporated it into a couple of my own books. Every generation picks out a group of no-good shits. In the Victorian age it was adolescent boys who masturbated, and now it's cigarette smokers. There's always got to be some no-good shits for people to denounce and persecute, and to the extent that ecology has degenerated into that, it arouses my satirical instinct. But of course the science of Ecology itself is tremendously important, and the more people who know about it, the better.

RMN: The methods of science and art are beginning to achieve some wonderful things together. What do you think created such a chasm between the two disciplines in the first place, and why do you think they are now merging?

ROBERT: Science and art. Now what created such a chasm between them? Why the hell did that happen? I think I'm going to go back and blame the Inquisition. Science had to fight an uphill battle against the Inquisition and this created a historical hangover in which scientists had acute hostility to every form of mysticism, not just to the Catholic church which had been persecuting them. I think that rubs off onto art, because there's something mystical about art no matter how much you try to rationalize it. If you get a bunch of artists together talking about where they got their creativity from, they sound like a bunch of mystics.

Then there was the rise of capitalism. I'm inclined to agree with Karl Marx about that, that every previous form of society has had different values, a hierarchy of values. Capitalism does tend to reduce everything to just one value—what can you sell it for? And as Oscar Wilde said, "All art is quite useless." The value of art depends on who's manipulating the marketplace at the time. It's spooky. Art is the Schrodinger's cat of economics.

All of a sudden, an Andy Warhol is worth a million, and nobody knows how that happened. Then it's somebody else the next year. Picasso never paid for anything in the last twenty years of his life. He just wrote checks which never came back to his bank. People saved them because they knew that the signature was worth more than the sum of the check. They knew it would be worth even more in twenty years, and so on.

> *Somebody asked a Zen master, "What's the most valuable thing in the world?" and he said, "The head of a dead cat."*

Somebody asked a Zen master, "What's the most valuable thing in the world?" and he said, "The head of a dead cat." The querent asked "Why?" and the Zen master said, "Tell me it's exact value." That's a good exercise if you're into creative writing. Write a short story where the hero's life is saved by the fact that he could find the value of the head of a dead cat. It could happen. Everything has a fluctuating value.

In capitalism, everything gets reduced to it's immediate cash value. *Citizen Kane*, to take one egrerious example, is generally considered one of the best films ever made. It lost money in it's first year, so Orson Welles had extreme difficulty for the rest of his life getting enough money to make other movies. Yet *Citizen Kane* made more money than any other movie made in 1941, if you count up to the present, because it gets revived more than any other movie. But the bankers who own the studios aren't interested in profit in twenty years, they want profit next June. They want *Indiana Jones* not *Citizen Kane*.

RMN: So, if the areas of science and art are merging it indicates a move away from the capitalist perspective.

ROBERT: Yes. I think information theory has probably done a great deal to bring science and art back together again. Norbert Weiner invented the basic equation for information at the same time Claude Shannon did. That's another example of things happening when they're ready to happen. Weiner explained information by saying that a great poem carries more information than a political speech. Information is the unpredictable. As we come to realize the value of the unpredictable, the value of art has become clearer.

You go through a museum and you look at a Leonardo, a Botticelli, a Rembrandt, a Van Gogh, a Cezanne, a Picasso, a Klee, a Jackson Pollock, and it's obvious the value of each of them is that they weren't copying one another. If Van Gogh were copying Rembrandt nobody would give a damn for Van Gogh. He had the chutzpah to paint his own vision. Somebody having their own vision instead of just repeating an earlier one in a different style—that's information. Information is the new and unpredictable, and information theory led to the computers which fascinate artists. Computers have opened up whole new areas of art.

DJB: Information is the unpredictability of a signal, but it's not quite chaos or randomness. It carries a message.

ROBERT: Yeah. When unpredictability gets too high, information turns into noise. That part of Shannon's theory involves very complicated mathematics and I'm not sure I fully understand it; I just more or less intuitively follow it. There has to be an information redundancy ratio where the highest grade of information is diluted with repetition.

DJB: Because it's so unpredictable one can't relate it to anything.

ROBERT: Yeah. Originality frequently looks like chaos until we learn how to deal with it, until we find the redundancy in it.

DJB: Have you had any experiences with lucid or conscious dreaming?

ROBERT: I've had a lot of lucid dreams, but I can't think of anything that's particularly worth discussing. I'd like to learn more about it. It happens spontaneously sometimes. I have a very rich hypnagogic and hypnopompic life, like Philip K. Dick. William Burroughs told me that his characters all manifest as voices in hypnopompic reverie before they have bodies, or names, or anything else. Robert Shea, an old friend of mine who's a scientific materialist of the most rigid sort, really blew my mind by admitting he hears his characters talking. I suspect all writers do. I think the difference between a writer and a channeler is that the channeler has found a way to make more money out of it than most writers ever do.

Originality frequently looks like chaos until we learn how to deal with it...

DJB: Synchronicity is a major theme that runs through most, if not all, of your books. What model do you use at present for interpreting this mysterious phenomenon?

ROBERT: I never have one model. I always have at least seven models for anything.

DJB: Which one is your favorite?

ROBERT: Bell's Theorem combined with an idea I got from Barbara Honegger, a parapsychologist who worked for Reagan. She wrote a book denouncing Reagan, Ollie North and the whole crowd, giving inside dirt about what she discovered while she was at the White House. Long before Barbara became a controversial political figure, she gave me the idea that the right brain is constantly trying to communicate with the left. If you don't listen to what it's trying to say, it gives you more and more vivid dreams and if you still won't listen, it leads to Freudian slips. If you still don't pay attention, the right brain will get you to the place in space-time where synchronicity will occur. Then the left brain *has* to pay attention. "Whaaaat!?"

I always have at least seven models for anything.

DJB: What do you think happens to consciousness after physical death?

ROBERT: Somebody asked a Zen master, "What happens after death?" He replied, "I don't know." And the querent said, "But you're a Zen master!" He said, "Yes, but I'm not a dead Zen master." Somebody asked Master Eckart, the great German mystic, "Where do you think you'll go after death?" He said, "I don't plan to go anywhere." Those are the best answers I've heard so far. My hunch is that consciousness is a non-local function of the universe as a whole, and our brains are only local transceivers. As a matter of fact, it's a very strong hunch, but I'm not going to dogmatize about it.

DJB: Could you share with us any experiences you might have had communicating with what you thought to be extraterrestial or non-human entities?

ROBERT: I've had a lot of experiences with what could be interpreted as extraterrestial communications. They could also be interpreted as ESP, or as accessing parts of my brain that are normally not available, or as contacting a non-local consciousness that permeates everything. There are a lot of different models for this type of experience. I got fascinated by the extraterrestial model at one stage in the early seventies, and still, every now and then, it makes more sense to me than any of the others.

Other times the non-local model makes more sense, which is a development of Bell's Theorem. This was stated most clearly by Edwin Harris Walker in a paper called *The Complete Quantum Anthropologist*. He developed a mathematical theory of a non-local mind, to which we can gain access at times. It's a complete quantum mechanical, mathematical model to explain everything that happens in mystical and occult experience. That makes a great deal of sense to me, especially when I found that Joyce was using the same model in *Finnigan's Wake*. I think it also underlies the *I Ching*. I explain this at length in my book *Coincidance*.

DJB: How do you see consciousness evolving into the twenty-first century?

ROBERT: It staggers my imagination. I get about as far as 2012 in my future projections, then I can't imagine beyond that. So much is going to change by then.

DJB: What do you see coming along up to 2012?

ROBERT: In Leary's terms, I think about one-third of the West now understands the neuro-somatic circuit, and some techniques for activating it. I think that's going to reach fifty to fifty-one percent pretty soon—and that will be a major cultural change. I think more and more understanding of the neuro-genetic and meta-programming circuits are coming along.

It's very obvious that quantum physics, parapsychology and all the work they're doing attaching brain scanners to Yogis and Zen masters means we're going to learn a great deal about the non-local quantum circuit. I think the history of mysticism has been sort of like a bunch of firecrackers with two or three going off every century. With the LSD revolution it became two or three every month and now it's moving up to two or three every week. I see a real acceleration in consciousness, just like in technology.

DJB: Soon it'll be fireworks every day. One final question, Bob. Tell us about any current projects on which you're presently working.

ROBERT: I've just finished a book called *Quantum Psychology* subtitled: *How Brain Software Programs Your Self and Your World.* I'm working on a movie, tentatively titled *The Curtain,* which may or may not ever get produced. I've been paid enough so that I'm not wasting my time, which is a good thing to know in Hollywood. There are all sorts of people around Hollywood who'll get you involved in projects without ever paying you a penny, if you're dumb enough to do that.

If the movie does get produced it'll have a tremendous impact. I'm also working on two possible television shows and I'm continuing my historical novels. I'm doing more lectures in more places than ever before, with workshops here and there, which involves a lot of travelling. Altogether, I'm very excited about what the next ten years will bring into my life.

Alice Springs

Timothy Leary

"To me the philosophy of the twenty-first century...is the philosophy of information."

Cybernautics & Neuro-antics
with Timothy Leary

Timothy Leary has been a public icon of extreme controversy for several decades. Because of all the sensationalized publicity he has received from the media, much of this man's real accomplishments have been obscured and his image distorted in many people's minds. Timothy was a highly successful research psychologist long before he had his first encounter with psychedelic drugs. He received his Ph.D. from UC Berkeley, was on the distinguished faculty at Harvard, and his book Interpersonal Diagnosis of Personality—*called "the best work in psychotherapy" in 1957 by the* Annual Review of Psychology—*remains a standard text in its field to this day. When his research with psychedelic drugs began to have an impact on the general public, and Leary refused to discontinue his research, he was dismissed from Harvard. Leary metamorphosized from academic professor to counter-culture folk hero. He continued his research in Mexico and the Millbrook estate in N. Y., working with many influential writers, artists, scientific researchers, and philosophers. Timothy's highly influential books and lectures made him extremely popular among young people and intensely feared by the establishment. He was sentenced to ten years in prison for less than a half an ounce of marijuana in 1970.*

He escaped from prison with the help of the Weather Underground, and lived the wild life of a fugitive in North Africa and Europe. He was kidnapped by DEA agents in Afghanistan, brought back to American prison, and was finally paroled in 1976. Through all this Leary never lost his sense of optimism, nor his sense of humor, which are trademarks of his charisma. Leary is the author of more than twenty-five books and computer software programs. He continues to lecture, write, perform, and design educational computer software. We interviewed Timothy on the patio at his home in Beverly Hills on June the 20th in 1989. Even in the hot, sticky heat of that afternoon, Timothy was buzzing with lively electrical energy, and his good-humored optimism was contagious. Timothy spoke with us about his eight-circuit model of consciousness, the sociobiological implications of the cyber-punk movement, information theory, computers, cyber-space, and his plans for cryonic suspension. Timothy has a wonderful ability to make people around him feel good about themselves. He looks you directly in the eye, listens carefully, and gives you full attention when you speak. Most of all, he made us laugh.

—DJB

DJB: What was it that originally inspired your interest in psychology? Was there an early event that sparked the interest?

TIMOTHY: From my earliest years of thinking about careers and futures, I always assumed I was going to be a philosopher. As early as ten, fifteen years old, I just assumed I was doing this. I've always been fascinated with communication. I was the editor of my school paper in high school, where I performed experiments in fissioning and collaging ideas. I edited this paper so that I filled it with works of writers who did not go to that high school, but whose works were necessary to fill it out.

I cite this as an example of my interest in communication, and new modes of communication. To me the philosophy of the twenty-first century, which is quantum philosophy, is the philosophy of information. We see this in the linguists, the seniticions, Korjipsky, Wittgenstein, and then the enormous breakthrough provided by the thought-digitizing appliance known as the computer. The history of the roaring twentieth century is the history of our becoming an information species, and you could hardly be a philosopher, or for that matter a scientist, in the twentieth century, if you're not working in this wave.

DJB: Just so that everyone is familiar with your eight-circuit model of consciousness, can you briefly explain the intention behind it and what it expresses?

TIMOTHY: Well, in the late 50s and 60s, a group of a hundred or so select psychologists and philosophers discovered the brain. That is, they discovered how to navigate and explore the brain, just like Magellan and Columbus did for the outer geography of the planet earth. People like Aldous Huxley, Alan Watts, and Albert Hofman used psycho-active vehicles to move around in the brain. One of the major philosophic tasks of the late twentieth century is mapping the different islands or hemispheres or continents in the universe of the brain.

I remember Huxley used the metaphor of the fire antipodes of the brain, or the mind—like Australia being discovered by Captain Cook. This is the first task of the psychedelic philosopher. So over the years I've produced dozens of sketch maps of the culvas circles, the circuits or the levels of consciousness. These were crude words to build up a vocabulary or a cartography of inner space. I don't use the notion of eight circuits now as much as I did, but that's why I did it.

RMN: Did you ever develop a holographic or integrational perspective for the model, to get rid of the higher and lower stuff?

TIMOTHY: By higher and lower I think you're referring to the notion of the linear or ordinal system of one, two, three, four, five, six, seven, eight. There's no implication here that seven is any higher or any better than six. An ordinal system just sets up location—it's the geometry of ideas or thought. Running through all the ordinal systems that we developed was the idea that they're recursive. Eight merges into one, like a double helix, in the sense of the DNA code, which is a wonderful model of an ordinal system.

Although I certainly agree with your rejection of the notion of hierarchy, I strongly defend the notion of ordinal. Because things do end up in chains of neighborhood location, and you have to get to six before seven. When you get to six you have a choice—you could go to seven or back to five, or you could go to north six or west six. But the notion of topography and, not linear, but ordinal relations, is the key to the digital language of computers, *which also happens to be the language of the universe.* Quantum linguistics is based upon zeros and ones. They're off and on just as computers are.

DJB: Timothy, could you give us a sociobiological perspective on the cyberpunk movement?

TIMOTHY: As a result of the many waves of acculturation and popularization of quantum philosophy in the twentieth century—modern art, jazz, digitizing ideas in the form of telegraph, teletype, telephone, and television—it is inevitable that towards the end of the twentieth century we're developing an entirely new culture. This is going to be an informational culture—a communications culture—in which most of the values, rituals, and certainly almost all of the laws of the tribal, feudal, or industrial societies no longer hold. We're taking thoughts and digitizing them so they can be hurled around the world at the speed of light. They can be duplicated. That's basically cybernetic or digital reality—digital language.

This new society has been described by Ted Nelson, who gives us the architecture of ideas in his *Xanadu System,* and Bedwood Fredkin, the quantum physicist, who has described the astro-physical algorithmic nature of reality. William Gibson has spelled it out in the most humanist, down, dirty, gritty, comprehensible, novel fashion. His books *Neuromancer, Count Zero,* and *Mona Lisa Overdrive* spell out some of the most important dimensions of the new culture that's emerging. There's a new theology, new ethics, and certainly a new psychology. The word cyber-punk—to get back to your original question—is an early and wonderfully vulgar concept of the role model of the twenty-first century.

The twenty-first century person is a cybernetic person. He or she accepts the Heisenberg principle that you create all realities. Therefore you're responsible for everything that you experience. This identification of yourself as a quantum entity certainly dissolves most of the identification chords to your former culture, your former nation, your former religion, or any other external structure, even to your family, unless family members are redefined as cybernetic entities. The cyber-punk, or the cybernetic person, is a free agent. By the way, nobody uses that term anymore; it's like one of those words that was wonderful for awhile, then it carried all the freight it could, and it was kind of co-opted by some high-falutin' literary types, and so forth. But no one uses that word anymore, although we certainly hang it up on the trophy shelf as a wonderful bumper sticker.

DJB: What role do you think it's playing in an evolutionary sense?

TIMOTHY: The cybernetic person spends a very high percentage of his or her time and energy in what's now called cyber-space, communicating, mutually creating new realities with other people, *on the other side of the screen.* The cyber-punk person is a free agent, and the new society is made up of free agents who link-up at a much different level of social connection than family, work, or religious commitment. So the cyber-society is a society of highly skilled, highly courageous, cybernetic people who mutually create what we call "cyberias" or cyber-architectures, on the other side of the screen.

RMN: I hear that you've made arrangements for your head to be cryonically suspended. Could you explain what this entails, what led up to your decision, and what fantasies you have concerning your future recoordination?

TIMOTHY: My motive is the obvious basic human motive that I want to have options as to my future. I have no intention of dying passively. I have not lived in a helpless, submissive, or passive way, and I certainly don't intend to make the next transition as a victim. There are many options to the passive role of just going belly up when your Blue Cross runs out. I've written papers on this subject of the options—the various forms of rejuvenation, and reanimation.

Of course on the negative side we know that death has always been controlled by religious organizations, by state and social organizations, and more recently by medical and legal bureaucracies. Death is the ultimate control mechanism by which human beings can be rendered helpless. It's very reassuring that all the Right people bitterly oppose cryonics and the reanimation option. Every religious person, of course, considers this the ulti-mate heresy of taking the function of God, to determine your own transition. All state organizations resist the individual's attempt to control any part of our lives, whether it's physical or neurological, through the medical monopoly.

> *Death is the ultimate con-trol mechanism by which human beings can be rendered helpless.*

This is the ultimate taboo, and it's, again, wonderfully reassuring to see how people just freeze, literally, when you suggest to them that there's any option that a courageous, thoughtful person and an industism can take to avoid just allowing your body to be eaten by maggots or burned. That's called the barbecue or maggot option. Just in the last two years that I have been talking to people about it, I've seen a wonderful openness in people who formerly, two years ago, would have reckoned it a *horror.*

We went through this same thing with the notion of psychedelic drugs, that you could actually take a drug that would change your mind. Your mind is supposed to be made up by God, by your parents, or by Freud, and the idea that you could take this reckless responsibility *shocked* people. On the other hand, it can't be acceptable, until it's at least comprehensible. I think you can explain the hibernation-reanimation option very clearly. See, the idea is you don't die, you hibernate, and you try to preserve as much of your body, and certainly as much of your brain as you can. This is a classic philosophic tool. It was used by the Egyptians, who probably produced the most scientific, the most aesthetic, and the most glorious culture, although they had human flaws.

I can explain the notion in three or four sentences. It's well accepted now that we have heartbanks, where people whose hearts are very healthy, but who are brain-dead, have their hearts stored and then given to other people who have healthy brains, but need a heart. We have kidney banks. We have liver banks. We have lung banks. So this concept is that there will be a brain bank. The option there is not cryonics, it is just to store it. It turns out the brain is much easier to store than the heart, because the heart has got all those muscles, and it's a pump, whereas the brain, as you know, has no mechanical parts and no sensation. The brain has no muscles, and there is very little hardware to it. So the maintenance of the brain is a piece of cake compared to the heart. Think of the kidney—ugh, my god, all that plumbing, and all those juices that you have to maintain.

The idea is that we can have a brain bank within twenty, thirty, or forty years—perhaps within five years if we had a crash program. If a healthy person tragically had an accident where they were brain dead, but their body was in good shape, we'd just go to the brain bank and pick up a new brain. If I donate my brain to a brain bank, I can suggest the parameters that I'd like to have. This time I'd like to have it put into a black woman. Everyone probably will have some sort of a medical thing saying that you don't want your brain to be taken over by a Romanian, or a Dodger fan.

There will be all sorts of protections that individuals can have so no one can do anything to anyone that they don't want. Just as now you can sign away your rights to have your organs given to somebody else—it's the same thing.

Again anything that has to do with the brain stirs up these incredible taboos.

Now, of course, when you transport a *brain* the consequences are different. Again anything that has to do with the brain stirs up these incredible taboos. Imagine a young healthy black woman running around with Timothy Leary's brain. I mean, think of it.

RMN: After transferring the brain into another body, do you think it will retain all of its memory? What do you think happens to human consciousness then after death?

TIMOTHY: Yes, that's the obvious and wonderful question. We're now getting into the concept of soul. The soul is defined in the dictionary as an immaterial entity which resides in the body—but is not the body, and can leave the body—which monitors, or is responsible for consciousness, thought, memory, emotion, and all that. It's almost the same definition as the brain. The brain is defined almost the same way as the soul, except for the immaterial entity part.

The answer to your question is now just a technological question. Yes. Memories are stored in the brain. Then the question is how can you recover them. Now, there are programs called the Neuro-beurtilities, in which you have these disks, in case you lose a memory on another disk. You see, you can have a computer disk, get all the work you've done in the last six months on it, and it crashes. But then they have these disks that allow you to go back and bring them back, because the memories are frozen in the grooves, or in the molecular combinations in the brain.

But you have to have that way of accessing, or booting it up, which is called life, what you'd call soul, or that which you call animation. But we are speculating about the soul—where does the soul go when it leaves the body? When you begin working in cryonics, and reanimation—particularly reanimation of the mind, memories, or personality—what formerly was you is either dead or alive. It's called irreversible involuntary metabolic coma; that's death.

Once you say, well no, it's reversible, and it's going to be voluntary, then you open up this enormous mid-frontier. We'll just call it No-Man or No-Woman's Land. What percentage of your memory could you get back? See, if we can get less than fifty percent of your memory back, we'd consider that, probably, a failure. But, you have the option. So when you sign up for this, you can say, well don't reanimate me unless you can bring back seventy-five percent of my memory. Because we could bring that back with nanotechnology, which is being taught by Eric Drexler.

We could clone or bring back another David or another Timothy. But then the question—if I had none of my memories, would I be just like a robot? It would be a tragedy and a horror, but it then becomes an option. You know, at my age I can tell you, you lose a lot of memories along the way. Well, of course, you probably lose a lot of the ones you didn't want anyway. So at least we've taken these areas of total taboo and religious fanaticism from the past, and converted them into a scientific discourse, with experimental probabilities, in which you have options, and can share these options.

I'm going to the cryonics center Friday at Riverside—that's ALCOR. I'm going there with Harry Nealson, probably with Ringo Starr, and a group of our friends. We're planning a reunion. We're going to sign up as a group for hibernation, and reanimation, possibly fifty years from now. We're having lunch at the St. James Club Friday with a group of people, and one of the things we're speculating is, we'd like to have lunch again in fifty years. The champagne will be chilled, there's no question of that.

Now what I'm doing there is I'm introducing a very powerful, comforting notion that cryonics is not you're being frozen like a stiff, like a frozen steak in a freezer, and you're popped out in cellophane, and popped in the microwave. We're talking about groups of people who have enjoyed being together in this first life, who would want to reanimate together. Because I don't want to wake up, frankly, fifty years from now, and not have any of my friends there. I'll be surrounded by these hot-shot scientists from the twenty-first century, and maybe a few of these scientists from ALCOR, who are nice people, but I don't hang out with them. I want my friends around too.

This, by the way, is agonizingly or heart-warming reminiscent of the Egyptians. Because when the Egyptians went into their reanimation laboratories, their wives, and then their pets, would join them. When their servants would die, then they'd do them too, and try to preserve them. The Christian archeologists said, well this is a Pagan policy, and they just wanted their servants there to wait on them in the future, the afterlife. But a more humanistic interpretation is that naturally they wanted to share this reanimation option with the people with whom they spent this life.

RMN: Have you heard about morphic fields?

TIMOTHY: Yes.

RMN: Sheldrake theorizes that memory is not even stored in the brain. What do you think of that?

TIMOTHY: Where is it stored?

RMN: Well, the idea is that there's access by the brain to these non-material memory fields, through which the brain picks memory up, but does not necessarily store it.

TIMOTHY: But the brain is a receiving instrument that picks it up? Yes. Well, there's no question. You don't have to say non-material. You're just referring to something we haven't been able to measure yet. See, the air is full of television signals, and to show a primitive person that, they'd think it was magic, or it's immaterial. It's not. It is material. Remember, almost everything that the former primitive religions called spiritual, you can redefine as being immeasurable right now by our level of equipment.

> *...almost everything that the former primitive religions called spiritual, you can redefine as being immeasurable...*

The planet earth is being bombarded by radio signals from outer space, none of which are comprehensible to us, and part of evolution is the increasing ability to detect information. You see, it's all information, everything is information. Morphogenetic information is information signals that we are now too crude and childish to pick up. I tend to resist strongly this notion that there's a spiritual thing that's outward beyond science, because then we have no options, we're just kind of helpless victims, and someone comes along and does it. So I have no quarrel at all with this notion. My only quarrel is with people who try to limit or moralize about different options.

DJB: What role do you see computers playing in the evolution of human consciousness, and do you think it's possible to down load, so to speak, human consciousness or brain software into a computer?

TIMOTHY: These concepts of computer and down load are really primitive, and they *lock* conversation at a certain level. The notion of cyber-space is that we are now creating this enormous universe of digital signals in the form of all the radio programs and television shows that have ever been produced, and all the traffic that's been going around in satellites. That actually there is an ocean. There's literally an ocean of electronic signals up there that's just as tangible as the Atlantic ocean. But before Magellan we couldn't access it. Now we're learning to explore this ocean of cyber-space and electric signals, and create within it. So that down-loading is just not a precise term.

I'm working with groups now that wear computers. You see, so that every time I move my arm there is a correspondence of movement on the screen. I can actually reach in and move and change things in the screen. And you can be there too—so we can shake hands, or we can dance, or we can even take each other's clothes off, or we can play tennis with each other. You can be the ball for that matter. So it's not a question of down-loading programs. Just as graphic art and books allowed us to communicate better, so too will the realities of digital creativity that we create. So there's no more computer.

Everything that I can do can be digitized, preserved, and then you can interact with it. It's robotry now because we're always aware that there's a breathing, living, juicy human being who's doing it. On the other hand, my self is stored there, so that a hundred years from now, even though I don't come back in

...a hundred years from now...anyone who wants to interact with Timothy Leary will be able to do it.

the physical form, my descendents, or anyone who wants to interact with Timothy Leary will be able to do it. We can actually play Frisbee, or we can probably fuck each other digitally on the screen, in years to come. This does not take the place of fleshy, juicy, interactions anymore than books took the place of touching, murmuring, and groping around.

As a matter of fact, you could argue that literature enriched human behavior. So that people fucked better, if they've read a few books, than if they had not. The same thing is true if you've had a hundred digital love affairs, digital tennis matches, or digital wars on the screen. You're going to be much more sophisticated, sensitive, and wise in your human and physical interactions—instead of being vulgarized, or even condemned, as they are now. The actual touch, like this, is considered this extraordinary, rare, and rich moment.

It's a high moment because Gosh, you know, we've been on the screen together, and we have been married three times, and you were a boy, and I was a girl, and we were gay, and this and that, and God knows what we've done, and now when we actually touch, we totally sanctify and glorify the rare opportunity of physical interaction, instead of just running around like animals. In the industrial age the concept of a body was of a messy machine. In the cybernetic age, the body is an incredible temple, bristling with sense organs, and information-sending output. So that's the down-load. I out-loaded your down-load.

RMN: As machines are comprised of earth-based products, Terence McKenna made the suggestion that it could be that through technological advancement the planet is organizing itself into a self-reflective conscious entity. What do you think of this idea?

TIMOTHY: That's fabulous. I'm a great admirer of Terence McKenna, and what he's doing. I must put a caveat here. All of our language is suspect as we move from a mechanical factory society, which is state-controlled, into a much freer cybernetic society. Now, all of us who grew up in the sixties have a terrible bias against technology, because technology was what was polluting the air, and grinding down the soil, and making a parking lot out of our planet. Much of this understandable contempt for technology has flipped over into a contempt for computers.

But there's a great difference between mechanical technology, which uses oil, metal, concrete, and is in material form, and the cybernetic technology which is invisible. Within two or three years of the computers, instead of the mainframe's enormous bar and building it will be as small as a cigarette box. So that the basic virtue and ethical goal in the cybernetic society is no longer big is better, and more is better, but smaller. Throughout, the lesson is learned from Hermes Trismagistus: as above, so below, as in the larger, so in the smaller.

The greatest wisdom is always housed in the smallest package. I think I even said that in the *Psychedelic Prayers* twenty-eight years ago. Look at the DNA code. The DNA code is invisible, and yet the DNA code has enough information to build you an Amazon rain forest, or build a hundred David Browns. I mean it's there. The point is certainly obvious. We've now learned that the atom is not just a bunch of billiard balls going around Bohr's solar system. The atom, we have every reason to expect, is charged with enormous miniaturized information. The fact that we can't decipher it is not the problem of the atom. That's what quantum physics demonstrates.

> *The greatest wisdom is always housed in the smallest package.*

See, matter and energy are frozen clusters of quarks. Matter is simply information which is frozen, and then it dissolves. So the smaller the information unit, the more efficient, and the more kindly, because you don't have to chop down a forest of trees to build books. It can just be put on tiny little silicon chip. See, we've gone from carbon to silicon, because carbon is much more precious. Carbon is organic, whereas silicon is cybernetic. You want to have the silicon do whatever you can to spare the carbon, because the trees, bees and flowers are carbon based.

DJB: How do you feel about scientific progress these days, and what do you think is missing?

TIMOTHY: There's been a wonderful surge of new and imaginative science in the last ten or fifteen years. Prigogine's system theory, for example. Sheldrake's morphogenetic resonance, and the notion of the hundred monkeys. Lovelock's Gaia hypothesis. Terence McKenna. I could go on listing. All of these wonderful intuitions growing out of science have been landmarks. There's just one little slip you have to add to it that makes it all click, and that is that all of these wonderful thinkers and prophets are talking about information. See, another thing I must say is that the key to information theory and quantum philosophy is the notion that *there are no laws of the universe*. That's such a typical Victorian British Empire piece of shit, because the Judeo God is up there—he's the judge, and he's emitting laws and commandments, of all things.

> *the key to information theory and quantum philosophy is the notion that there are no laws of the universe.*

DJB: How do you see the process of evolution working?

TIMOTHY: The way that evolution works at the level of astro-physics, or at the organic level, and even the level of human knowledge, is that it's all based on algorithms. I won't go into the details, but algorithms can be summed up as: if, if, if, if, if, if, if, if, if—then. So, if the sunlight is such, if the temperature is this, if the water level is this, if the meteorological stuff is this, and if there is enough nitrogen—Click—then it happens in every island around, all the leaves turn green. See, they're programmed that way.

DJB: Have you thought about Bell's Theorem, how the mechanism of non-locality occurs?

TIMOTHY: This notion of the non-locality of cause—Bell's Theorem and all that—seems kind of mysterious, unless it's all information, of course. If you program an algorithm, you don't set laws; you're the program, and if the program is if, if, if, if—then, the same thing's going to happen on the other side of the galaxy if it's going to happen here. That's the non-locality of cause. It's totally comprehensible and inevitable if you understand it's all information chains and codes, and they all pop up if, if, if, if—then. This is not in any way a reductionist perspective. Another one of the problems of a soft philosophy and hard philosophy is reductionism.

There's no reductionism here because if you've played around with algorithms, like fractals for example, you realize that you never know what's going to happen. They asked Fredkin—who's the great prophet of all this—"Are you saying that God is some crazed computer hacker in the sky, who's writing all these programs for stars, and atoms?" If there are two of you, and one of me, and you're hydrogen, and I'm oxygen, we get water, see? But, *if* that's the if.

Fredkin said, "Well, I don't know about trying to identify the intelligence that set these algorithms up; we're too crude right now to speculate, but I'll tell you one thing about it. Whoever he, she, it, or they were who wrote these algorithms, they're surprised as hell every time because—quick—oh my god—look what they're doing now!" If you've ever seen how a fractal program operates, you know that these incredible forms develop, and yet they always come back to the basic forms of cosines, which are like the linings of the esophagus, which are like the clouds.

See, coastlines and coast-like phenomena are wonderful, because they are a way of miniaturizing information. If you took a coastline and pulled it out, it'd be like ten miles long, but not if you crunch it together, like the DNA code is. It's a way of miniaturizing and packaging. Now, the notion of

> *It's so comforting to know that everyone is right.*

algorithms account for non-locality of cause. Whether it's Bell's physical experiments, or Sheldrake's hundred monkeys. It's so comforting to know that everyone is right. It's just that we can improve the theories, and make Sheldrake and Bell more precise and comprehensible.

DJB: Can you tell us about any current projects on which you're working?

TIMOTHY: Yes, I'm working on a series of educational programs that allow us to convert education into exciting performance. I've recently been appointed a professor at Penn State. You don't teach courses, you coach. The stars in this metaphor of learning, naturally, are the students, just like baseball. The coach or the teacher—he's the one who just tells you how to use your bat. The stars are the players, who we formerly called students. So I'm coaching students at Penn State via computer. I'm also preparing to nationally syndicate a daily five-minute radio commentary and a weekly half-hour television talk show.

Rupert Sheldrake

"...the regularities of nature I think of as more like habits ,
than as things governed by eternal mathematical laws..."

In the Presence of the Past
with Rupert Sheldrake

Rupert Sheldrake is best known for his controversial theory of "formative causation" which implies a non-mechanistic universe, governed by laws which themselves are subject to change. Born in Newark-on-Trent, England, Rupert studied natural sciences at Cambridge and philosophy at Harvard, where he was a Frank Knox Fellow. He took a Ph.D in biochemistry at Cambridge in 1967, and in the same year became a Fellow of Clare College, Cambridge. He was Director of Studies in biochemistry and cell biology there until 1973.

He was a Rosenheim Research Fellow of the Royal Society and at Cambridge he studied the development of plants and the aging of cells. From 1974 to 1978, he was Principal Plant Physiologist at the International Crops Research Institute for the Semi-Arid Tropics (ICRISAT) in Hyderabad, India, and he continued to work there as a Consultant Physiologist until 1985.

Rupert is the author of A New Science of Life *and* The Presence of the Past, *in which he presents his theory for explaining the mysterious process of morphogenesis. In 1981 the British science magazine,* Nature *described* A New Science of Life *as "the best candidate for burning there has been for many years," while the* New Scientist *called it "an important scientific inquiry into the nature of biological and physical reality."*

In The Rebirth of Nature, *Rupert examines the philosophical implications of morphogenesis, and in* Trialogues on the Edge of the West, *which he wrote with Terence McKenna and Ralph Abraham, he debates and interweaves many ideas concerning the nature of reality.*

On September 15, 1989, we met with the Sheldrakes and their young son Merlin at the Esalen Institute, where Rupert's wife, Jill Pearce, was teaching a workshop in the art of overtone chanting. Rupert spoke to us about the subtle processes involved in the evolution of nature through time, painting a simultaneously intricate and simple picture of a dynamic universe where previously unrecognized functions of space-time are constantly at work interacting with every aspect of life on earth.

—RMN

DJB: Rupert, what was it that originally inspired your interest in biochemistry and morphogenesis?

RUPERT: I did biology because I was interested in animals and plants, and because my father was a biologist. He was a natural historian of the old school, with a microscope room at home and cabinets of slides, and so on. And he taught me a lot about plants, and I learned about animals through keeping pets. I was just very interested in biology. One reason I did biochemistry was because it was one of the very few sciences you could do which was still covering all of biology. Biochemistry covered plants, animals, and microorganisms. That appealed to me. It was a kind of universal biological science. I saw, of course, quite soon, that biochemistry was no way of understanding the forms of animals and plants, and I spent a lot of time thinking about how to make the bridge between embryology, plant development, and what was going on on the biochemical level. And this was the subject of research for some ten years that I did at Cambridge.

DJB: Just so that everyone is familiar with your theoretical work, can you briefly define for us the basic intention behind, and the basic elements of, the theory of formative causation?

RUPERT: The theory of formative causation is concerned with how things take up their forms, or patterns, or organization. So it covers the formation of galaxies, atoms, crystals, molecules, plants, animals, cells, societies. It covers all kinds of things that have forms, patterns, structures, or self-organizing properties.

> *An atom doesn't have to be put together by some external agency. It organizes itself.*

You see, all these things organize themselves. An atom doesn't have to be put together by some external agency. It organizes itself. A molecule and a crystal are not assembled by human beings bit by bit, they spontaneously crystalize. Animals spontaneously grow. All these things are different from machines, which are artificially put together by human beings.

So, what my theory is concerned with is self-organizing natural systems, and it deals with the cause of form. And the cause of all these forms I take to be organizing fields, form-shaping fields, which I call morphic fields, from the Greek word for form. The original feature of what I'm saying is that the forms of societies, ideas, crystals and molecules depend on the way that previous ones of that kind have been organized. There's a kind of built-in memory in the morphic fields of each kind of thing.

> *...forms of societies, ideas, crystals, and molecules depend on the way that previous ones of that kind have been organized.*

So the regularities of nature I think of as more like habits, than as things governed by eternal mathematical laws that somehow exist outside nature.

RMN: Could you give a specific example of, and describe the morphogenetic process in terms of, the development of a well-established species, like a potato, for example?

RUPERT: Well, the idea is that each species, each member of a species draws on the collective memory of the species, and tunes in to past members of the species, and in turn contributes to the further development of the species. So in the case of a potato, you'd have a whole background resonance from past species of potatoes, most of which grow wild in the Andes. And then in that particular case, because it's a cultivated plant, there's been a development of a whole lot of varieties of potatoes, which are cultivated, and as it so happens potatoes are propagated vegetatively, so they're clones.

So each clone of potatoes, each variety, each member of the clone will resonate with all previous members of the clone, and that resonance is against a background of resonance with other members of the potato species, and then that's related to related potato species, wild ones that still grow in the Andes. So, there's a whole kind of background resonance, but what's most important is the resonance from the most similiar ones, which is the past members of that variety. And this is what makes the potatoes of that variety develop the way they do, following the habits of their kind.

Usually these things are ascribed to genes. Most people assume that inheritance depends on chemical genes and DNA, and say there's no problem, it's all just programmed in the DNA. What I'm saying is that that view of biological development is inadequate. The DNA is the same in all the cells of the potato, in the shoots, in the roots, in the leaves, and the flowers. The DNA is exactly the same, yet these organs develop differently. So something more than DNA must be giving rise to the form of the potato, and that is what I call the morphic field, the organizing field.

An example of how you'd test the theory would depend on looking at some change in the species that hadn't happened before, a new phenomenon, and seeing how it spreads through the species. So, for example, if you train rats to learn a new trick in one place, then rats of that breed should learn it more quickly everywhere in the world, just because the first ones have learned it. The more that learn it, the easier it should get.

RMN: What about how the morphic field develops in a new system, like a newly synthesized chemical, or a drug? How would the field evolve around that?

RUPERT: Well, the first time the chemical is crystallized, there won't be a morphic field for the crystals, because they would not have existed before. As time goes on, it should get easier to crystallize, because of morphic resonance from previous crystals. So, however the first pattern is taken up—this is a question of creativity, but assume, for example, it's random—whenever the first lot of crystals crystallize that way, out of the other possible ways they could have crystallized, then that pattern will be stabilized through morphic resonance, and the more often it happens, the more likely it will be to happen again, through this kind of invisible memory connecting up crystals throughout the world. There's already evidence that new crystals, new compounds, do get easier to crystallize as time goes on.

DJB: What are morphic fields made of, and how is it that they can exist everywhere all at once? Do they work on a principle similiar to Bell's Theorem?

RUPERT: Well, you could ask the question, what are any fields made of? You know, what is the electromagnetic field made of, or what is the gravitational field made of? Nobody knows, even in the case of the known fields of physics. It was thought in the nineteenth century that they were made of ether. But then Einstein showed that the concept of the ether was superfluous; he said the electromagnetic field isn't made out of ether, it's made out of itself. It just is. The magnetic field around a magnet, for example, is not made of air, and it's not made of matter. When you scatter iron fillings, you can reveal this field, but it's not made of anything except the field. And then if you say, well maybe all fields have some common substance, or common property, then that's the quest for a unified field theory.

Then if you say, "Well, what is it that all fields are made of?" the only answer that can be given is space-time, or space and time. The substance of fields is space; fields are modifications of space or of the vacuum. And according to Einstein's general theory of relativity, the gravitational field, the structure of space-time in the whole universe, is not *in* space and time; it *is* space-time. There's no space and time other than the structure of fields. So fields are patterns of space-time. And so the morphic field, like other fields, will be structures in space and time. They have their own kind of ontological status, the same kind of status as electromagnetic and gravitational fields.

DJB: Wait. But those are localized aren't they? I mean, you sprinkle iron fillings about a magnet, and you can see the field around it. How is it that a morphic field can exist everywhere all at once?

RUPERT: It doesn't. The morphic fields are localized. They're in and around the system they organize. So the morphic field of you is in and around your body.

The morphic field around a tomato plant is in and around that plant. What I'm suggesting is that morphic fields in different tomato plants resonate with each other across space and time. I'm not suggesting that the field itself is delocalized over the whole of space and time. It's suggesting that one field influences another field through space and time. Now, the medium of transmission is obscure. I call it morphic resonance, this process of resonating. What this is replacing in conventional physics is the so-called "laws of nature," which are believed to be present in all places, and at all times.

So, what is the substance of a law of nature? And how are laws of nature present in all places and at all times? These are the alternative questions to the idea of morphic resonance. It's not as if ordinary physics has something that's more "common sense" than morphic resonance; it has something that's less common sense. It has the idea of invisible mathematical laws, which are not material or energetic, yet present everywhere and always, utterly mysterious. Morphic resonance is mysterious, but it involves not a pattern imposed from outside space and time everywhere, but rather a pattern that can spread through space and time, by the process I call morphic resonance.

RMN: You suggest that the hypothesis of formative causation does not refute orthodox theory but actually incorporates and complements it. How is this so?

RUPERT: The orthodox theory in biology and in chemistry, and indeed in science, is the mechanistic theory of nature that says all natural systems are like machines, and are made up of physical and chemical processes. What I'm saying is that you can, if you like, think of aspects of nature as being machine-like, but this doesn't explain them. Nature isn't a machine. You and I are not machines. We may be *like* machines in certain respects. Our hearts may be like pumps, and our brains, in some sense, like computers.

Nature isn't a machine.

Mechanistic theory is providing machine analogies for nature, and it's true that you can look at some aspects of organisms in this machine-like way. But in other important respects, nature in general, and organisms in particular, are not machines or machine-like. So, what I'm suggesting is that the mechanistic theory is alright as far as it goes. Its positive content is alright when it tells us about the physics of nerve impulses, or the chemistry of enzymes; that's fine, this is useful information, and is part of the picture.

If it says that life is nothing but things that can be explained in terms of regular ordinary physics, that already exist in physics textbooks, if it says life is nothing but that—and this is what most mechanistic biologists do say—then I think it's wrong, because it's too limited. It's taking a part of the picture, and assuming it's the whole. It's a half-truth.

RMN: You've incorporated that into your theory, and just taken it to another level...?

RUPERT: Yes. There are still enzymes and nerve impulses in the kind of world I'm talking about; all the things that are in regular biochemistry and biophysics are still there. What isn't still there is the assumption that these aspects of the process are all there is. To take an analogy, it's like trying to understand a building. If you want to understand a building, one level of looking at it is to say, well it's made of wood and other things, metal and frames, and so on. And then you can say we can measure, we can analyze the wood and other components.

You can find out exactly what chemicals are in the wood, the exact molecular composition, the exact constituents of the whole building. But when you grind it up or break it down to analyze the parts, the form of the building, the structure of the room, the *plan* disappears when you're analyzing the constituents, especially if you have to knock it down to do that. And usually to analyze the chemical constituents within an organism, first you have to kill and destroy it. So the plan of the building is also part of the building, it's the formative aspect of the building, the form. And you'll never understand the plan of a building, its form or its function for that matter, just by analyzing the constituents. Although without the constituents, the wood and stuff, you can't have a building.

DJB: What are the implications of the theory of formative causation? How do hypothetical morphic fields affect things like the sciences, the arts, technologies, and social structures?

RUPERT: Well, I've written an entire book on this subject—*The Presence of the Past*—so it's difficult to answer it extremely briefly. But, first of all, it gives a completely different understanding of formative processes in biology and in chemistry. It gives a new understanding of instincts and behavioral patterns, as being organized by morphic fields. It gives a new understanding of social structure, in terms of morphic fields, and cultural forms, and ideas. All of these I see as patterns organized by these fields with an inherent memory.

In the human realm, for example, it leads to the idea of a collective human memory on which we all draw, which is very like Jung's idea of the collective unconscious. In terms of social groups, it gives rise to the idea that the whole social group is organized by a field. And that that field is not just an organizing structure in the present, but also contains a memory of that social group in the past, a group memory—and also, through morphic resonance, a memory of other similar social groups that have existed before.

So, a football team, for example, will tune into its own field in the past. The individual players on the football team will be coordinated not just by observing each other, but by a kind of group mind that will be working when the game's going around. And this will in turn have as a kind of background resonance the morphic fields of other similar football teams.

RMN: On the one hand it is reassuring that a certain pattern or order is being maintained, and yet options must be available for change if that pattern ceases to function effectively. In what ways does nature supply the necessary conditions for this balance of repeatability and novelty?

RUPERT: Well, the universe is not in a steady state; there's an ongoing creative principle in nature, which is driving things onwards. Cosmologically speaking, this is the expansion of the universe. If the universe had been in a steady state at the moment of the Big Bang, it'd still be at billions of degrees centigrade. We wouldn't be here. The reason we're here is because the Big Bang involved a colossal explosion, an outward movement of expansion of the whole universe, such that it cooled down, and virtually created more space for new things to happen. And in the ongoing evolutionary process, there's a constant destabilization of what's there through the fact that the universe is not in equilibrium.

This ongoing process in the whole of nature in itself tends to break up old patterns, and prevent things just stopping where they were. You see it in the history of the earth, the ongoing evolutionary process, through the catastrophic changes that have happened to the earth through the impact of asteroids and so on.

The cumulative nature of the evolutionary process, the fact that memory is preserved, means that life grows not just through a random proliferation of new forms, but there's a kind of cumulative quality. You start with single-celled organisms, and you end with complex multi-cellular ones, like there are today. New species arise usually when new opportunities appear, and the biggest bursts of speciation that we know about in the history of the earth are soon after great cataclysms, like the extinction of the dinosaurs, which create new opportunities, and all sorts of new forms spring up. Thereafter they tend to be fairly stable. So, quite often, the reasons for creativity depend on accidents or disasters that prevent the normal habits being carried out.

RMN: When a system hits an evolutionary dead end, an organism becomes extinct or an object obsolete. What happens to its field? Does it kind of just breakup and merge with other similar fields?

RUPERT: Well, I think in a sense the ghosts of dead species would still be haunting the world, that the fields of the dinosaurs would still be potentially present ... if you could tune into them. If a dinosaur egg could be reconstituted, you could get them back again. I think that in the course of evolution these past forms do indeed reappear. They're known in the biological literature as atavisms, the process by which the forms, or patterns, or behaviors of extinct species reappear in living ones. Like babies being born with tails.

DJB: Or parallel evolution?

RUPERT: Well, parallel evolution would involve a similar process, but what I'm talking about is the influence of extinct species traveling across time and these features reappearing. Parallel evolution would be where you have the features of some species traveling across space, and similar patterns evolving somewhere else like, for example, the evolution of forms among marsupials in Australia that parallel those of placental mammals elsewhere.

DJB: You said before that there could be a sort of collective memory, and you said that was analogous to Jung's notion of the collective unconscious. Do you think it's possible then that morphic fields are, or can be, actually conscious?

RUPERT: I don't think that morphic fields are conscious. I think that some aspects of morphic fields could become conscious in human beings. I think that the underlying patterns of mental activity that are ideas, thoughts, etc., depend on our morphic fields. I think they become conscious in us. But most of the collective unconscious, most of our habits, and most of the habits of nature, I think, are unconscious, and most of nature, I think, works much more like our unconscious minds than like our conscious minds. And after all, 90%, maybe 99%, of our own activity is unconscious. We don't need to assume that the kind of unconscious memories that we ourselves have are any different from the rest of nature.

We needn't assume that just because we have some conscious memories, all of the memory of nature must be conscious. In fact, most of our memories are unconscious, as are most of our habits, like the habit of speaking English, for example, the way one speaks, one's mannerisms, one's accent, or the habit of driving a car. When you drive a car, you don't have to be conscious of every muscular movement, or everything you're doing. Those habits unfold spontaneously. And the more deep-seated biological habits, like the functioning of our bodies, and our heartbeat, and the way our guts our working are completely unconscious to most of us.

DJB: In your book *The Presence of the Past* you offer the suggestion that memories are not actually stored in the brain, but rather they may be stored in an information field that can be accessed by the brain. If this should prove to be true, do you believe then that human consciousness, our personal memories and sense of self, may survive biological death in some form?

RUPERT: Well, certainly the idea that memories aren't stored in the brain opens the way for a new debate or new perspective on the question of survival of death. Most people assume memories are stored in the brain, simply because this is the mechanistic paradigm that's very rarely challenged. There's hardly any evidence for memory storage in the brain, as I show in my book, and what evidence there is could be interpreted better in terms of the brain as a tuning system, tuning into its own past. So that we can gain access to our own memories by tuning into our own past states. The brain is more like a TV receiver than like a tape recorder or a video recorder.

> *...the idea that memories aren't stored in the brain opens the way for a new debate...on the question of survival of death.*

If memories are stored in the brain then there's no possibility of conscious, or even unconscious survival of bodily death, because if memories are in the brain, the brain decays at death, and your memories must be wiped out through the decay of the brain. No form of survival in any shape or form, even through reincarnation, would be possible in such a scenario. That's one reason why materialists are so attached to the idea of memory storage in the brain, because it refutes all religions in a two line argument. But, in fact, there's very little evidence they're stored in the brain.

So if they're not stored in the brain then the memories won't decay at death, but there'll still have to be something that can tune into them, or gain access to them. So could some tuning system, could some non-physical aspect of the self survive death and still gain access to the memories? That's the big question. I regard it as an open question. I myself think that we do survive bodily death in some form, and that some aspect of the self does survive with access to memories. And that's a personal opinion. The theory as such leaves this question quite open.

DJB: Do you think there is a morphic field for dreams, mystical experiences, and other states of consciousness?

RUPERT: I think that any organized structure of activity—which includes dreams and some mystical experiences, and altered states of consciousness—any pattern of activity has a structure, and in so far as these mental activities or states have structures, then these structures could indeed move from person to person by morphic resonance. And indeed, in many mystical traditions, it's thought that people through initiation are brought into that particular tradition and resonate, or in some sense enter into communion with, or connection with, other people who followed in the tradition before.

So, in Hindu and Buddhist lineages, you often get the idea that through initiation and the transmission of the right mantras, and so on, the initiate comes into contact with the guru, the teacher, and the whole line of those who'd gone before. There is a similar idea in Christianity, the idea of the communion of saints. Those who participate in the Christian sacraments, particularly the Eucharist, are in contact, not just with other people doing it now, or other people who happen to be around, but somehow in some kind of resonant connection with all those who've done the same thing before.

RMN: What have your ideas been on the hierarchical systems of morphic fields, of the fundamental fields of nature or life, and the basic morphic fields that have influenced that, or the morphic fields of morphic fields? I've been wondering about that.

RUPERT: I think all such fields are organized holorarchically or hierarchically. They're hierarchical in the sense of nested hierarchies. Cells are within tissues, and tissues are within organs, and organs are within your body. There's a sense in which the whole, the body and the mind, the whole of you, is greater than the organs in your body, and those in turn are greater than tissues, those in turn greater than cells, those in turn greater than molecules. The greater is a spatial context, the more embracing field.

If you think about the way nature is organized, you can see the same pattern at every level. Our earth, Gaia, is included in the solar system, the solar system is in the galaxy, the galaxy within a cluster of galaxies, and ultimately everything is included within the cosmos. So you could say the most primal basic field of nature is the cosmic field, and then the galactic fields, and solar system fields, planetary fields, continental fields, and so on in this nested hierarchy. At each level the whole organizes the parts within it, and the parts affect the whole; there's a two-way influence.

> *At each level the whole organizes the parts within it, and the parts affect the whole...*

DJB: Do you think it's possible that morphic fields from the future may be influencing us, as well as those from the past? If not, why?

RUPERT: Well, I think that is related to the question of creativity; how do new patterns come into being? There may possibly be some influence from the future. But the habitual fields, which I'm mainly talking about, are not influenced by the future, at least as far as this theory is concerned. It would be possible to have a theory that said the future and the past exerted equal influences, but that theory would be different from the one I'm suggesting, which is that the past is influencing the present through morphic resonance. If future and past influenced it equally, the theory would be virtually untestable, because we don't know what will happen in the future, so we wouldn't know what influences we'd be testing for.

If the future influenced things as much as the past, then the experiments I'm suggesting, like rats getting better at learning something all around the world, shouldn't work. Rats should start off just as good as they continue, because they'll always be limitless numbers in the future, which would be influencing them. So this is actually a testable possibility.

I think that habits and memories come from the past. This is just common sense. We have memories of the past, and we don't have memories of the future in the same way. Occasionally some people have pre-cognitive flashes. But we don't have memories of the future. We may have hopes, plans, desires, inspirations, insights, etc., but they're not memories in the same sense that memories from the past are memories. We don't get habits from the future, we get them from the past.

RMN: Could the presence of the future be described as the potential state of the system, the virtual state, as it moves along the pathways or access routes towards it?

RUPERT: Yes, I think so. I think there are two ways of thinking about it. One is there's a kind of aura around the present stretching out into the future, which is the realm of hopes, fears, possibilities, dreams, imaginings about what can happen. But then there's a further question, and a more fundamental one, as to whether the whole evolutionary process is being pulled from the future, rather than being pushed from the past. And the idea that it's all being pulled from the future is a very traditional view, and so is the idea it's being pushed from the past.

The traditional Judeo-Christian view of history is that history is being pulled from the future, there's something in the future—which Terence McKenna calls the transcendental object, Teilhard deChardin calls the omega point, what the *Book of Revelation* calls the new creation, what metanarians have thought of as the millenium. That some future state of perfection is drawing the whole cosmic evolutionary process towards itself in some mysterious way. And that, therefore, the whole cosmic evolutionary process has a kind of goal or purpose. Well that's a view which many people subscribe to, and it's a view that lies at the root of the doctrine of progress, which dominates our whole society.

So this view isn't just a philosophical view; in a secularized form, it dominates both capitalist and communist societies—the dream of a better future. Most traditional societies haven't had that dream, they haven't been motivated by that, they looked to the past for a model of the way things should be, how it used to be in the golden age. They haven't tried to create a new kind of future golden age. And our society represents an ambitious global attempt to do just that through conquering nature by means of science and technology. The inspirational basis for the destruction of the environment, the development of the tropical forests, etc., is this dream of a future state on earth that progress will lead us towards, where there's peace, prosperity, and plenty through man's conquest of nature.

And many of us now think that dream is a kind of chimera, a vision that is utterly destructive in its consequences. But the fact is that it still comes from that same dream of a future pulling things along. I think all forms of western thought are under the influence of this particular attractor, as one could call it. The idea of a future goal attracting things towards it is utterly dominant in almost every area of western thought I know. The New Age communists with their millenarian vision—it's just part of our culture.

RMN: Yeah, that leads on to the next question I have about how to use the concept of attractors, as expressed in the current research of dynamical systems, in the theory of formative causation.

RUPERT: Well, the idea of attractors, which is developed in modern mathematical dynamics, is a way of modeling the way systems develop, by modeling the end states toward which they tend. This is an attempt to understand sytems by understanding where they're headed to in the future, rather than just where they've been pushed from in the past. So, the attractor, as the name implies, pulls the system towards itself. A very simple, easy-to-understand, example is throwing marbles, or round balls into a pudding basin. The balls will roll round and round, and they'll finally come to rest at the bottom of the basin. The bottom of the basin is the attractor, in what mathematicians call the basin of attraction.

The basin is, in fact, their principal metaphor. So the ball rolls down to the bottom. It doesn't matter where you throw it in, or at what speed you throw it in, or by what route it takes—what this model does is tell you where it's going to end up. This kind of mathematical modeling is extremely appropriate, I think, to the understanding of biological morphogenesis, or the formation of crystals or molecules, or the formation of galaxies, or the formation of ideas, or human behavior, or the behavior of entire societies. Because all of them seem to have this kind of tendency to move towards attractors, which we think of consciously as goals and purposes. But, throughout the natural world these attractors exist, I think, largely unconsciously. The oak tree is the attractor of the acorn. So the growing oak seedling is drawn towards its formal attractor, its morphic attractor, which is the mature oak tree.

RMN: So, it is like the future in some sense.

RUPERT: It's like the future pulling, but it's not the future. It's a hard concept to grasp, because what we think of as the future pulling is not necessary what will happen in the future. You can cut the acorn down before it ever reaches the oak tree. So, it's not as if its future as oak tree is pulling it. It's some kind of potentiality to reach an end state, which is inherent in its nature. The attractor in traditional language is the entelechy, in Aristotle's language, and in the language of the medieval scholastics. Entelechy is the aspect of the soul, which is the end which draws everything towards it. So all people would have their own entelechy, which would be like their own destiny or purpose. Each organism, like an acorn, would have the entelechy of an oak tree, which means this end state—entelechy means the end which is within it—it has its own end, purpose, or goal. And that's what draws it. But that end, purpose, or goal is somehow not necessarily in the future. It is in a sense in the future. In another sense it's not the actual future of that system, although it becomes so.

RMN: Perhaps the most compelling implication of your hypothesis is that nature is not governed by eternally fixed laws but more by habits that are able to evolve as conditions change. In what ways do you think the human experience of reality could be affected as a result of this awareness?

RUPERT: Well, I think first of all the idea of habits developing along with nature gives us a much more evolutionary sense of nature herself. I think that nature—the entire cosmos, the natural world we live in—is in some sense alive, and that it's more like a developing organism, with developing habits, than like a fixed machine governed by fixed laws, which is the old image of the cosmos, the old world view.

> *...the idea of habits developing along with nature gives us a much more evolutionary sense of nature herself.*

Second, I think the notion of natural habits enables us to see how there's a kind of presence of the past in the world around us. The past isn't just something that happens and is gone. It's something which is continually influencing the present, and is in some sense present in the present.

Thirdly, it gives us a completely different understanding of ourselves, our own memories, our own collective memories, and the influence of our ancestors, and the past of our society. And it also gives an important new insight into the importance of

> *The past is continually influencing the present.*

rituals, and forms through which we connect ourselves with the past, forms in which past members of our society become present through ritual activity. I think it also enables us to understand how new patterns of activity can spread far more quickly than would be possible under standard mechanistic theories, or even under standard psychological theories. Because if many people start doing, thinking, or practicing something, it'll make it easier for others to do the same thing.

RMN: And the way different discoveries are found simultaneously.

RUPERT: Yes. I mean, that's another aspect. It will also mean things that some people do—will resonate with others, as in independent discoveries, parallel cultural development, etc.

RMN: When you were talking about the individuals' destinies being ruled by some kind of morphic field of their own. Individuality—does that resonate through their ancestral heritage and their environment?

RUPERT: Well, it was in a quite limited sense that I was using the term. When you're an embryo there's a sense in which the destiny of the embryo is to be an adult human being. There's a sense in which the growth and development of an embryo and a child are headed toward the adult state. That's a relation to time, of heading towards an adult or mature state that we share in common with animals and plants. This is a basic biological feature of our life.

   Then there's a sense in which there is a kind of biological destiny that's common to all animals—you know, having children and reproducing. Not everybody does it, but it's obviously pretty fundamental. Most people do it. If they didn't we wouldn't have a population problem, and that's something that's pretty fundamental to the human species today. Then there's the more psychic, or personal, or spiritual kinds of destinies. Here one gets a whole variety of opinions as to what these are.

RMN: Could you expand on that?

RUPERT: The thing is that most of us aren't at all original. We mostly take on opinions from the available variety on the market, and when you come to the question of individual destiny, you know, there's several traditional theories. One is that when we die, that's it, everything just goes blank, and so the only purpose of life is to enjoy it while it's happening. There's nothing beyond. This is the classic materialist or epicurean view of life.

   Then there are those who think that after death we go into a kind of underworld, and our destiny is to join the ancestors, and that basicaly we're just cycled back into a kind of eternally cycling pool of life. This is found in traditional societies where it's not believed that things change much over time, so the ancestors are constantly being recycled among the living, and they're a living force. But people don't have any individual destiny other than becoming merged with the ancestors. So that would be another option.

   Then there's the reincarnational theories, that you're reincarnated, and that the ultimate destiny is liberation from the wheels of reincarnation. The boddhisatva ideal in Buddhism is to become liberated and then help others to become liberated. But if you don't aspire towards that end, which is the ultimate human end, namely liberation, then through karmic activities and involvement with this life you'll simply be reborn and keep being reborn until you move towards this end or goal which may take many lifetimes to achieve.

Then there's the view you find among Christians and Moslems, which is that there's another realm after this life in which you can undergo continued development or some further destiny, different destinies, depending on how you behave and what you want in this life. So, I mean there are many choices, and that's one of the areas in which choice or freedom comes in. We choose which of these kinds of destiny we want to align ourselves with. Or if we don't think about it or don't choose, then we just fall to the lowest common denominator.

DJB: What types of research experiments do you think need to be done that would either prove or disprove the existence of morphic fields?

RUPERT: Well, I outline quite a number of them in my books. There's a series of experiments that can be done in chemistry with crystals, in biochemistry with protein folding, in developmental biology with fruit fly development, in animal behavior with rats, in human behaviour through studying rates of learning tasks that other people have learned before. So there's a whole range of tests, the details of which I suggest in my books, which could be done to test the theory in a variety of areas: chemistry, biology, behavioral science, psychology. Some of these tests are going on right now in some universities in Britain. There's a competition for tests being sponsored by the Institute of Noetic Sciences, tests to be done by students. The closing date's in 1990. So these are just some of the tests that I'd like to see done to test the theory.

DJB: Could you tell us about any current projects on which you're working?

RUPERT: Well, I'm doing two main things at present. One is that I'm helping to coordinate research on morphic resonance, organizing tests in the realms of chemistry and biology. And secondly I'm writing a book called *The Rebirth of Nature*. It's a book about the ways in which we're coming to see nature as alive, rather than inanimate, and how this has enormous implications: personally for people in their relationships with the world around them; collectively, through our collective relationship to nature; spiritually, the way this leads to a reframing or re-understanding of spiritual traditions, and politically through the Green Movement, which is now an influential political force, especially in Europe.

Moving from the exploitive mechanistic attitude to a symbiotic attitude, we

> **...*we realize that we're not in charge of nature*...**

realize that we're not in charge of nature, we're not separate from nature and somehow running it. Rather we're part of ecosystems, and part of the world, and our continued existence depends on living harmoniously with the planet of which we're a part. It's an obvious thing, this Gaian perspective, but it hasn't been taken seriously in politics. But now it is being taken seriously, and so I would say the idea of nature as alive has become a very important force in our society through its political manifestations as well as its scientific ones.

Dennis Wyszynski

Carolyn Mary Kleefeld

"...when artists are working directly from their emerging
consciousness, their art is their most honest mirror."

Singing Songs of Ecstasy
with Carolyn Mary Kleefeld

On September 14, 1989, in her candlelit living room at around midnight, we interviewed poet and painter Carolyn Mary Kleefeld at her home in Big Sur, perched on the crest of a mountain cliff high above the sea. Carolyn was born in Catford, England, and raised in Santa Monica, California. Fueled by a life-long fascination with psychological transformation and a passion for creative expression, she is the author of three internationally acclaimed, award-winning poetry books that address these archetypal themes: Climates of the Mind, Satan Sleeps With the Holy: Word Paintings, and Lovers in Evolution. Her influential books received the rare honor of being translated into Braille—so as to give vision to the blind—by the Library of Congress, and are used worldwide at many universities and human potential centers. Carolyn is currently completing her sixth book— The Sixth Dimension:Architecture for Ecstasy.

During the Summer of 1990 the Gallerie Illuminati in Santa Monica featured a dazzling series of Carolyn's visionary paintings in an exhibit entitled "Songs of Ecstasy," and an art book of the same title was simultaneously published. Since then her work has been featured in galleries all over the world. A selection of her paintings is also available as a line of fine art cards, from Atoms Mirror Atoms of Carmel. Her painting "Neuro-Erotic Blast-Off" appears on the cover of my first book, Brainchild, and her piece "Fluorescent Sunset of the Future" is included in a textbook on visual art called Unique Journeys, by Professor James Schinneller of the University of Wisconsin. Carolyn spoke to us about the relationship between art and consciousness, expanded awareness and creative expression, and personal and universal transformation, and muses with us about the living secrets of nature. She looks as though she danced right out of one of her own paintings. Her eyes and smile have a luminous mystery about them that is present also in much of her work. She has a graceful and elegant manner about her, and one is easily enchanted by her poetic style of expression.

—DJB

DJB: What was it that originally inspired your interest in creative expression?

CAROLYN: It is the discovery of my relationship with the universe, the unknown, that propels my translation. The spheres explored radiate a spectrum of seed-images. The wilderness of the unconscious is lush with the gems of infinity. The ancient codes lie in the seams between worlds. They only await the radiance of our conscious light to be illumined, recognized.

> *It is the discovery of my relationship with the universe...that propels my translation.*

For example, at seven years old, I wrote and illustrated my first book entitled, *The Nanose.* Many years later I found out that my experience then, which was triggered by dust particles dancing in a sunbeam flooding my bedroom window, actually had its inherent meaning in my poetic translation of it, rather than in the external event itself.

Through my impression of the dancing dust particles I had my first recorded interaction with atomic life. My art was the bridge, translating localized conception (dust particles) into atomic theory. I thus experienced intimate dialogue with the vaster universe.

Today my reading of science tells me that the Nanose in my childhood book were monads, or cellular/atomic entities that underlie our contemporary concepts of biology and physics. Even the title *Nanose* essentially is the Greek word "nano," meaning very small, as in the contemporary innovation called "nanotechnology."

So art acts as a prescient translation from the unconscious mind, revealing the codes—the consciousness of the underlying forces of nature.

DJB: So, it was basically a need to express powerful experiences?

CAROLYN: Well, it was my interaction with inner experience, rather than the exterior event itself, that propelled the creative expression.

DJB: What do you think triggered these experiences?

CAROLYN: It is in the dynamics of discovery that innovation occurs. I also am saying that I "respond" from the inside out. Rather than having the exterior world give me its reality, I interpret the reality from within myself.

The experiences are woven and sculpted by my particular nervous system. Those certain experiences that need to be lived as part of one's evolvement are the ones to leave the deepest impressions. These impressions imprint their design within me and are the songs that emerge in my tides of creative expression.

> *Even the mistakes that are birthed instigate further invention.*

Also, it is out of the foundation of my own philosophical architecture that I germinate my art, with subsequent reflection, consciousness. Out of this constant processing within me, which is my life's work, my visible art reveals the seeds, buds, blossoms, fruits, the pollen of my interplay with the unknown. Even the mistakes that are birthed instigate further invention. The propulsion of innovation wings me beyond localized sight.

This last idea intimates the possibilities of developing "laser sight" in the future. This means to inhabit a transparency of being that is so open a system as to let radiance flood it. The vision of our futures could possibly allow us to see through the density that now blocks our vision.

From the architecture of a new way of perceiving, we will peer from the infinite spheres and see into the gossamer connections of our electric loom of being. Our cosmic eyes will see immediately into the true laws that be. Instantaneous perception will bloom in this smoldering symbiosis. Our cellular beings will manifest our consciousness in new sight and technologies of life.

RMN: To what extent is your work autobiographical? How do you use it as a tool by which to access, understand, and integrate your inner processes?

CAROLYN: Being an artist, I am the translator of my experience and thus am the author of my life. Since each of us experiences something in our own unique way, everything we create is essentially autobiographical. I am at once the tool, and the work. The universe is strumming the strings of my nervous system and I record the songs. After the songs are born, either in my paintings, drawings, prose, or poetry, I study and endlessly see different perspectives depending on my own state of being, or cycle of evolvement.

Last Fall, I gave a reading in Monterey at the Cafe Portofino titled "Art as Evolution's Mirror"—my theme being that when artists are working directly from their emerging consciousness, their art is their most honest mirror. I mean, when the work comes from the inner development of the artist, rather than from imitation. Most artists are like engineers reproducing the familiar. This type of art, from the outside in, is not the same art as art that is being created as part of an emerging consciousness. If artists are not involved in the inner consciousness of their work, they can't learn by it.

But each of us has a unique path, and none are to be judged. It's just that for me the conscious reflection is part of the fun of discovery, so I'm blessed with this tool which shines light on my work. Symbolic poetry, which is my bridge of translation, offers a kind of insight similar to the *I Ching*. It reflects back to the participant-viewer or reader. It is a kind of Rorschach, revealing from the truth of the unconscious one's inner shadow.

This way of living requires constant preparation, keeping oneself clear enough to create the space to ride the constant waves of invention. The process is one of digestion, assimilation and integration of the universal flux.

RMN: Do you think you benefited by having a formal art training, and how have you incorporated that?

CAROLYN: In both my painting and poetry, I learned what didn't inspire me. It served to tell me I was to sculpt my own path, sing my own unique song. "Find your own voice," as Anais Nin wrote to me while I was writing *Climates of the Mind.*

RMN: How easy do you find it to be objective about your own creations, and what do you think are the most important qualities that a good critic should have in order to evaluate something from a non-biased standpoint?

CAROLYN: There is no such thing as being objective. Every observer has a particular set of prejudices and preferences, so it isn't possible for myself or a critic to be non-biased. The most essential quality for a critic to have is to be aware of this.

DJB: When you're in need of inspiration, where do you turn?

CAROLYN: It depends on what cycle or season I'm in. It could range from quiet meditation in a beautiful environment, to dashing somewhere for social stimulation. It's all in my relationship to the internal dialogue that the inspiration comes. So, I will draw to me that which mirrors me. The outside inspiration comes from a projection, which later I may say "inspired me," or was the "stimulus." Actually it's the interplay of myself with that which mirrors me. The company distributing my art is called "Atoms Mirror Atoms," which reflects this idea. We are nature's forces translating, in human terms, our existence. Art is my bridge of translation. That is why art is the "international language," as it has the myriad tongues of its artists' voices.

DJB: Are there any particular authors or musicians that have inspired or influenced you?

CAROLYN: Yes, my first mentor was Dr. Carl Faber, then came the writings of Anais Nin. Other influences include: Herman Hesse, Marie Rainer Rilke, William Blake, Vincent Van Gogh, Marc Chagal, Gustav Klimt, D.H. Lawrence, Baudelaire, Dylan Thomas, Benjamin de Casseres, Aldous Huxley, and Mozart. Then there is the current powerful influence of my friends and contemporaries.

DJB: How do you experience and describe the stages of the creative process?

CAROLYN: To begin with, creative expression requires an overflow of energy. It requires me to be a canvas or open page. I offer myself as the film for being photographed by the sublime. It is always out of a random spontaneity. That is why I have paints in different areas outside as well as in my living room. I carry a pen and paper on my hikes. I draw some of my best work while in a car. As to the length of time of the stages, it varies from very quickly to a few months, or longer. Sometimes there is a fermentation or incubation; other times, the flame seems to be ignited in the darkest night.

DJB: How do you see consciousness evolving in the next century?

CAROLYN: Progress is painfully slow. We are still existing on a biological survival level. Nature will use us as its tools

...the word "universe" means united verses.

to continue its galactic body. For us to survive, we will have to refine ourselves as one with this endless expanding universe. Notice that the word "universe" means united verses. When in harmony, life is a symphony of united verses; when discordant, there is cacophony.

RMN: How do you compare the creative process involved in writing poetry with that of painting?

CAROLYN: My painting and drawing, being visual, are pre-lingual. Poetry and prose, being verbal, are more restricted in their word-clothes. I enjoy both translations, the freedom of the non-verbal in painting, and the architecture of words. They are in constant dialogue, a harmonious chord ascending my song.

DJB: In your three books, there seems to be an evolution of consciousness that is being expressed: a progression from states of psychological difficulty and struggle to ecstatic mystic revelations. How would you describe this archetypal journey from darkness to light?

CAROLYN: I would say the darkness is there before the "witness of oneself" is developed. It's in the capacity to reflect, that one illuminates one's experience and thus can move into the light. The light is one's own star in orbit amongst the galactic systems in constant electrical interplay. The dialogue, the information, the secret messages come from being deeply in reception of these infinite channels. It is a lying back in the embracing arms of infinity, having all in expecting nothing. My books are the charting of this voyage of experiences, the currents in the wake of navigation. Presently I am editing and completing my first prose book titled *The 6th Dimension: Architecture for a Esctasy*. It represents the recordings of my own particular vessel as it rides the waves of existence, a vessel united in verse with the universal.

RMN: Many of your paintings reveal mythic combinations of humans and animals. Does this arise from your own experience of inter-species communication?

CAROLYN: Yes, we have an aviary here with thirty-six lovebirds, parakeets, and cockatiels. We're living with owls, hawks, peregrine falcons, chipmunks, squirrels, mice and many other unique creatures. The creatures and I are in daily dialogue. I make a special whistle sound when I paint which I also use to communicate with the birds. They seem to tune in to the resonance.

RMN: Are they usually friendly?

CAROLYN: Yes, unless put on the defensive, which we avoid. In Nature one can see into the ancient wisdom, the order that governs our greater existence, our interactions with one another.

DJB: So you feel that you can talk to Nature sometimes, or that Nature talks to you?

CAROLYN: Yes, I do commune with Nature. It may be necessary for others to also experience a less literal, more poetic language for this to happen. Incidentally, we've discovered that lovebirds aren't necessarily monogamous and that falcons can carry grudges.

DJB: Free-love birds?

CAROLYN: Well, their behavior exposes our misconceptions about their monogamy. The creatures' instincts are the same as ours, except that we are far more complex and lethal. Even though our birds have all their needs met in the aviary, they are still programmed in a survival code, and will fight if territory or sex is involved.

DJB: How has your location influenced your artwork?

CAROLYN: We are living 500 feet above the sea, with a 360-degree view. This serves to keep a lid off our heads. The beauty is a never-ending, changing spectacle. We receive the winds from every direction, which can be quite a challenge to live with. The wildly divergent energies, forces of the "dragon's crown" where we live, are all translated into my art through the instrument of myself in concert with it all.

DJB: How has being in Big Sur in particular influenced your work?

CAROLYN: It's a unique place to be. It has accelerated my internal journey, and simultaneously my art, to be in a place where I can create the space and time to let all that's possible happen. It's an enigmatic and challenging environment. It's been essential for me to be in the constant inspiration of nature, where I can be in

> *...we have so few places left that can mirror the human soul.*

a position to live my own natural rhythms, and define my own nature. Previously, I didn't have the time to do so. Here, I'm able to create a world where I can live in my imagination as much of the time as possible.

This wilderness is a place that allows me to be in a receptive and vulnerable state of being. Because I'm not dealing with the daily traffic of a city, I'm not having to use the defense mechanisms that dull my sensibilities. My sensitivities and sensibilities can have the freedom to play, experiment, and just be. Big Sur is a mirror for a beautiful state of mind, hence the real importance of keeping it unpolluted can't be stressed too much, since we have so few places left that can mirror the human soul. Of course, one's internal environment always creates one's perception of the external environment, wherever one is, and can eventually reshape the external.

DJB: So you're saying that there's a reflection or a synchronistic parallel between your own inner experience and the environment here?

CAROLYN: Yes, I'm attempting to live in a conscious process with my experience, weaving this integration into my artwork. Of course I'm also dealing with many business issues, social issues and other demands while I live here. So, I'm not able to be totally in meditation. But in dealing with the world, I can see how other people are relating to the universe. There are enormously divergent climates, conflicting psychological warfares, and assumed prejudices that take different cruel forms of human expression. This does not make for a healthier world, and drags our evolutionary force downward like gravity, instead of evolving us into an ideal future.

DJB: What's dragging the evolutionary force downward?

CAROLYN: I see us as the clothed forces of nature in our vast geometric diversity. Our greatest limitation is our closed minds, our limited perceptions.

This causes us to live from survival fears, and prevents us from realizing that we have everything that we need, here on this glorious planet. If all people were to cultivate themselves, the way they think, we could grow out of this survival mentality. But human beings have been raped of their self-rights, and have allowed this to happen. For some reason they've given up their original birth-rights.

> *If all people were to cultivate themselves...we could grow out of this survival mentality.*

DJB: Why do you think they've done this?

CAROLYN: There's a temptation to hand over self-responsibility, first to familial hierarchies, then to the influences of educational and governmental "authorities." On the other hand, we are tools in the hands of nature, and the world uses us according to our strengths and susceptibilities. The jungle needs its mechanics to go on, just as the inter-galactic intelligence needs its imagination.

DJB: So what do you think we can do to help wake people up? Or maybe you're saying we shouldn't, because if we're all part of a larger super-organism, and some people play the role of liver or stomach cells, maybe they don't need to wake up—but then again you said before that they're hindering or pulling back on the evolutionary process. So what do you think people can do?

CAROLYN: Ideally, all people would develop a self-referencing point to comprehend themselves and their universe well enough to guide their own vessel with awareness. Otherwise all you have is sleeping, dazed nuts and bolts, endless repetitions of people in reproduction. A certain amount of this is obviously an ingredient of evolution, but at this point in history we can see that a total regeneration of inner, thus outer values is necessary for all of our survival. The exploitation, the murderous lies of our leaders, must be rec-

> *The collective is only as great as every individual.*

ognized, and the individual must reclaim their rights to harmony. Everything that's going on outside is also within us. It's up to us to navigate our forces, unify to a greater harmony. The collective is only as great as its every individual.

DJB: The idea being that the more people that do it, the easier it is for other people to do it. It creates a stronger field, and then there's more of a resonance?

CAROLYN: Yes, for instance, once an athletic record is broken, then it's psychologically easier for others to do the same. The resonance is in the expanded consciousness.

DJB: And you think part of the problem is that the bureaucratic systems discourage people from living their highest integrity?

CAROLYN: The word integrity has been lost to a dysfunctional fragmentation. The comprehensive whole has become disconnected, schizoid. There is no prominent ethical reality in our society to serve as a model for a healthy way of being. I consider it truly pathetic that the leaders chosen by the people are the most aggressive, vicious and deceitful of the population. This shows we are on a bare survival, fear level and choose the most murderous dogs to defend us. The people have to think differently and demand a voice that gives them their basic rights to a healthy existence. They must not agree to having their hard-earned money used for defense instead of progress.

As Einstein said, the problem is the way we think. I think everyone has been constricted by a non-culture that is dollar-crazed, where the churches have been replaced by the banks. People are enslaved by their fears, by the stress that they're under financially. You know, I'd like to see everybody in America all stand up together demanding to have a voice, right on their tax form; as to how their money is spent. The most humiliating thing the government does is to levy a tax so hard on the people that they have to work everyday under stress, and then their money is used to build systems that kill them.

So, here you have an example of what I was speaking of earlier. If you take the individuals' rights away, you make them completely dependent on you. Once people submit to having their birthright, their individual rights, taken away, they've sacrificed themselves to a system that swallows their integrity. That's the end of them, because they've lost their capacity to grow as individuals beyond that social survival level of existence, and that's not where anyone's ever going to find fulfillment. Out of the relentless need for exterior power and exploitation can only come the damaging imbalance of needs and greeds.

DJB: Do you foresee a major change coming along soon?

CAROLYN: Well, I think that generally everything happens very gradually, just like Nature. But Nature also can do some very extreme things that are the opposite of gradual. An asteroid or comet could crash into Earth, for example, and there would be instant evolution, in a direction that we may not recognize!

DJB: Without warning there are earthquakes, volcanic eruptions, and genetic mutations. Things happen all of a sudden sometimes.

CAROLYN: I think that the earth is, as we are, a transforming entity. We are planets unto ourselves, the same as the earth.

DJB: Planets are really people?

CAROLYN: Planets are really people. They have transformations, they go through illnesses, and everything just like we do, on every level. Right now this planet is in a health crisis, and it will do whatever it has to in order to move to the next stage. So I think that there will an increase in natural and peculiar physical disasters, including increased volcanism, or at any moment we could be hit by asteroids from outer space.

DJB: Wow. You really think that something like that could happen?

CAROLYN: Well, anything is possible with Nature. Its design in undesign goes beyond our localized conceptions.

DJB: In the way that we're like cells in a larger body, planets are also like cells in a larger body, and our planet is sending out SOS signals?

CAROLYN: Yes, every atom in every universe is in response from another alchemical stage of transformation. We are part of an expanding intergalactic system and what the interplay of all this will mean is very complex and speculative. I see it as in our molecular biology, where different enzyme combinations have a uniquely specified part to play.

DJB: Have you had any experiences that you thought to be communications with beings from another planet or not of this world?

CAROLYN: Well, I feel as if I'm in touch with what I call the "ancestral resonance." This would be a poetic translation for receiving information from everything that's ever happened. Within one's every breath lives every beginning.

DJB: It sounds like what Philip K. Dick called Valis—the Vast Active Living Intelligence System, or what the Hindus called the Akashic Records, or Alyha Vijnyana, where all the information in the universe is stored.

CAROLYN: Yes, if you listen to the sounds of the tides of the oceanic pulse, you hear the music of all that's ever been. Everything that's ever been has a sound, and the sound is still reverberating from its origin. Of course the eternal symphony is forever expanding with each new cellular note of sound. I have a poem about this idea called "The Lost Language of Unheard Sound."

DJB: The way that each sound is connected to its whole ancestral past, and carries within it the whole history, and maybe even the future...

CAROLYN: Yes, it can be the exquisite music I heard in deep meditation that inspired my poem. It is the lost language of unheard sound because it's lost in the infinite until we open our ears and deepen our silence to hear and receive it.

DJB: Have you ever thought that you are translating music into visual forms?

CAROLYN: Yes, the fluid media I use allows the musical colors and rhythms to form a circulation of patterns and forms through me. The fusion of the varied colors and chemicals creates a form of its own, paralleling the synthesis of musical textures.

As the example of the dolphin's ultrasonic communication teaches us, you can remake the form if you have its sound. So, out of the currents and colors of the music I paint to comes the form through my translation. The sound I make is dolphin-like and tunes me in mantra-like to the unknown, carrying back images like a dolphin's sonar.

DJB: You've refrained from imposing a kind of internal structure onto the natural flow?

CAROLYN: It's more like I become the empty canvas, empty mind, and in becoming one with the atomic energies that be, these energies, this consciousness, uses my nervous system for its translation. Rather like an Aeolian harp being brought to sound by the winds.

DJB: It seems like a musical instrument, your body or nervous system?

CAROLYN: True, an instrument that lets itself be played by nature, but it isn't that I'm not guiding. I'm very much in charge of what I'm doing. But I'm also completely not in charge. It's like all the opposites are happening—because that's the only way you can get perfect balance, meaning the balancing of opposites. I wear ballet slippers when I paint. At an early age I was a prima ballerina, so I was always involved with balance.

As in our living, we must be the navigator of our energies, the balancers of the flow of atomic information. As a conductor I stand above my paintings and work as the skies and winds as a torch of current. I dance and leap about quite unconsciously, letting us form each other, the work and I, as one. Thus, in the inherent order of my particular integration, consciousness, the gossamer order, underlies the freedom of chaos.

DJB: Because you are unique, your works have their unusual originality.

CAROLYN: Thank you. Originality has its origin in its freedom and the only way true liberation is possible, is through inherent order. So I am spinning and weaving my thoughts constantly into my art, into order. The bliss of inventing keeps me in tune.

DJB: Yes, being a musical instrument is a beautiful metaphor for the process of creative expression.

CAROLYN: Also, it is a unique circulation, a poetic metabolism. I've noticed the imagination has beautiful sounds when in tune; it hums. The metabolic intensity of creating is hypnotic, like an unfurling chant, chord in accord.

I once experienced my body as being a nanotechnological factory in which I heard the buzzing and repairing of my system. Atomic elves regenerating all my parts.

DJB: So your work expresses, through poetic metaphor, atomic life?

CAROLYN: Yes, the language of poetic symbolism is multi faceted, offering a kaleidoscopic view of life that is ever moving in possible perception. It is connected to a deep comprehension of the question of reality, not limited in the linear, or one-reality concepts. You can see from this overview the theater of our existence, its pageantry of absurdity. There is the cosmic eye with all its clarity and humor. In my drawings, I have a character called "the Witness of the More." This is the self-referencing director who sifts out the superfluous in the editing room of one's consciousness.

There are some of us who live in the imagination, in the crown of the universal consciousness. There are others essential to the industry, the mechanical. Unfortunately most people have become enslaved by the rusty mechanics of our times, the stale and massively re-broadcast thoughts, and operate as robotized ants.

DJB: Slaves?

CAROLYN: Yes, liberation requires people to wake up, see the illness of their planet, of themselves, their leaders, and rise to a higher more conscious integration. Through abrasion there is refinement. So the brave, the bold, the adventurers will put themselves out there, and invent these possibilities for higher existence. Like being a diamond or crystal through their strength of vision, their capacity to see through life, they illuminate the genes of life's potential, the ideals of themselves. Since this planet is in a crisis stage, it will call on its healthiest instruments to bring it to its next stage of evolution. Of course this is all happening in integration with an ever-expanding intergallactic system.

> ...*every atom of our consciousness is being involuntarily mirrored throughout space.*

Remember, every atom of our consciousness is being involuntarily mirrored throughout space. That's why each individual is so important; if they are living from their highest potential, it is automatically transmitted, radiated. Today we must replace the "arms race" with a "race to hold hands." Atomically speaking, we are anyway, even though our defenses block the natural harmony of really holding hands.

DJB: What do you foresee happening to the evolution of human consciousness in the future? Where is the human race going in terms of how it's evolving in say ten years or fifty years?

CAROLYN: I saw a small waterfall of sand sifting down from a huge sand dune at the beach the other day. I thought about the fact that it took all of time for that one movement to happen just the way it did.

If we can move out of our "survival mode" and put our resources, imagination and money into medical science and technology, we could hold immortal life sooner than we might think. Nature already does it, and through nanotechnology we can.

DJB: What effect do you think immortal physical bodies would have on the evolution of consciousness?

CAROLYN: We could evolve beyond our constant preparation for death. This could liberate people from many of the exploitative emotions. In the prose book I'm writing, that's what I write about—the dimension that doesn't have to have death for life to exist.

DJB: So your latest book is about going beyond physical limitations?

CAROLYN: Yes, it's architecture for a new philosophy, a new way of thinking: a spiritual technology which, hopefully, will manifest in our scientific advancements.

DJB: Spirituality. What does the word spiritual mean to you?

CAROLYN: It means to go beyond the limited, physical conception of oneself, one's personality, to unify with the greater order. This requires shedding the many superficial needs, desires and myriad other ego-enslavements. It also means having a reverence for life, a passion that takes you beyond the limits of self-imposed "will-power" into a space that is effortless and yet animated by the greater forces that be, that are within each of us.

It takes giving oneself the time and space to recreate one's life and self. It requires much re-structuring to eventually regain the essential simplicity. When you are living in your unconditioned being, in the

> *It requires much re-structuring to eventually regain the essential simplicity.*

rhythms of your Tao, life becomes a surfing of reality, of the waves and cycles of the infinite seasons. It is action through non-action. The circles of our cycles bring us back to a beginning that makes everything possible, where again imagination may ride the crest of our highest potential.

Colin Wilson

"...we possess all kinds of unknown powers, and the science
of the future will be an exploration of these powers."

Outside the Outsider
with Colin Wilson

Colin Wilson was born in Leicester, England, in 1931, the son of a boot and shoe worker. He left school at the age of sixteen, spent some time working in taxes and the Royal Air Force, then became a tramp and did various laboring jobs for several years while writing his first novel Ritual in the Dark *and then his first book* The Outsider. *Living on almost no money, he would sleep outside at night in London, and spend his days writing in the British Museum. After his first book became a best-seller in 1956, he took to writing full-time and moved to Cornwall, where he lives to this day. In the mid-1960s, he was commissioned to write a book about the "paranormal," became fascinated by the subject, and has written a number of books on paranormal phenomena. He has also written several works on criminology, psychology, and numerous novels with science fiction and fantasy themes.*

Colin is incredibly prolific, and has produced over sixty books to date. Some of his well-known titles include The Occult, Mysteries, The Mind Parasites, *and* The Philosopher's Stone. *His favorite recreation is listening to music and at his home he has a large collection of opera recordings. Except for occasional lecturing trips abroad, he lives near Mevagissey in Cornwall with his wife and two sons. I interviewed Colin, while Rebecca was abroad, outside the cafeteria at the Esalen Institute on the afternoon of September 16, 1990. There is a laser-beam-like intensity to Colin, and he has an extremely focused and well-disciplined mind. Colin spoke eloquently about his interest in the paranormal, the relationship between sex and creativity, certainty and ambiguity, life after death, and the new emerging species that he believes is evolving out of humanity.*

—DJB

DJB: Colin, what was it that originally inspired your interest in the occult and the paranormal?

COLIN: I was simply asked to write a book about the paranormal by a publisher in 1968. At first I was not very interested, although I'd always been mildly interested in the occult. I would buy books in American airports about ghosts, weird coincidences, or whatever. Never the less I took it on as rather a light-hearted thing, and I would not have been the least upset to discover that the whole thing was just a tissue of nonsense and wishful thinking.

However, when I had agreed to write the book for the sake of money, and I began to go into the subject, I became increasingly fascinated as I saw that there's as much evidence for the paranormal as there is for atoms and electrons. Moreover, what excited me so much was that my work had all been about this recognition that we possess powers that we do not normally know about or use. This appeared to be the perfect example of all kinds of powers that we don't know about or use. So it was a direct extension of my work in *The Outsider*, as it were. I stumbled upon it at just the right moment.

> *...there's as much evidence for the paranormal as there is for atoms and electrons.*

DJB: Aha, or it stumbled upon you. Why do you think that magic is the science of the future?

COLIN: In a way this supplements the last question that you asked. Because what I was saying is that we possess all kinds of unknown powers, and the science of the future will be an exploration of these powers. But at the present science does not accept the unknown powers, and it's still putting up a terrific struggle against the paranormal. You know this Society for the Investigation of the Claims of the Paranormal, and so on. It seems to me that this is old-fashioned science, of the most narrow and materialistic kind. You have just got to be tolerant, and open up to this other possibility of unknown powers, which at the moment, we do not fully recognize.

DJB: I believe that you have said that if your first book made millions, you may have stopped writing at that point, implying that a lack of money motivated you to write more. Now I have always thought just the opposite—that a lack of financial freedom actually inhibits many people from creative expression. Are you saying then that it was money that motivated you to write your first book, and if not, what was it?

COLIN: Oh no, of course not. The first book, in any case, *The Outsider*, was written simply out of this compulsion that I have been speaking about all weekend. It was this basic fascination obviously that motivated me, not money. Neither have I said that if I had become a millionaire I would have stopped writing. I most certainly would not have. What I have said is, that if my first novel *Ritual in the Dark* had been turned into a movie, as it almost was in 1960, all of my subsequent novels would probably have been filmed and I would have been very comfortably off. But certainly I would not have been driven in the way that I have been driven, and I can not help feeling when I look back on this that the way that I have been driven is not necessarily a bad thing.

Once, Fritz Peters turned to Gurdjieff in a state of depression, and Gurdjieff was forced to make a terrific effort to get him out of this depression. Then at this moment crowds of people arrived, and Gurdjieff, from looking exhausted, suddenly looked absolutely, magnificently full of vitality. He said to Peters, you have forced me to make a terrific effort, but this has been very good for both of us. Thank you for reminding me. Now, very often the very efforts we do not want to make prove to be the very best that we could make. So, in a sense, being too successful would simply remove some of that inner pressure. You would slip into what I have been calling ambiguity.

> *...often the very efforts we do not want to make prove to be the very best that we could make.*

DJB: What similarities and differences do you see between pathological or criminal minds and the creative process?

COLIN: Shaw said that we judge the criminal by his lowest moments, and the creator by his highest moments. So obviously, in a sense, they are absolute opposites, and that is what's so interesting about them. And yet you can also see very often that the criminal may be, particularly nowadays, a quite interesting intellectual creative sort of person. And that when he explodes, as let's say Bundy did, into crime, he's choosing a path just as much as let's say a painter, like Picasso, or more Van Gogh, chooses to create this kind of thing.

The explosive sort of force behind Van Gogh's painting is obviously a force based upon a sort of frustration, and it's the same frustration that you would find in a criminal. The only difference is, of course, that Van Gogh deliberately makes the effort to transmute that to a much higher level. The criminal merely says, oh the hell with it, lets go, and invariably destroys himself in doing so, destroys something essential in himself.

There's a play by Pushkin called Mozart and Salierie in which he explores this myth that Salierie murdered Mozart. One of the main points of the play is the discussion in which they state that a man who is a criminal cannot also be a great creator. When Salierie has poisoned Mozart, it suddenly strikes him that he's poisoned Mozart because he considers him his chief musical rival. But, in a sense, by poisoning him, he's proved that he himself is no Mozart. He's a second-rater.

DJB: You said this weekend that it is mathematically provable that "head consciousness is the answer." Do you think that the intellectual mind is superior to the emotional circuit in regard to solving the problems of human existence, as you seemed to imply here this weekend at Esalen? Don't you agree that one should integrate many ways of "Knowing," as you say, besides the intellectual mode of interpretation? For instance—sensory, emotional, phermonal, intuitive, perhaps telepathic, etc.

COLIN: What I have said basically is that up to now, the twentieth century culture has tended to emphasize these other modes you mention. So that, for example, someone like D. H. Lawrence said, what we have to do is go back to the solar plexus, to sexuality, and mistrust the intellect. Henry Miller would have said the same kind of thing. Walt Whitman also was saying in a way, trust the body. Now, all of this is perfectly correct in its way, but if Walt Whitman had said trust *only the body*, or D.H. Lawrence had said trust *only the solar plexus*, then they would have been totally wrong.

Now what I'm trying to say is that the body, the solar plexus, and all of the rest of them, play their part in this synthesis. You know the old Latin tag, *men sarne encal porsano*, a sane mind in a sane body. But, at the same time we have to recognize that the ultimate arbiter is the mind, and that when you see something to be true, as it were, you can see that it is true intellectually. Now it is this intellectual recognition of truth that *must* be the foundation of all these other things. No good having this D.H. Lawrence attitude that you should not trust the intellect because it will always tell you lies. This is the reason that Lawrence's novels, particularly ones like *Women in Love* and so on, always end with a strange feeling of bitterness, defeat, and futility.

DJB: What do you think happens to human consciousness after physical death?

COLIN: As a result of writing the book *Afterlife*, and studying this, I came almost reluctantly to the conclusion that it does survive, that there is survival after death. It would not worry me terribly if there weren't, because it seems to me logical that when I fall asleep, I disappear. I could not really complain if that happened to me after I died.

> *...I came almost reluctantly to the conclusion that...there is survival after death.*

It would seem natural to say that the solution to the problem of human existence lies elsewhere than in the notion that we have got to continue to exist. And yet the evidence is that we do continue to exist. And I don't think that there's any possible doubt about it.

DJB: Why do you think there's such a fear of death then?

COLIN: For the obvious reason that most people are not aware of this. I'm not even sure that it would be terribly good for them to be aware of it. As it is, people who have near-death experiences say that it's so exquisite that they are often resentful about being pulled back. It would be too bad if *death* became, as it were, the outlet for everybody in the way that drugs or alcohol can be.

DJB: That sounds like a good design for the universe. Have you ever had any experiences communicating with beings that you felt were extraterrestrial in origin, or not from this world?

COLIN: No.

DJB: You have said that evidence for free will stems *not* from recognizing that we robotically fulfill desires like hunger and sleep, but from the recognition that we can think what we want. But how do you know that you can think what you want—especially in light of the knowledge that by changing neurochemistry we change consciousness?

COLIN: I said that William James' proof that he was not *just a machine*, that he possesses free will, was this recognition that you *can think one thing rather than another*. And there's no doubt whatever that we can do that. You may feel that everything else is mechanically determined, that what I do next can be explained in completely mechanical terms. I am going to dinner because I am hungry, and so on and so forth. But there is that one thing that makes it absolutely certain that we do possess free will, and that is the fact that you can think one thing rather than another. You can change in mid-stride, so to speak, and think something else.

DJB: Why do you view the psychedelic experience as a step backwards in evolution—to our instincts, as you say—when so many people seem to claim just the opposite?

COLIN: If Tim Leary's claim was that you could, use the psychedelic experience to find your way into new realms of subjectivity, and *then* use it to find your way *back* there *without* the psychedelic, I would agree, it would be extremely valuable. What tends to happen is that when people get into these realms they find that there are no words to express what they are seeing, and so in a sense the experience is useless. They can just say, well it was wonderful. And what's more, of course, this kind of experience of—it was wonderful, but I can't express it—tends, I think, to cause a kind of pessimism, a feeling that the only way I can get the experience is by taking the psychedelic again. Which is the reason, you see, that, as I say, after taking it once myself, I would not dream of taking it again.

DJB: But if people were able to integrate it into their lives in a meaningful way?

COLIN: Yup. If they were able to integrate it, I would entirely agree.

DJB: How do you see human consciousness evolving in the future, and what do you think the next stage in human evolution will be?

COLIN: That is something that I've been trying to explain all weekend. At the moment we have passed through centuries in which the pendulum has swung backwards and forwards between total materialism and a curious desire of human beings to explore their own potentialities, a weird feeling that you know there's far more than the material world. Succeeding movements from the platonic movement in ancient Greece, right down to Romanticism in the nineteenth century, and this present consciousness explosion that you're now getting in America—all of these are back swings.

You see, when I wrote *The Outsider* most people were determinedly sort of Left-Wing. Any sort of intellectual you would talk to was almost certainly a Marxist or a Left-Winger. And they thought the only sensible question to ask was, how can we get a fairer, more balanced political system. In the sixties all that disappeared, and you suddenly began to get the consciousness explosion, which is still continuing. Now the swing is towards the recognition that the consciousness explosion is the answer. We have got to keep moving in that direction.

> *...we have now reached a point in human evolution where...we could go forward, and permanently get up to the next step...*

There must be no back swing into total materialism. This, you see, is the really interesting and exciting thing that's happening. We've got to stop thinking in terms of possibly going back. Whatever happens now, we must go forward. I think that we have now reached a point in human evolution where we could go forward and *permanently get up to the next step* on which we would stay.

DJB: Do you know of any techniques to maintain what Maslow has termed "peak experiences" in our day-to-day lives?

COLIN: No, except as I say, knowing this; you see, the business about techniques, once again, means trying to do it the easy way. Obviously psychedelics would be one technique, and alcohol is another technique. Various yogic meditation exercises are another technique. But what's so important is to have the precise knowledge of what you want to achieve, and then to calculate how to get there. Now you must *know* what you want to achieve. So I keep emphasizing you have got to know in advance. This *is* what I am after.

It seems to me that what we are all aiming at is what Jean Gebser called "integral consciousness," these levels of consciousness in which you find yourself perfectly contented with the present moment. So if everytime we experience that feeling of tiredness, that feeling of, oh god what the hell, and so on, what we must do is to recognize *clearly* that this is telling us lies. Whereas, of course, what we very often tend to do is not only to accept it, but let ourselves therefore get into a state of discouragement, and then suddenly into *negative feedback*, where as it were, you're rolling down hill. This is the real danger— to go into depression.

DJB: You have stressed the importance of people having a strong sense of certainty about things in their lives. But we know from quantum physics that we can never really be certain of anything, because everything that exists, exists as vibrating waves of probable possibilities. What are you certain of?

COLIN: Now, as I say, that is not true in quantum physics. That is the Copenhagen Interpretation. All that Heisenberg stated is you can not know both the position and the speed of an electron. And Einstein said, well yeah, maybe that's true simply because we are dealing with sub-atomic events. In order to observe a sub-atomic event, you would need some way, as it were, of getting inside the atom or the electron, which is not possible without affecting it. So, in point of fact, it just appears to be a simple consequence of the fact that you are observing something so small.

On the other hand, Einstein did not believe there is any fundamental uncertainty about this. He went on to say, if you could devise an experiment in which you could somehow bombard something so that two particles shot off in opposite directions, you could in theory, measure the speed of one and the position of the other. And if they're identical particles shooting off in opposite directions, you would in fact have this double measurement. Of course this whole Bell's Theorem business seems to recognize that this is so. As far as I'm concerned, like Einstien, I do not believe in Bohr's Copenhagen Interpretation.

DJB: Do you see the non-local effect postulated by Bell's Theorem as being an explanation for such unexplained psychic phenomena as telepathy?

COLIN: No, I just don't know. I don't think that the two electrons are telepathic.

But on the other hand, I have noted in my book *Beyond the Occult* cases of identical twins, where you get absolutely absurd similarities in their lives, even though they have been separated from birth. They have married people of the same name, on the same day. They go to the same place for holidays, and all kinds of other preposterous things like this. They fell down and broke their leg on the same day. I do not know how you explain this. It does seem to me that there is something very weird going on.

DJB: What kind of relationship do you see—if you do—between sexuality and creativity?

COLIN: Well, I don't know. It seems to me tremendously important because sexuality is one of these examples where we experience ambiguity so often. This sudden feeling of—oh my god, is this really what I want? You know the old Latin tag about after sex one feels sad, because you suddenly feel—oh it's gone. There never was anything there in the first place. It's what I call the Ecclesiastes effect. There is nothing new under the sun—vanity of vanities, all is vanity. Which is the state we get into, when we get something we badly want, as Shopenhouer says. But on the other hand, you don't let it depress you that when you have eaten your dinner, you no longer want to eat another dinner. You just accept it and take it for granted, and it seems to me the same thing applies in this case. That the pessimism that Shopenhouer and Ecclesiastes believed is simply a sort of logical howler.

It seems to me that obviously sexuality can play an important part in creativity. But not simply because one feels that the essence of sexuality is so immensely important, like D.H. Lawrence. You see, William Barrett, writing about existentialism, used this phrase about return to the sense of power, meaning, and purpose inside us. We all recognize that somehow that's what it's all about—to get back to that sense of power, meaning, and purpose inside us. Now sex does tend to do that for us. It will jar us instantly, for example, into a sense of meaning.

If a man is feeling rather bored, and then suddenly catches a glimpse of a girl pulling up her stocking, instantly he's wide awake. You can learn from this to see your way, for example, through the kind of pessimism we have been speaking about. But on the other hand, what I have been saying today about this romantic revolution is the fact that I feel that human evolution can be explained, to a very large extent, in terms of woman and man's romanticism about woman. That may well explain the brain explosion. I feel that the romantic revolution, Gurter's eternal woman, draws us upward and on. This is really related to the creative process.

> *...human evolution can be explained, to a very large extent in terms of woman, and man's romanticism about woman.*

DJB: You have just begun to touch upon what I was going to ask you in the next question. What role do you think having a sense of purpose—or a lack thereof—plays in our lives?

COLIN: Obviously people are simply going to mark time. I mentioned yesterday, one of the things that struck me a long time ago, is that if you look at writers, the ones who produced something interesting and significant have been, in fact, the writers who have been forced to struggle like mad from difficult beginnings. So there's no question of them suddenly saying, oh what the hell, and letting go. They have a very powerful sense of purpose.

Proust is an example of a writer who started off from a pleasant middle-class beginning, and although he is a great novelist, *A la recherche du temps perdu*, is basically a vast pessimistic cathedral that I personally have never succeeded in reading all the way through, particularly the *Albertine disparue* volume, which really gets me down. What I am saying is that if you've gone through extremely difficult experiences that have forced you, whether you like it or not, to make efforts, then from then on, you never fall back into this facile pessimism.

DJB: Could you tell us about any projects on which you are currently working?

COLIN: I have just finished a book on serial killers. I intend to do two more equally big parts to my *Spider World*—the first four volumes of which are out in America, and which in a sense is complete in itself already. That, as it were, is the first part. So that when it is finished it will be a twelve volume work, about twice as long as *The Lord of the Rings*. This sort of fantasy novel, which I started a long time ago, strikes me as one of the most interesting things I have ever done. I have a feeling that one day all kids will know my *Spider World*. They will know me as the author of *Spider World*, in the way that they know Lewis Carroll as the author of *Alice in Wonderland*. Apart from that, I want to write a book called *New Pathways in Human Evolution*, to summarize all the kinds of things I have been saying this weekend, and I'm intending to write a study of the Female Outsider.

Lisa Law

Oscar Janiger

"I get more from what great minds have written
about human behavior, than any psychiatric text."

Psychiatric Alchemy
with Oscar Janiger

Oscar Janiger was born on February 8, 1918, in New York City. He received his M.A. in cell physiology from Columbia, and his M.D. from the UC Irvine School of Medicine, where he served on the faculty in their Psychiatry Department for over twenty years. His research interests have been wide, and he describes himself as a "tinkerer." He established the relationship between hormonal cycling and pre-menstral depression in women, and he discovered blood proteins that are specific to male homosexuality. His studies of the Huichol Indians in Mexico revealed that centuries of peyote use do not cause any type of chromosomal damage. He is perhaps best known for establishing the relationship between LSD and creativity in a study of hundreds of artists. In addition to his research interests he has also maintained a long-standing private psychiatric practice, which he continues to this day.

Back in the late fifties and early sixties when LSD was still legal, Oscar incorporated LSD into some of his therapy, and is responsible for "turning on" many well-known literary figures and Hollywood celebrities, including Anais Nin and Cary Grant. More recently Oscar has been involved in studying dolphins in their natural environment, and is the founder of the Albert Hofmann Foundation—an organization whose purpose is to establish a library and world information center dedicated to the scientific study of human consciousness. He has also just completed a book entitled A Different Kind of Healing, *about how doctors treat themselves. Jeanne St. Peter and I interviewed Oscar in the living room of his home in Santa Monica on January 3, 1990. Surrounding virtually every wall in his house is the largest and most interesting library I've ever encountered. Oscar spoke to us about his scientific research, creativity and psychopathology, the problems he sees with psychiatry, and his discovery of the psycho-active effects of isolated DMT. Oscar is an extremely warm, highly energetic man. There is a deep sincerity to his manner. He chuckles a lot, and one feels instantly comfortable around him.*

—DJB

DJB: Could you begin by telling us what it was that originally inspired your interest in psychiatry and the exploration of consciousness?

OSCAR: I was about seven years old and I was living on a farm in upstate New York. The nearest neighbor was a mile away. I would go for a walk, visit them, play, and then come home in the evening. This was a wild kind of country setting, and I had to get home before dark. Some evenings I would be coming home and the scene around me on the path was filled with menacing figures: pirates and all kinds of cut-throats ready to grab me and do me in. There was a place I called the sunken mine, where people had supposedly drowned and there was a frayed rope hanging from a tree. All of these menacing things gave the evening a very sinister cast, and I'd finally run to get home.

Certain evenings I'd make the trip, and everything was just light and airy. Things around me were filled with joy and pleasure. The birds were singing: rabbits, squirrels and other animals were having a wonderful Disneyland time. So one day I was thinking, My God, that's a magic road! One time it's this way, another time it's that way. So I puzzled over that. I finally came to the conclusion that, if it wasn't a magic road, then I was doing something to these surroundings and if I was doing it then *I could change it.*

So the next time I came back from my neighbor's place, and everything got murky, strange and sinister, I said, "No! If I'm doing this then bring back the rabbits, bring back the squirrels, bring back the fairies and let's lighten this thing up." Sure enough, it changed. That was the beginning of my interest in consciousness. It was all crystallized into a marvelous saying from the Talmud—"things are not the way they are, they're the way *we are.*"

From then on, when I'd get into situations, I'd determine what aspect was within me that was being projected outward, and what was a reflection of the world that others can validate along with me. That, of course, has been the theme of my work in therapy and as a scientist. The important distinctions regarding projection are among the fundamental things that one has to solve to understand how people behave and the contradictions in their behavior. Other inspirations are simply those of curiosity. I was enormously curious about how things worked. I was always asking Why? Why? Why? Then I got to medical school and the why extended to the brain and the activities of the nervous system, which seemed to me to be the largest why of all. Also, I had personal experiences with people who had become, I guess you'd say, psychotic, or who acted bizarrely or strangely. These matters have been of great interest to me.

DJB: How do you define consciousness?

OSCAR: Well, I was afraid you were going to ask me that. When you say define something, I'm caught between what I recognize as the accepted definition—the sources that come out of dictionaries, legal definitions and all that stuff that belongs in the pragmatic world—and the definitions that come from my intuition. The Oxford English Dictionary offers at least six or seven varieties of definition for consciousness, and several have entirely different connotations. When you get

> *When you get down to contradictions like being conscious of one's unconscious, it get's pretty strange...*

down to contradictions like being conscious of one's unconscious, it get's pretty strange and labyrinthine.

I would say the conventional definition contains the idea of being aware of one's self—a sort of self-reflection. Or you can describe it operationally as being the end product of a complex nervous system that eventually produces a state that allows us to be in some way cognizant of ourselves and the environment. It allows us to extrapolate into future events, into past events, and allow us to take a position in our imagination so we can examine realities that are not responsive to the ordinary, daily context of the world around us. Many of these things require qualifications, but let me then stay with the word as something that gives us a feeling that distinguishes us as individuals, that gives us a sense of self, and sense of self-reflection and awareness.

JSP: Many years ago, while you were studying at Columbia, you had some problems with your high school teaching job. What happened?

OSCAR: Well, I was practice-teaching at the same high school that I had attended, Erasmus Hall in New York, the second oldest high school in the country. I was teaching general science with the lady who taught me, Miss Thompson. I took over her class, and she would sit in the back of the room. So, I was teaching astronomy to these sophomore or junior students. I borrowed a ladder from the custodian and I bought a bunch of gold stars. I spent the entire night pasting them on the ceiling in the form of the constellations. When I wound up it was getting light outside, and I thought I had done this incredible job. So the next day when we had the class, I said with a grand gesture, "We're studying the stars - look up." All the kids looked up, everyone was fired up and we had a good time learning about all the stars.

That evening, as I was going home, I discovered a note stuck in my letterbox from Mr. McNeal, the principal of the school. It said, "See me." So the next day I went to see him. He said, "The custodian told me that you pasted things on the ceiling." He shook his head and said, "I'm afraid you're going to have to remove those, that's defacing school property," and he just waved me aside. I spent all the next night scraping the stars off the ceiling, thinking about the errors of my ways.

A week later, I decided that we would study eclipses. I said to the kids in the first row, "You bring in the lemons." To the second row I said, "You bring oranges." The third row I told, "You bring in grapefruits." To the fourth row I said, "You bring in knitting needles." So they were all very eager and they came back with these required things. I said, okay, the grapefruits are the suns, the oranges are the planets, the lemons are the moons, and the knitting needles go through the planets to make them tilted and spin around accordingly. So we had a ball, but a big commotion ensued. During this general upheaval, the door opens and McNeal puts his head in and pulls back again. So sure enough, in my little box, there's a note that says, "See me immediately."

So I see him, and this time he's very unhappy. I said, "Dr. McNeal let me explain about the sun and the moon and the oranges and the lemons," but I couldn't explain it. He said, "Did you know that the teachers on the floor were complaining about you? You were making a lot of noise." I said, "Yeah, well, you know it's very difficult to get the spatial relationships right." He said, "I don't understand. You come from Teacher's College, that's the finest college in the country for teachers, it's the cradle of American education. It was Dewey's shrine. Don't they teach you about discipline in the classroom?" I said, "Gee, yeah, I guess so." He says, "Well, your classroom was in chaos!" I said, "Gee, I…but let me tell you about the oranges and the lemons." He said, "What are you talking about?!" The guy was ready to explode, he just couldn't handle it. He said, "I don't understand this, Mr. Janiger, but I'm sure that we can work it out. Now please understand we're here to keep discipline in our classrooms." I said, "Okay."

So I continued teaching and one day we had to study fermentation. That was my undoing. I brought into class that day a loaf of bread, which was covered with penicillin mold, a flask of vinegar, a few pieces of blue cheese and a little flask of wine. I put them out on the laboratory table and I said, "These are the useful and harmful results of fermentation. Then after class I said, "If any of you want to come up, you can sample a little bit, you can see how the cheese tastes, and so on. So one kid came up and nothing would please him, but he had to have a slug of the wine. Then I get the note, "See me immediately!" I went to see McNeal. He shook his head and said, "I've been a principal for twenty years and I've never run into this in my life. You will have to go back and see your professor because you're under suspension right now." I said, "What's wrong?" "Wine, wine! You brought spirits into the classroom!" I said, "Now let me tell you about fermentation." "Please!" He said, "don't tell me about it, I don't want to hear about it!" He was apoplectic.

So I go back and see my professor, the holy of holies, the teacher of teachers. He was perplexed and then said to me, "There's something you should know. We're here to teach children, *not to entertain them*." Well, that phrase broke loose in me and I got very upset. I got up and said, "You know what professor? You can take your goddamn class in general science and stuff it." For weeks after, he'd call me and write me letters saying, we can work this out, but I refused. That was my stint at teaching in high school. It was the best thing that ever happened; I'd still be teaching high school today if it hadn't.

DJB: You've used the term "dry schizophrenia" in describing a creative artist. Could you explain what you mean by this and what similarities and differences you see between certain aspects of madness and the process of creativity?

OSCAR: Well, of course that's always been on my mind. I remember that I could make the wallpaper do all kinds of tricks when I had a fever, and I could sit—if you'll excuse me—on the john, and watch the tiles recompose themselves and make patterns. Therefore I suspected that there was a part of my mind which had a certain influence over the world around me, and that, under certain conditions, it can take on novel and interesting forms. The dreams I had were very vivid, very real, and there were times when I found it hard to distinguish between the dream life and what we might call the waking life.

So there was a very rich repository of information that was somewhat at my disposal at times, sometimes breaking through at odd moments. I later on thought that could be a place that one could draw a great deal of inspiration from. So I studied the conditions under which people have these releases, breakthroughs, or have access to other ways and forms of perceiving the world around them and changing their reality.

When I studied the works of people who profess to go to creative artists and ask them how they did it and what it was about, I realized that what we had by way of understanding creativity was a tremendous collection of highly idiosyncratic and subjective responses. There was no real way of dealing with the creative process as a state you could refer to across the board, or how one could encourage it.

That's how I got the idea for a study in which we could deliberately-change consciousness in an artist using LSD, given the same reference object to paint before and during the experience. Then I would try to make an inference from the difference between the artwork outside of the drug experience and while they were having it. In doing so I was struck by the fact that the paintings, under the influence of LSD, had some of the attributes of what looked like the work done by schizophrenics. If you would talk to the artists in terms of the everyday world, the answers would be very strange and tangential.

Then I began to look into the whole sticky issue of psychopathology and creativity. I found that there are links between the creative state and certain qualities that people say they have when they're creating, that were very much like some of the perceptions of people who were schizophrenic or insane. I began to notice what made the difference. It seemed that the artists were able to maintain a certain balance, riding the edge, as it were.

> *The artist was able to ride his creative Pegasus, putting little pressure on his ability to control the situation.*

I thought of creativity as a kind of dressage, riding a horse delicately with your knees. The artist was able to ride his creative Pegasus, putting little pressure on his ability to control the situation, enabling him to just master it, while allowing the rest to flow freely so that the creative spirit can take its own course. The artist is faced with the dilemma of allowing this uprush of material to enter into his conscious mind, much like trying to take a drink from a high-pressure fire hose. This allows him to integrate his technique and training, and *still be able* to keep relatively free of preconceived ideas, formulated notions or obligatory reality.

In that state they were able to harness it enough so that the overriding symptoms of psychosis were not present, but every other aspect of their being at that time seemed as though they were in a semi-psychotic state. So I evoked the term "dry schizophrenia" where a person was able to control the surroundings and yet be "crazy" at the same time, crazy in the sense that they could use this mode of consciousness for their work and creative ability.

There's a lot of documentation about psychopathology and creativity but I think its all from a central pool, kind of a wellspring of the creative imagination that we can draw from. It equally gives it's strength to psychosis in one sense, or breaks through in creativity, or in the theological revelation in the world of the near-dying and people who are seriously ill, and so on. All of that provides us with a look into this cauldron, this very dynamic, efficacious part of the brain, that for some reason or other is kept away from us by a semi-permeable membrane that could be ruptured in different ways, under different circumstances.

I recall reading that James Joyce had a daughter named Lucia who was schizophrenic. She was the sorrow of his life. Upon persuasion from Joyce's patron, both of them were brought to Carl Jung. This was against Joyce's wishes because he didn't like psychiatrists. Jung examined Lucia, then finally came in and sat down with Joyce. Joyce said to him that he thought Lucia was a greater artist and writer than he was. Can you imagine? So Jung said, "That may be true, but the two of you are like deep-sea divers. You go into the ocean, a rich, interesting, dramatic setting, with your baskets, and you fill them up with improbable creatures of the deep. The only difference between the two of you is that you can come up to the surface, and she can't."

DJB: Basically it's like the difference between being able to swim in the ocean or being...

OSCAR: Caught by the waves and dashed to pieces. There's a wonderful book that describes the process of this ever-changing remarkable flux of consciousness that Sherington called "the enchanted loom." It's called *The Road to Xanadu* by John Livingston Lowes. I recommend it highly as an exercise in the ways of the imagination.

DJB: Could you tell us about the thought-experiment that you devised to categorize what you refer to as "delusions of explanation?"

OSCAR: Imagine that someone is taken quietly at night while they're sleeping, out of their bed, and are then deposited in one of the most unearthly places on the planet—Mammoth Cave. We found by repeated experiments that upon awakening, there are only five explanations that someone in a Western culture would come up with, and I refer to these main headings or rubrics as "delusions of explanation." They are: (not in order of frequency) I must be dead, I must be dreaming, someone or something has played a trick on me, I've gone crazy or I am in Mammoth cave.

Through my experience in mental hospitals, I've found that schizophrenics will try to explain the extraordinary nature of their experience by using one of these basic rubrics. In our culture explanations for unexplainable phenomena are rather sparse. My supposition is that other cultures may have different explanations for such phenomena.

JSP: What are your thoughts on the mind-body problem?

OSCAR: This is related to the problem of consciousness, but isn't quite the same thing. The mind-body problem is, I guess, as old as the human race. It has to do with how the "soup becomes a spark." How is it that the material world, and the material substrate of ourselves, can give rise to something that seems to be of a different universal order, that of thought? Obviously consciousness stands somewhere between this maneuver of going from material things to thought.

> *...consciousness stands somewhere between this maneuver of going from material things to thought.*

There are several different propositions that occur. Brain function simultaneously coexists with thought processes, and this interacts in a dynamic fashion. That's one theory. Another theory is that the brain, being so complex and convoluted, spawns or gives rise to what we experience as thinking, which seems to have a semi-independent existence. This is a dualistic approach to the problem.

The third notion is simply that mind is also spirit, and this is imposed on the brain from the outside in some strange way. This is a theological sort of explanation. The vitalist notion claims that the life-force gives rise to, or at least

> *I've never had a problem with the notion that material substance could give rise to immaterial energy.*

coexists with, the soul, which after the death of the material host, leaves and finds somewhere else to reside.

I've never had a problem with the notion that material substance could give rise to immaterial energy. It's not odd to conceive of the fact that you can build a machine out of material substances and that out of it comes electrical energy, or that you can press a button and out of these batteries comes a beam of light from your flashlight. So the light doesn't seem to me any more miraculous in relationship to the batteries than does the thought process coming out of the material aspect of the brain.

DJB: Or the same goes for magnetic fields. They're defined as non-material regions of influence on the material world.

OSCAR: Yes. You could make a machine where the electricity could turn itself back on and regulate it's own existence to some extent. When I worked with Barbara Brown in her bio-feedback laboratory in Sepulveda Virginia, I was able to see my brainwaves in the form of patterns on a screen. I got the notion that as I'm watching my brainwaves, I'm changing them at the same time. They're constantly being influenced by my watching them, so I'm never really seeing the objective evidence of my own brain.

You could argue that if someone else was watching my brainwaves they might get a different notion, but *I'm* watching them, I'm taking that information in and in turn sending out something else which is subtly influenced by what I just took in. This has been called the auto-cerebroscope, a device where you see something happening that projects what your brain is registering, but in witnessing it, you change its content. Do you ever see things as they *really* are? This philosophical dilemma is never more clearly outlined than when under these conditions.

DJB: What are some of the main problems that you see with the state of psychiatry today and how do you think we can improve it for the future?

OSCAR: Boy, you've really got a tiger by the tail there! I think that the material emphasis of psychiatry and neuropathology of the last century, where everything was reduced to the simplistic notion of the mind as a switchboard, and all illnesses were the result of pathological processes in the brain itself, didn't set well. It did not provide a dynamic framework for understanding human behavior. So when the emphasis changed, and Freud and others came on the scene for modern dynamic psychology, I suspect the pendulum swung equally too far in the opposite direction.

The heyday of psychoanalysis and depth psychology then ushered in a kind of behavioral construct that seemed to be dependent only upon the dynamic thought process, and left very little to any kind of physical explanation. So I think we were trapped in constant psychological formulations of all our behavior. This was mirrored very well in my own studies. I was interested in finding out the way that the chemistry of the brain and the state of the body influences our thoughts and the way we feel.

The trouble was I couldn't find a suitable research prospect. I couldn't get a definitive case where I could show that the state of the body influenced thinking and feeling in a specific way. That was supplied serendipitously by a lady who came in and told me that a week prior to her period she experiences profound depression. Suddenly a light went on and I said, "That's what I'm looking for!" I realized that an optimal experimental subject for human behavior was a woman because of her menstrual period. She is a wonderful biological metronome that you can count on because of this reliable episodic lunar event.

So using that concept, I began to plan a series of behavioral events employing this strategy. I found that some women regularly, about a week before their period, have terrible changes in their general demeanor: their behavior, feelings and thinking. I made a study of three or four good clinical subjects, who went into serious states of mental change around that time. In studying them I was struck by the fact that all of them seemed compelled to give me *psychological* explanations of their behavior.

For example, a woman would say, "Well, I had a fight with my husband yesterday; that's what made me depressed." And I said, "Yes, that's interesting because you had a fight with him last week and it didn't make you depressed. And every month you have a fight with your husband exactly at the same time and you get depressed." She agreed it seemed very odd.

So then I went to the psychoanalytical texts. They explained this phenomena by saying, well, a woman is afraid that in a week or so she's going to bleed. This suggests to her that she is being castrated and her penis was removed, so why shouldn't she be depressed? Another analytical interpretation is that this fear is a ubiquitous reminder of her feminine identity and that she was therefore inferior. That's a good one.

I decided to use progesterone as a means of seeing if I could break into the problem of premenstrual depression. I took this woman and I presented her case to my residents when she was depressed. I said, "I'm going to allow you to ask her any question you want, except one, which I'll keep to myself." At the end of the presentation I asked the group, "Well, what do you make of this woman?" These residents, who knew quite a bit of psychiatry said, "There's no question that she has classical clinical depression."

Since pure progesterone is not absorbed through the gut, you have to give it either by injection or vaginal suppository. So I devised an experiment. I double-blinded my progesterone. I injected the material randomly and didn't know which was which. Then I charted the symptoms and found, when I broke the code, that progesterone had an extremely salutary effect in relieving these women of pre-menstrual symptoms. I began to see clear evidence of a substance in the body that, in short supply, was markedly influencing the behavior of these women.

I gave a talk before the Medical Society and outlined what I had done. I said that premenstrual depression could best be treated by looking at this as a hormonal problem, and that it had certain implications for the way the body influences the mind. The people in the group were skeptical and some said, "How do you know that it isn't some unconscious factor that's still operating regardless?" They said, "You haven't proven that she still isn't worried about her castration fears. You've only proven that if you give her progesterone, that could be modified, but you haven't attacked the basis of the problem."

> *...the people in the group were skeptical and some said... "You haven't proven that she still isn't worried about her castration fears."*

How could I do that? Psychoanalysis has an answer for everything. I went to two of my brightest women medical students, and I asked, "How would you like to spend the summer in Europe? I want you to go to all the primate centers there, and find out: do great apes have a menstrual cycle similar to humans? I want you to talk to the keepers and find out if they have any reason to suspect that their behavior is any different during their menstrual cycle." For the next three months I had letters from all the European zoological gardens. We were excited to discover that in the Berlin zoo, Fritz, who took care of a female gorilla named Olga, said, "A week before her period I can't get near Olga, she's just a mess. All she does is throw all kinds of shit at me."

At my next opportunity to present I said, "Ladies and gentlemen, I have discovered that the gorillas have feminine identification problems, and they also have castration fears, because they can get very upset before their period." Everyone applauded and started to laugh. That was the beginning of my under-standing of how mental and emotional difficulties could be correlated with one's biochemistry. This is the basis for the treatment of depression by altering one's neurochemistry.

DJB: So part of the problem was that people were locked into the idea that the mind could only be affected by the body and not the other way around?

OSCAR: Yes. I think the over-emphasis on psychodynamics, in deriving every-thing from psychological theory, retarded us from reaching the same conclusions that the British made. For a long time this perspective stalemated progress in American psychiatry. In fact, it was difficult to achieve any academic status in psychiatry without having taken psychoanalytic training. At present, psychiatric residents are less inclined to enter psychoanalytical training programs, which may reflect their opinion on pscyhoanalysis as an effective treatment.

JSP: So in American psychiatry, there was a initial reluctance to use drugs to treat emotional problems.

OSCAR: Right. In that sense European psychiatry was much more progressive. In fact, most of the innovations in psychiatry came from Europe. And you would wonder why, considering the status of American medical research and the abundance of psychiatrists. The British were making strong gains with psychotropic medication that we adopted later on. When you come to think of it, Freud was European, as well as Jung. Menduna in Hungary and Bini and Cerlucci in Italy were the first to use insulin and electro-shock therapy. Neuroleptic drugs were first developed in France. Psycho-drama and Gestalt therapy had European and South African origins. The basis for Behavioral therapies originated in Russia.

It's quite remarkable how *little* innovation we have brought to the field. We're good at taking what they give us and grinding it out, but we have a poor record at innovation in the field of psychiatric treatment. Also, psychiatrists have been more locked into their therapeutic systems with little flexibility. In my LSD experiments we ran close to a thousand people, and we found that psychiatrists tended to have negative experiences. The ministers were next. The artists had the most positive experiences. It would seem that the psychiatrist has a strong investment in a particular norm or standard of reality.

JSP: What about in the field of psychobiology and psychopharmacology?

OSCAR: In psychobiology the situation is a little different. I think a lot of the research in psychobiology is relatively freer of the psychological bias than the clinical work, and in that respect, more progressive. Psychopharmacology is where the action is. The medicines have been remarkable. Even so, there's been no remarkable new anti-depressants. There's been a span of about twenty years between the last ones, which were the tricyclics, to the new ones of Prozac and Zoloft, which came out recently. All in all, the psychologists have stolen a great march on the psychiatrists. They're more accessible and they speak a language which the public finds easier to understand, and they pander to the public's fear of medicines and pills.

DJB: Why do you think that there's such a fear and resistance against using chemicals to heal the mind?

OSCAR: We're a drug-phobic culture. It's a contradiction in terms because we

We're a drug-phobic culture.

consume more drugs than in any other country. We make a strange distinction between various kinds of pills. Somebody ought to do a research paper on that, on why certain pills are acceptable and others are not. You see people who take handfuls of vitamins in the morning, and they go to a herbalist and take herbs which they know nothing about. But many have great reservations about "drugs."

DJB: I was talking to a friend about the anti-depressants. He said, "I think people should be able to do it by themselves and not rely on drugs." But then at the end of the phone call, he starts telling me about this herbalist that recommended something for his allergies that he felt had an amazing effect.

OSCAR: Yes. We have this funny schizophrenia about pills.

JSP: What is your view on bridging alternative medical modalities, such as acupuncture and herbalism, with modern methods?

OSCAR: For ten years I was Research Director on the board of an organization call the Homes Center. We gave sums of money to scientifically validate unconventional and unorthodox treatment methods. So you can see where I'm at. The Homes Center was the first and, for a long time, the only organization to be doing that.

One of the grants was for Stephen LaBerge's work in lucid dreaming. Some of the other work we funded was in support of energy healing, biofeedback and acupuncture. So I'm very much in favor of the scientific exploration of alternative methods, but not just accepting them unreservedly without discrimination.

DJB: You told me about the theory of an emoting machine that embodied the complex array of emotions. Could you explain this concept to us?

OSCAR: It was an extension of things I had seen and read, but I put it in a new form, which hypothesized that emotions have a kind of quantitative nexus. That means that they are composed of particles, just like photons in a beam of light. In the final analysis emotions are a form of energy that have a pulse or quanta like the electrons in an electrical field. Once you assume that emotions can be quantified and measured, then they no longer need to be seen as this vague, amorphous thing that just pours over you, that seems to arise in some strange, spontaneous way, and has no form or substance.

I see emotions as relating to cognitive experience in the same way a music score relates to a movie.

We know something of that part of the

brain that specifically regulates emotions—it's called the limbic system. Here, emotions are engendered, and in some way made appropriate for the occasion. I see emotions as relating to cognitive experience in the same way a music score relates to a movie. The musical score is not discursive, it doesn't tell you anything about the specific action, but it lends a kind of overtone, a richness to the experience that fleshes it all out. For example, it's hard to imagine seeing *Chariots of Fire* without the musical score. I think emotions act in very much the same way. I believe that emotions can be traced and channeled.

Some day we may have a way of regulating emotions, and devise a system of emotions just like we have a grammar of logic or cognitive effects. In theory, it is possible that a machine could be made that could emote, but we're a long way off from that. In order to do this, emotions would have to be reduced to some formula, using the analogy of color. They are like the three primary colors. Out of red, blue and yellow, every other nuance of color is created. I think somebody once said that it runs into the thousands, the discernible hues we can see. Thousands, can you imagine that?

So I figured you can get a vast array of emotions from three primary emotions. Fear, anger and love would seem to be the most basic and reasonable choices. Out of fear, love and anger, mixed in the proper tinctures and proportions, you might get such complicated emotions as indignation, apprehension and so on. All these fancy sounding ones. But there are two which don't seem to fit in. One is curiosity and the other is disgust. I had a lot of fun with this, it's really off-the-wall stuff.

Let's assume that this is possible, that the body is equipped to create fear, love and anger in some way. The limbic region may be the generator. We found that emotions are mediated through the nervous system and they are transmitted through specialized neurons in the form of chemical messengers called neuro-transmitters which seem to carry an emotional charge.

It is a very elegant way of thinking, that emotions are transmitted through this chemical interchange. That was proven by the fact that if you alter the chemistry, then you alter the emotional content of the mind or the brain. So you now have a beginning theory for emotions as having some substrate in material things that could be quantified. This leads to some way of building an emotional model that may work.

JSP: What is your view with regard to the evolutionary process of male-female relationships?

OSCAR: The word relationship in this context is a bothersome one. I think men and women have certain attributes that are native to their individual biology. How they manage to coordinate them is something that requires a tremendous amount of tolerance and understanding for what is unfamiliar to the other person.

I think that men and women have to somehow appreciate the differences between them, and not assume that either of those differences have a more superior quality than the other. And there *are* differences; I think the danger is assuming there are none. I think it's an issue of how mature the human race gets. It's the difficulty in discriminating between the biological and cultural differences and their resolution. The problem here is that they are hopelessly mixed up, and that has to be sorted out before you can say anything definitive about it. For example, all kinds of cultural values are placed on behavior which has nothing to do with biology.

DJB: Well culture and biology are quite intertwined.

OSCAR: Yes, they're intertwined, but there is a way of studying this in relative respect to the circumstances involved. Now you have a group of people who feel that men and women live differently in different conditions. That is to say, there was a time in the world when things were primitive and presumably better, and our modern problems are really the result of industrialization and male supremacy and egotism. Women, in an effort to become compensatory have become goddesses.

These changes in historical conditions made these differences exaggerated, but I wouldn't go any further with that, because it's too easy to fall into established prejudices on this issue. I think basically women make an extraordinary contribution in their own biology, so to speak, and its mental equivalence, and men make their contribution.

JSP: What kind of philosophy do you think people should adopt in regard to social responsibility in general?

OSCAR: I think what we need more than anything else is *enlightened self-interest*. This is not the same as selfishness. Selfishness is gaining something at the expense of others. Enlightened self-interest is somehow nourishing and gaining something in terms of ourselves and what we need, not at the expense of others. Unfortunately, instead of that we have charity and sacrifice which only compounds the problem. You can see clearly that I'm not one of the holy types.

> *I think what we need more than anything else is enlightened self-interest.*

Let your mothers and fathers take care of themselves. Freud said the most important story he every heard was of a mother bird carrying a little bird on its back. There were three little birds and she carried them across the channel. In the middle of the channel the mother bird said, "When I am old and sick, would you carry me on your back?" The first bird said, "Yes, mother, I'd be happy to." And the mother turned over and dumped the bird. The second bird, the same problem. The third bird, however, said, "No, I won't carry you on my back, I'll carry my *children* on my back."

Think about it. If everyone here did that, we'd have no more problems. Your obligation is to carry your children, not your mother on your back. If she did the right thing, you wouldn't have to carry her. She would have already prepared, like you're going to prepare for your children. That's what I'm talking about— enlightened self-interest.

DJB: Oz, you've worked with and interacted with many of the outstanding minds of our time. Who have been some of the most important influences in your development and where have you found inspiration when you needed it?

OSCAR: Well, Aldous Huxley has been a real source of inspiration to me. Let me give you an example. I was on the stage of the Ebel Theater as part of a three doctor team, to examine a man who professed to be able to lower his blood pressure, stick pins through his cheeks, and remain buried alive in some way where he could get no air. I was to examine him, along with the other two doctors, to see that he wasn't faking.

He stuck a hatpin right through his hand. It didn't bleed, and we reported that dutifully to the audience. He said he would then lower his blood pressure to 50 over 30, a level at which I felt a person couldn't live. I took his blood pressure and it was high—about 180 over 110, and I reported that. Then he huffed and puffed and went into a trance. He got rigid, and then we took his blood pressure again. It was 110 over 70 and I reported that to the audience.

That evening we met with Aldous, his wife Laura, Anais Nin and her husband Rupert, and this issue came up and I recounted my experience at the theater that morning. And then I said, "So you can clearly see that this man was faking. He said he would lower his blood pressure to 50 over 30, and he didn't." I went on to lament that so many of these so-called miracle workers are charlatans. I was very self-righteous. Then Aldous looked at me. He said, "Dr. Janiger." I said, "Yes?" He said, "Don't you think it was remarkable that he was able *to lower it at all!*" A light went on in my head. From that moment on, I got a lesson that I always remembered.

Then there was Alan Watts, who I had the good fortune to know and to be his physician for part of his life. He was a remarkably intelligent man, probably the best conversationalist I ever met. A witty, very open, candid person - great guy. He lived his life to the hilt. We went to see one of his television shows in which he was a featured guest. The audience was filled with hippy-type kids and everyone was fascinated. During the performance he was smoking these little cigarellos; they're like little round cigars.

So at the end of the performance a hand shot up. "Mr. Watts. You tell us about life, and how to be free and liberated. Then why are you smoking these terrible cigars?" Old Alan, when he would get excited, one of his eyes would drift over to the corner of his head. He had this funny look and I knew something was coming. He looked at the young man and he said, "Do you know why I smoke these little cigars? *Because I like it!*" So that's Alan for you, and it tells the story of his whole life. If that's Zen, more power to him.

Another incomparable man was Gerald Heard. He could get up, give a lecture, and you could transcribe it, with footnotes and all, and it was ready for publication. It came out flawlessly. It was a seamless performance. Somebody in an audience once asked him, "Could you say a few words on architecture?" So Gerald replied, "What kind of architecture?" He said, "Oh, British architecture." "What year of British architecture?" He said, "Well, let's say about the end of the nineteenth century." "Precisely what period are you referring to young man?" He said, "Well, the 1890's." Gerald said, "Would you say the first half of the 1890's?" He said, "Yes." Then Gerald went off for an hour and a half on architecture in England during the first half of the 1890's. It was a virtuoso performance. Aldous said to me that he thought Gerald was the best informed man alive. Coming from Aldous, that was quite a compliment.

Then there were people I didn't know, but read. Great influences were Joyce, Camus and Bertrand Russell. These were people who meant a lot to me. An incomparable writer named B. Travin added a lot to my understanding of human nature. I get more from what great minds have written about human behavior, than any text. Sometimes I feel that I have learned more psychology from Dostoevsky and Conrad than I have from Freud. I approach my practice that way; by interacting with people as if they were protagonists in their own dramas. That way you can't be biased.

It was the way Proust described the Tower of Combrey. He said, if you really want to know the tower you must see it in the morning light, and in the evening light. You must see it in the winter time covered with snow. You must see it in the summer time. You must see it in the mist, and you must see it sometimes with eyes half closed. You must see it from above and from below. You must see it from the east, north, south and west. Then you'll begin to know the Tower of Combrey.

DJB: Oz, have you ever given any thought to what happens to human consciousness after physical death?

OSCAR: I've given a lot of thought to it, but I'm afraid not much productive thought. My bias is that when the current is shut off, we somehow lose our sense of individuality. That is the only way I can put it. Shakespeare called death "that strange bourne from which no traveller doth return." No traveller has ever returned from this journey, so there's no direct evidence, except people who say they have. Well, you can decide for yourself whether they have or not.

> *I always remember the Big Bang as the biggest orgasm in history.*

In any case, my thought is that, for myself only, that I'm simply shut down in my present state, and that somehow I—which is now a kind of fruitless phrase—am somehow restored to the earth, or to the matrix, or to what the Germans called the urschlime, or the fundamental substrate of all things, the fundamental primitive primordial stuff of which we are constituted. We go back to before the Big Bang. I always remember the Big Bang as the biggest orgasm in history.

JSP: How has your experience with psychedelic drugs influenced your life, your work and your practice?

OSCAR: In a word—*profoundly*. It really took me out of a state in which I saw the boundaries of myself and the world around me very rigorously prescribed, to a state in which I saw that many, many things were possible. This created for me a sense of being in a kind of flux, a constant dynamic equilibrium. I used a phrase at that time to designate how I thought of myself at any given moment. It's a nautical term called a "running fix." It means that when you report your position in a moving vessel, you are only talking about a specific time and circumstance —the here and now.

The illusion of living in one room has now given rise to the illusion that there are a great many rooms. All you have to do is get out into the corridors, go into another room, and see what's there. Otherwise you'll think that the room you're living in is all there is.

DJB: Could you tell us about your discovery of DMT?

OSCAR: Yeah! It is a psychoactive ingredient of the hallucinogenic brew they use in the Amazon called Ayahuasca. An analysis by chemists revealed that it contained a substance called dimethyltriptamine, DMT. This was unusual because it was almost identical to a chemical found naturally in the body, and it didn't make sense that we'd carry around with us such a powerful hallucinogen. Nevertheless, a friend of mine, Parry Bivens and I, purified some dimethyltriptamine. We had it all set up one evening. It was thought to be inactive orally by itself. To be on the safe side, we thought we'd inject it into one another the following day. So Parry said he'd see me in the morning and we'd go ahead and try it out.

We had nothing to go by as it had never been used before. So when Parry left me I was in the office looking at these bottles, and I got this devilish thought that I should take a shot of this stuff. But I had no idea of how much to take. So I said, like Hofmann, I'll be conservative and take a cc. I backed myself up to the wall until I could go no further so I had to inject myself in the rear. And from then on—*man, I was in a strange place,* the strangest. I was in a world that was like being inside of a pinball machine.

The only thing like it, oddly enough, was in a movie called *Zardoz,* where a man is trapped inside of a crystal. It was angular, electronic, filled with all kinds of strange over-beats and electronic circuits, flashes and movements. It looked like an ultra souped-up disco, where lights are coming from every direction. Just extraordinary. Then I'd go unconscious; the observer was knocked out. Then the observer would come back intermittently, then go back out. I had a sense of terror because each time I blacked out it was like dying. I went through this dance of the molecules and electrons inside of my head and I, for all the world, felt like the way a television set looks when on between pictures.

> *I was in a world that was like being inside of a pinball machine.*

Finally I lay on the floor; time seemed endless. Then it lightened up and I looked at my watch. It had been forty-five minutes. I'd thought I had been in that place for two hundred years. I think what I was looking at was the archetonics of the brain itself. We learned later that that was an enormous dose. Just smoking a fraction of this would give you a profound effect. So in that dose range I think I just busted everything up. Parry came back the next day, and he said, "Well, let's try some." I said, "I got to the North Pole ahead of you."

DJB: That took a lot of courage.

OSCAR: Well, it was foolhardiness.

DJB: I hear you've been doing some interesting work with dolphins and Olympic swimmers. Perhaps you could tell us a little about this project.

OSCAR: Albert Stevens, Matt Biondi and I got the idea several years ago that we might find an innovative way of approaching wild dolphins, by using Olympic swimmers—the best in the world. It is difficult to study wild dolphins because they are free-ranging and peripatetic. We went to where the dolphins were reported to be, fifty miles off the coast of Grand Bahama Island. We waited. When they came we jumped in with them, and did a great deal of underwater filming. We studied the film to try to find out how the dolphins behave, and we're still in the process of doing that now.

We did it for three years and developed a good working relationship with these dolphins whom we were now able to identify. Dolphins are strange and beguiling creatures. Their language seems totally incomprehensible, as we know our own language to be nothing like it whatsoever. It appears to be a different order of communication. What stories the dolphins could bring back from their alien world of water if we could only communicate with them.

DJB: The final question. Could you tell us about the Albert Hofmann Foundation and any other current projects that you're working on?

OSCAR: Well, I co-founded the Albert Hofmann Foundation about three years ago. I was involved in LSD research from 1954 to 1962. During that time I accumulated a large store of books, artwork, papers, correspondence, tape-recordings, newsclippings, research reports and memorabilia which probably represented a fair sample of what went on in the psychedelic history of Los Angeles and elsewhere. I was aware that there is a great deal of this kind of information that is scattered and isolated and in danger of being lost or destroyed. Collected and organized this would provide an extremely valuable resource for future research and historians.

I was approached by several people who were committed to preserving these unique records. We formed a non-profit organization that we felt was fitting to be named in honor of the man who discovered LSD and psilocybin— Albert Hofmann. He was most gracious in his acceptance and pledged his whole-hearted support. It is based in Los Angeles and functions solely as a library, archives and information center at this time. We have collected a great deal of relevant material from the pioneers of psychedelic research; e.g. Laura Huxley, Allen Ginsberg, Stan Grof, Humphrey Osmond and many others.

I got back an enthusiastic response from most of the leaders of this movement. The foundation provides the only open forum for the legitimate discussion of these issues. It offers a place where people can discuss ideas about their own experiences under these various agents. I was surprised to learn how many people out there are closet psychedelic graduates. I've talked to people who I thought that never in a

> *"Oh my, it was a wonderful experience!" said a sixty-five-year-old professor of Medieval French...*

million years would understand what I was talking about. "Oh my, it was a wonderful experience!" said a sixty-five-year-old professor of Medieval French, and I couldn't believe that she had said that. There's plenty of them out there, so we're bringing them together and many of them have become members in our organization.

Other projects? I've been working in several non-profit organizations that have some concern for the ecological welfare of the Earth. One is called, "Eyes on Earth," and another is called, "Earth Anthem." Eyes on Earth involves a scientific visualization of the Earth and it's resources. It is the only true cloud-free picture of the Earth, projected electronically onto a huge globe. It was painstakingly assembled by the photographs of the Earth without clouds taken by satellite and it depicts how different resources are dwindling and being depleted.

Earth Anthem is a contest for people throughout the world, to find an anthem that represents the earth. This project will culminate in a program designed to celebrate the finalists of this contest. We want to find a song that is representative of the earth, one that we could sing if the Martians come. In addition, my new book, *A Different Kind of Healing*, is in publication by Putnam and is to be released shortly. So that's what I'm up to, and I keep moving. I think Einstein said it: "Keep moving!"

John C. Lilly

**"The explanatory principle will save you from the fear
of the unknown. I prefer the unknown…"**

From here to Alternity and Beyond
with John C. Lilly

Combining thirty-five years of academic training with a stubborn refusal to play by academia's rules, John C. Lilly has become something of a New Age icon. Ridiculed as a cosmic trickster by some and lauded as a pioneer in human consciousness by others, Lilly's refusal to be pigeonholed makes him hard to pin down. He is a neurophysiologist, neuroanatomist, biophysicist, computer theorist, dolphin researcher, inventor, drug experimenter, and consciousness explorer. He is the author of ten books, hundreds of scientific articles, and was the prototype for two Hollywood films, Altered States *and* The Day of the Dolphin. *After earning his M.D. at Dartmouth Medical School, Lilly pioneered scientific research in the areas of electrical brain stimulation, sensory deprivation, and human-dolphin communication. He invented the isolation tank in the 1950s, and began using psychedelics such as LSD and ketamine in the solitude of the tank about a decade later. Lilly's seminal work with cetaceans, recounted in the books* Man and Dolphin, The Mind of the Dolphin, *and* Lilly on Dolphins, *inspired a generation to rethink the relationship between humans and other species.*

His incredible journeys through inner space were documented in popular books such as The Center of the Cyclone *and* The Scientist, *and his guidelines for using psychedelics were published under the title* Programming and Metaprogramming the Human Biocomputer. *We interviewed John at his house in Malibu on the night of February 16, 1991. John spoke enthusiastically to us about how his early scientific research influenced his later explorations in consciousness, the distinction between insanity and outsanity, ECCO (the Earth Coincidence Control Office) and he discussed his ideas about how ketamine makes the brain sensitive to microwaves, so that it can pick up television and radio signals. John has a reputation for being extremely unpredictable, and he has this sometimes disconcerting tendency to make one continously redefine their basic assumptions. John's child-like curiosity and ruthlessly analytical mind make him both playful and profound. He seemed like an extraterrestrial Zen master, and was in high spirits when we interviewed him.*

—DJB

DJB: John, what was it that originally inspired your interest in neuroscience and the nature of reality?

JOHN: At age sixteen, in my prep school, I wrote an article for the school paper called "Reality," and that laid out the trip for the rest of my life—thought versus brain activity and brain structure. I went to CalTech to study the biological sciences, and there I took my first course in neuroanatomy. Later I went on to Dartmouth Medical School where I took another course in neuroanatomy, and at the University of Pennsylvania I studied the brain even further. So I learned more about the brain than I can tell you.

RMN: In what ways do you think your Catholic background influenced your mystical experiences?

JOHN: At Catholic school I learned about tough boys and beautiful girls. I fell in love with Margaret Vance, never told her, though, and it was incredible. I didn't understand about sex so I visualized exchanging urine with her. My father had one of these exercise machines with a belt worn around your belly or rump and a powerful electric motor to make the belt vibrate. I was on this machine and all the vibration stimulated my erogenous zones. Suddenly my body fell apart and my whole being was enraptured. It was incredible.

I went to confession the following morning and the priest said, "Do you jack off?." I didn't know what he meant, then suddenly I did and I said, "No." He called it a mortal sin. I left the church thinking, "If they're going to call a gift from God a mortal sin, then to hell with them. That isn't my God, they're just trying to control people."

> *I left the church thinking, "If they're going to call a gift from God a mortal sin, then to hell with them."*

RMN: What is your personal understanding of God?

JOHN: When I was seven years old I had a vision alone in a Catholic church. Suddenly I saw God on his throne: an old man with a white beard and white hair surrounded by angels and the saints parading around with a lot of music. I made the mistake of asking a nun about the vision and she said, "Only saints have visions!" I assumed that she thought I wasn't a saint.

So I kept that memory, and on my first acid trip I relived it completely to Beethoven's Ninth Symphony. And suddenly I realized that the little boy had constructed this to explain the experience he had. I realized that one has to project onto an experience if one is going to talk about it because the experience itself can't be said in words. But if you are going to talk about it you choose words

> *...one has to project onto an experience if one is going to talk about it because the experience itself can't be said in words.*

which you feel are most appropriate. I understood that, as a seven year old I had done that. I saw an old man with white hair because the pre-programming was there. It wasn't physiology; it was something inside, the inner reality.

RMN: Has your understanding or idea of God evolved over time as a result of your changing experiences?

JOHN: Well, when I started going out on the universe with LSD in the tank, I'd come to a certain group of entities and I'd say, "Are you God?" And they'd say, "Well, we say that to some people but God is way up there somewhere with the angels." And it turned out no matter how big they were, God is bigger. So finally I got to the Starmaker. But as Olaf Stapledon says in his book, it's impossible to describe the Starmaker in human terms. He was well aware of the bullshit of language.

I call God ECCO now. The Earth Coincidence Control Office. It's much more satisfying to call it that. A lot of people accept this and they don't know that they're just talking about God. I finally found a God that was big enough. As the astronomer said to the Minister, "My God's astronomical." The Minister said, "How can you relate to something so big?" The astronomer said, "Well, that isn't the problem, your God's too small!"

DJB: Do you think that the concept of objectivity is valuable, or do you think that separating the experimenter from the experiment is impossible?

JOHN: Objectivity and subjectivity were traps that people fell into. I prefer the terms "insanity" and "outsanity." Insanity is your life inside yourself. It's very private and you don't allow anybody in there because it's so crazy. Every so often I find somebody that I can talk to about it. When you go into the isolation tank outsanity is gone. Now, outsanity is what we're doing now, it's exchanging thoughts and so on. I'm not talking about my insanity and you're not talking about yours. Now, if our insanities overlap then we can be friends.

DJB: How would you define what a hallucination is?

JOHN: That's a word I never use because it's very disconcerting, part of the explanatory principle and hence not useful. Richard Feynmen, the physicist, went into the tank here twelve times. He did three hours each time and when he finished he sent me one of his physics books in which he had inscribed, "Thanks for the hallucinations."

So I called him up and I said, "Look, Dick, you're not being a scientist. What you experience you must describe and not throw into the wastebasket called "hallucination." That's a psychiatric misnomer; none of that is unreal that you experienced." For instance he talks about his nose when he was in the tank. His nose migrated down to his buttonhole, and finally he decided that he didn't need a buttonhole or a nose so he took off into outer space.

DJB: And he called that a hallucination because he couldn't develop a model to explain it?

JOHN: But you don't have to explain it, you see. You just describe it. Explanations are worthless in this area.

RMN: How do you feel about the role that discipline has to play in the process of self-discovery?

JOHN: It's absolutely essential. I had thirty-five years of school, eight years of psychoanalysis before even going into the tank. So I was freer than I would have been had I not had all that. Everybody could say, "Well, that was dissonant," and I would say, "Yes, but I learned what I don't have to know." I learned all the bullshit that's put out in the academic world and I would bullshit too. This bullshit is an insurance that I don't remember the bullshit that the professor says, except that which is really worthwhile and interesting.

RMN: What guidelines do you use when travelling through innerspace?

JOHN: My major guideline when I go in the tank is, for God's sake don't preprogram, don't have a purpose, let it happen. With ketamine and LSD I did the same thing; I slowly let go of controlling the experience. You know some people lie in the tank for an hour trying to experience what I experienced. Finally I wrote an introduction to *The Deep Self*, and said, if you really want to experience what it is to be in

...if you really want to experience what it is to be in the tank, don't read any of my books...just go in there and be.

the tank, don't read any of my books, don't listen to me, just go in there and *be*.

RMN: So you don't ever try and go in with a mission or an idea of what you want to accomplish?

JOHN: Why should I? I'd only have gotten more ridiculous. Every time I took acid in the tank in St. Thomas it was entirely different. I think that I couldn't even begin to describe it. I only got 1/10 of 1% of it and I wrote that in books. The universe prevents you from programming and when they take you out, they tear you wholly loose and you realize that these are massive intellects, far greater than any human. Then you really get humble. When you come back here you say, "Oh well, here I am, back in this damn body again, and I'm not as intelligent as when I was out there with them."

I took an acid trip in the Carlisle Hotel in Washington, near the FBI building. I turned on the tape recorder and I just lay down on the bed. I was a tight person but it was an incredible trip. They took me out and showed me the luminous colossus, and then the Big Bang that they created three times. And they said, "Man appears here and disappears there." And I said, "That's awful. What happens to them?" And they said, "That's us." I went into a deep depression because I didn't identify with that. Then, about a week later, I suddenly realized they're also talking about *me*. You see all this in the introduction to *The Center of the Cyclone*.

DJB: John, let me ask you, how did your earlier inter-species communication research with marine mammals influence your later work where you experienced contact with extra-terrestial or inter-dimensional beings on your psychedelic travels?

JOHN: Let me say how I got to work with dolphins first. I was floating in the tank for a year and wondering, who floats around twenty-four hours a day? I went to Pete Shoreliner and he says, "Dolphins. They're available. Go down to the Marine Studios in Florida." So I did, and I immediately fell in love with them. Then we killed a couple of dolphins to get the brains, and when we saw them we said, "Oh boy! This is it. This is a brain bigger than ours!" And I thought, this is what I want to do.

Well, I didn't kill any more dolphins. I studied their behavior and interactions. I was working alone at Marine Studios and I had a brain electrode in one dolphin, which I regret immeasurably. Anyway, when I would stimulate the positive reinforcement system he would just quietly push the lever and work like mad, and if I stopped he would vocalize immediately. I knew monkeys wouldn't do that. And if we stimulated the negative system he would push the lever, shut it off, and then he'd scold us. See? Then he broke the switch and just jabbered away.

So we then took the tape of this over to a friend of mine's house and his tape machine ran at only half the speed of what we had recorded in. It was incredible. Dolphin making human sounds. We didn't believe it at first. What he was trying to do was to say, "I can talk your language, let me talk to your leaders, then we can really get this straightened out about positive and negative reinforcement."

So when I got my lab organized in Miami I turned to Ellsbrough and I said, "I'm going in there to try this with Elvar." So I went and shouted at the dolphin we called Elvar, "Elvar! Squirt water!" He zoomed right back immediately, "Squouraarr rahher." And I said, "No. Squirt water." And finally after about ten times, he had it so we could understand it. It was just an amazing experience.

DJB: Do you think that he had an understanding of what he was saying, or do you think he was just mimicking the sounds?

JOHN: If you're experiencing a foreign language, what do you do?

DJB: Well, the first thing you do is mimic.

JOHN: That's right. And slowly but surely, your phenome system masters the sounds, right? And it doesn't make any difference whether it makes sense or not. Then the next thing you have to do is hook the phenomes up and make words. And then you have to hook the words up to make sentences. And then the meaning, the semantic system in your brain, starts working. So we have to go through all these steps and if you're at all smart you'll realize that you have to have intensive contact with the other language, with someone who speaks it very well. I learned Swedish that way and that's what we did with the dolphins.

DJB: Right. So this work with the dolphins, how did it influence your experiences with ketamine in the isolation tank?

JOHN: Well, I discovered that dolphins have personalities and are valuable people. I began to wonder about whales which have much larger brains, and I wondered what their capabilities are.

There's a threshold of brain size for language as we know it, and as far as I can make out it's about 800 grams. Anybody below that, like the chimpanzee or the go-

> *...the dolphin's life is probably as complicated as ours.*

rilla can't learn to speak a language. But above that language is acquired very rapidly, as in a baby. Well, this means that the dolphin's life is probably as complicated as ours. But what about their spiritual life? Can they get out of their bodies and travel? Are they extraterrestials? I asked those kinds of questions. Most people wouldn't ask them.

So I took ketamine by the tank at Marine World in Redwood City. I got in to the tank and I had a microphone near my head and an underwater speaker that went down into the dolphin tank. My microphone hit their loudspeaker under water. So I waited. Then I began to feel that I was in direct contact with them and as soon as I felt that one of them whistled, a long whistle, and it went from my feet right up to my head. I went straight out of my body. They took me to the dolphin group mind. Boy, that was scary! I shouted and carried on. I said, "I can't even handle *one* dolphin, much less a group mind of dolphins!"

So instead of that they put me into a whale group mind and when you have an experience like that, you realize that some of the LSD experiences may have been in those group minds, not in outer space at all. Since then I suspect that they're all ready to talk and carry on with us if we were not so blind. So we open up pathways to them with ketamine, with LSD, with swimming with them, with falling in love with them and them falling in love with us. All the non-scientific ways.

RMN: Why did you stop doing the English experiments with the dolphins?

JOHN: Because I didn't want anyone to speak to them. So I did it more esoterically with ketamine in the tank, and so on, which these idiots in the Navy wouldn't do. I was appalled by what they were doing.

RMN: Have you ever managed to learn enough of their language to communicate with them on their level?

JOHN: No, because they're too fast and too high frequency. They're ten times as fast as we are and ten times the frequency. So if you record it on tape and then slow it down ten times you can get an idea. When they're working on human speech, at first they're too fast for you, and then they suddenly realize it so they slow down.

DJB: Have you ever given ketamine to a dolphin?

JOHN: No. I gave them acid to see if it would knock out their respiration. It didn't. I couldn't understand what was happening to them on LSD except for one thing they did. They turned around along the tank at the same time, and suddenly they turned their beaks down and turned on their sonar straight downwards. I remember on my first acid trip that suddenly the floor disappeared and I saw the stars on the other side of the earth, so I stamped my foot on the floor to find it. That's what they were doing.

Also, the dolphin Pam had been spear-gunned three times by Ricco Browny in the "Flipper" series. The first time, Pam went over to Browny and pulled the spear from him. The second time, she took one look at him and turned away. The third time she ran like mad and wouldn't go near him or any humans. It was just awful. So when we got her she was staying away from us with the other dolphins. So I gave her LSD and she climbed all over us. It was marvelous.

Boy, I've been trying to stop talking about dolphins. I was enslaved by them for twenty years and now I'm trying to avoid them for a while. But I can't. People like you come out and remind me of them.

RMN: That's wonderful. Okay, let's get back to people. Could you tell us, in what ways you think the exploration and mapping of the human psyche can help to improve the quality of people's lives and what about people with mental disorders?

JOHN: Do you know Thomas Szaz's book, *The Myth of Mental Illness*? Well that's where I'm at. I don't believe any of this mental health stuff; it's all bullshit. Having been through psychoanalysis with a doctor of physics, Robert Beltim from Vienna, that's what I've come to think. He used to analyze analysts, Anna Freud and so on. I started quoting papers from psychoanalysis and finally he said, "Dr. Lilly, we're not here to analyze Freud or the psychoanalytic literature; we're here to analyze *you*, and you're just avoiding yourself. I learn more from you and you learn more from me than we'll ever get in the literature." So that's the way I've looked at everything. Wide open.

RMN: What do you think about people who suffer from a disruption of their interior reality? People who experience problems in coming to terms with their inner process in relation to the world around them?

JOHN: Do you know Candice Pert's work? Well, she's found fifty-two peptides in the brain that control mood. As Pert said, "Once we understand the chemistry of the brain there will be no use for psychoanalysis." She said that the brain is a huge, diverse chemical factory. We cannot make generalizations about any one of these yet but, for instance, if you give an overdose of this one people get depressed, if you give an overdose of that one they get euphoria, and so on. If you OD on cocaine your brain changes its operation, but if you're aware of this and you pay attention you realize that yes, it modifies some things, but it doesn't always do it in the same way. So there's this continuous modulation of life versus brain chemistry. So I gave up long ago trying to figure out how the brain works because it's so immense and so complex. We don't yet know how thought is connected to operations in the brain!

DJB: Do you think it would be possible to create some kind of window into the brain to see the dynamics of how thoughts arise and what their interaction is by using some kind of highly precise combination of EEG and MRI scannings?

JOHN: No. It's impossible. The Positron Emission Topography or PET scans show the changes in various parts of the brain and of various substances. When the observed person is learning, a compound acts one way, and then another way. But what's that? That's one compound that they're looking at. Imagine what else is going on.

DJB: Years back you helped to pioneer the original electrical brain stimulation research. With the understanding that you've gained in this area, do you think that it will eventually be possible to directly stimulate brain centers without using electrodes, in order to create psychedelic experiences?

JOHN: Electrical stimulation of brains is very poor without brain electrodes and with electrodes you wreck the brain when you put them in there. That's why I quit.

DJB: So you think then that it is possible to stimulate brain centers without using electrodes?

JOHN: Yes. A friend of mine at the University of Illinois showed me a set-up in which he was stimulating a brain at minute spots with focused ultra-sound and electrical interference.

RMN: Do you think that men and women's brains operate in a very different way?

JOHN: You know, I've been researching that for years, and finally I admit that you are another universe that I can't possibly be in because you're female and I'm male.

DJB: What directions do you think neuroscience should be taking? What are the most important avenues of exploration?

JOHN: The most important things to do in science is to figure out who the human is and how he operates biochemically. We're never going to understand how the brain works. I always say that my brain is a big palace, and I'm just a little rodent running around inside it. The brain owns me, I don't own the brain. A large computer can simulate totally a smaller computer but it cannot simulate itself, because if it did there wouldn't be anything left except the simulation. Consciousness would stop there.

> *The most important things to do in science is to figure out who the human is and how they operate biochemically.*

DJB: Could it not be possible for human beings to create a computer system large and complex enough that, although it may not be able to understand itself, it would be able to understand the human brain?

JOHN: No, because we don't know the basis for the human brain. As Van

Neumann said, it was strictly by accident that we discovered multiplication, addition and subtraction first. If we discovered the mathematics of the brain we'd be way ahead of where we are now.

DJB: You mean the binary language?

JOHN: There's no way to tell what the hell language the brain uses. Sure, you can show digital operations of the brain, you can analyze neural impulses travelling down your axons, but what are those? Well, as far as I can see they are just a recovery from a system that's in the middle of the axon, and that's operating at the speed of light. Neuronal impulses going down the axons are just clearing up the laser points so that it's ready for the next one, continuously. It's like sleep. Sleep is a state in which the human biocomputer integrates and analyzes what went on the previous time it was outside, throws out all the memories that aren't going to be useful tomorrow and stores only those memories which will be useful. So it's a process like a big computer in which you have to empty memory and start over. We do this all the time.

DJB: Along these lines, I'm wondering, do you think memories are actually stored in the brain or do you agree with Rupert Sheldrake's theory that memories are stored in information fields or something similar.

JOHN: I've read some of Sheldrakes's stuff and he's too glib. He's got an explanation for everything. The universe is much more complicated than he's trying to make it out to be. People tend to do this— I've tried to avoid it. I make fun of my own theories. I say, what I believe to be true is

> *I make fun of my own theories.*

unbelievable, so that I don't believe in anything, you see? Temporarily I may in order to talk with somebody. Memories are stored in the feedback with ECCO and ECCO takes care of all this. I don't know how they operate, but Sheldrake calls stuff memory which isn't memory; it's living program.

DJB: Do you think that the brain acts as a transceiver?

JOHN: Yeah, that's right. The brain, the bio-computer is a huge transmitter/receiver and we're just beginning to see what it is. Have you ever seen anything like a TV show on ketamine?

DJB: Yeah, with commercials even.

JOHN: Well, they're real. The first time I saw that I thought, my God, all we're doing is increasing the sensitivity of the brain to microwaves. And the problem with microwaves is that they're influencing us below our level of awareness all the time. Well, this morning for instance, on ketamine, I went into this place where all these people were interacting and I got involved. When I came back I realized that I had got into a soap opera on TV and was taking part in it as if it were reality!

Now kids must do this all the time. Marvelous! But you got to watch out because you may be taken in and think they're extraterrestial or something, unless you can see something that cues you in that this is a TV station.

DJB: Have your experiences with ketamine and your near-death encounters influenced your perspective on what happens to human consciousness after biological death?

JOHN: I refuse to equate my experiences with death. I think it's too easy to do that. When I was out for five days and nights on PCP, the guides took me to planets that were being destroyed and so on. I think ECCO made me take that PCP so they could educate me. And they kept hauling me around and I tried to get back but they said, "Nope, you haven't seen all the planets yet." One was being destroyed by atomic energy of war, one was being destroyed by a big asteroid that hit the planet, another one was being destroyed by biological warfare, and on and on and on. I realized that the universe is effectively benign; it may kill you but it will teach you something in the process.

> *...the universe is effectively benign; it may kill you but it will teach you something in the process.*

DJB: Do you think that there is actually some kind of learning process that's going on as a result of ECCO's positively or negatively reinforcing certain behaviors so that humanity's evolution is guided in certain directions?

JOHN: I had the illusion that humanity is making progress in certain directions, yes.

DJB: Do you feel that when synchronicity happens, that it's actually being arranged either by ECCO or by us?

JOHN: The only place that Jung defined synchronicity at all well was in the introduction to the *I Ching*, and he talks about controlling coincidences. He fell into the same trap I did. Synchronicity doesn't mean anything; it's an explanatory principle.

RMN: Do you think that ECCO is concentrating on humans?

JOHN: Of course not! ECCO is the one that's running everything on the whole planet.

RMN: So they have no particular interest in our survival, we're just a minute part of what's going on?

JOHN: They? You're personalizing. I used to personalize. I saw angels, extra-terrestials, then I called them guides and finally I called them ECCO and it's totally impersonal. It's way beyond what people can understand except in a ketamine or LSD state. Then they tell you, well we're at a low level, there are influences above us. It would be nice to meet these entities that experience these various states. They won't take human form, though; it's a waste of their time. And once I joined them and realized that that's where I came from and that I had gotten bored and become human in order to have some different experiences with a smaller intelligence. It's like becoming a cat or something, to find out what's going on with the cat.

RMN: I feel that my dog, Safety, might have done that very thing. She's more human than many people I know.

JOHN: Well a dog finally convinced me of this, that there are levels that these entities choose to be, dolphins or whatever. When I experienced level +3 (refer to *The Center of the Cyclone*), I was part of a huge consciousness that was creating from the void. It was taking energy and creating a form, life and so on. It wasn't me. My ego afterwards wanted it to be me but of course it wasn't.

DJB: Do you have a hard time bringing information back?

JOHN: Oh, of course. It isn't hard to bring it back, it just doesn't come back. It's in you, though; ECCO put me straight on that. They said, "Well, everything that's happened is stored and when it's important that you know it, you'll know it."

RMN: When you're ready for it.

DJB: Bringing information back from my ketamine experiences is a real struggle for me.

JOHN: You've got to be more passive. If you struggle, then all you'll see is your struggle. It's like trying to do something instead of doing it.

DJB: Let me ask you John, how do you, or do you, distinguish between mind and body, spirit and matter?

JOHN: Those are all explanatory principles.

DJB: How about in terms of descriptive principles. How would you describe the difference between them?

JOHN: Naming such things is a dichotomy. The only dichotomies are in language and in the eye of the observer. Until you can describe the system of mathematical continuous process, or stepless process, then you aren't really saying anything. As I keep saying in every workshop I give, "For the rest of this week you are going to hear a lot of stuff and all of it is bullshit." You know why? Because language itself is bullshit. It's a way of spending your time without experience or experiment.

DJB: But what other alternative do we have besides language for communication?

JOHN: Well, if you don't know, I can't explain it to you. No, I told you about it; on the ketamine experiences you're going through reality experiences and they're experimenting on you and you're experimenting and there's no way that language has anything to do with this. So what's happening is so fast and continuous that you don't have a chance of describing it.

DJB: But don't you think it's important that people write books and map out the territory?

JOHN: Only if they tell you, "There's a territory over there. Go see it." That's all.

DJB: What do you think of the notion that Terence McKenna talks about a lot, that language actually creates reality?

JOHN: No, it doesn't. Language creates reality? That doesn't make any sense at all.

RMN: Maybe he means that language creates our *experience* of reality, because it programs us to think in certain ways.

JOHN: The experience in the tank, for example, is a continuous paragraphic process and that's true of life in general. You can't describe me, for instance, you can't even remember me in your video memory, right?

RMN: I can't remember you? I haven't forgotten you yet.

JOHN: No, no. That's a simulation. You haven't forgotten your simulation of this, whatever it is. See, I can't describe me and I can't describe you.

RMN: Right, I see that. But if somebody were to ask me about you later on, the language I used to recall and describe you then would effect how I re-experienced you.

JOHN: My book, *The Simulations of God: The Science of Belief,* explains all of this.

DJB: Explains? Isn't that the notorious explanatory principle creeping in again?

JOHN: All we do is construct simulations. I construct the simulation of you, for instance, and I turn this into words. But that simulation is nowhere near who you really are. Then I tell you what my simulation of you is and you correct it, and on and on. You cannot substitute words for the action of the brain, the action of thought or the action of mind When I say mind I'm talking about the whole universe of stuff, see? It's not that simple.

> *All we do is construct simulations.*

RMN: Why do you think we have this desire for meaning, this compulsion to explain things all the time?

JOHN: Childishness. The circle. The explanatory principle will save you from the fear of the unknown; I prefer the unknown, I'm a student of the unexpected. Margaret Howe taught me something. I went over to St. Thomas one time and she said, "Dr. Lilly, you're always trying to make something happen. This time you're not going to make something happen, you're going to just sit and watch." You know what I'm saying?

DJB: Yeah, I get caught in that one a lot.

JOHN: So, if I can't make something happen I get bored sometimes. But if I don't get bored and I just relax and let it happen, you show up. Now I can afford to do this, I don't have to earn a living, but if you know how to do it you can earn a living and be passive as hell.

DJB: What's the trick to doing that?

JOHN: You become an administrator who doesn't know anything, so people are always explaining to you what's happening. My father was the head of a big banking system; he taught me something about passivity. He said, "You must learn to be *as if* you're angry, and then you'll always be ahead of the guy who really gets angry." And I said, "Well, what about love?" And he said the same thing. All those powerful emotions—you can act as if you're experiencing them, but you're not involved, you see, you haven't lost your intellectual load.

DJB: You think that if people get overwhelmed by emotion they lose their ability to think clearly?

JOHN: Well, I had a lesson in that. I got really angry at my older brother, and I threw one of those cans that have calcium carbide in them and spark, because he was teasing me so much. He teased me an awful lot. So I threw this can at him and it missed his head by about two inches. And suddenly I stopped and thought, "My God, I could have killed him! I'll never get angry again."

RMN: What do you think about America's involvement in the Gulf War and what are your thoughts about the causes of war in general?

JOHN: Well, the Gulf War happened because Russia and the United States made peace. So the United States Defense Department had to have something to do, because they have this huge budget. Luckily the Russians didn't have that huge budget as their economy is falling apart. If our economy was falling apart then there wouldn't be any war. As Eisenhower said, industrial establishment and the Defense Department are in control of this country.

RMN: Why do you think it is that politicians and national leaders so often reflect the darker side of human nature?

JOHN: It isn't the darker side. It's the busy side. They get bored so they have to do these things. I started a book called, *Don't Bore God or He Will Destroy Your Universe*. Nobody knows they're doing this to avoid boredom; they make other excuses for it. You've never been bored?

RMN: I've been bored but I don't feel like going out and bombing somebody because of it.

JOHN: No, no. You're not one of those people. If you took PCP you wouldn't kill anybody. Sidney Cohen, who died last year, was the head of the committee of the Mental Health Institute for Drug Abuse. He said, "How is it that PCP and ketamine have similar molecules. Have you ever seen any violence with ketamine?" I said, "No." He said, "Well, with PCP we see it all the time." I said, "Look Sidney, you've forgotten that there's a selection of people who take PCP and a selection of people who take ketamine. All the people that I know who take ketamine are professionals who have respect for their own minds and brains. They're knowledgeable and educated and they're not violent. But the people who take PCP are violent in the first place; peaceful people who take PCP don't get violent.

RMN: What do you think needs to happen before war becomes an obsolete activity?

JOHN: It won't happen. Something must make people busy together and war does that.

RMN: Does busy have to mean war? Are there no alternatives?

JOHN: Now Kennedy tried to make a space program. I think if we started a colony on the moon, and then on Mars and we got sufficiently involved we could redirect all our boredom.

RMN: Do you think that aggression is inherent in the human psyche?

JOHN: No. I once wrote a chapter called, "Where do Armies Come From?" Do you know where they come from? Tradition. Kids learn that history is war, so they're all pre-programmed. If you read some of the history books, it's all about war, it's incredible! In my Latin class I learned about the wars of Caesar, when I took French I learned about the wars of Napoleon and on and on and on. What did we learn from Caesar? That you don't divide Gaul into three parts. What did we learn from Cleopatra? The you may have to kill yourself with an asp. If you start reading Italian history and you come across Leonardo Da Vinci or Galileo then the whole thing falls apart. They're individuals doing their thing and it's magnificent. And that's the only part of history that's interesting.

RMN: What do you think about the current theories of evolution?

JOHN: I looked into the paleontology of humans. Paleontology is the only science that could take an observation here, and a million years later another one here and draw a straight line between the two. Every time I read Leaky or Gordon Danier or any of those other people I look at it and say, well those are good observations but are they necessarily connected at all? Maybe a spaceship came and put a colony in at this point. But they don't think of the obvious, you see.

I have a concept called "alternity." From here to alternity. I came back from Chile and sat in Elizabeth Campbell's living-room on acid and started evoking ECCO. Suddenly the energy came out from above and went straight down my spine and on all sides of me were these divisions like a pie. And I could look down this one and see a certain future and then right over here another future and on and on. So this was alternity that I was sitting in. Now actually, unconsciously, we sit in alternity all the time, we have to or you wouldn't know how to get anywhere, right? But you don't know it.

DJB: You mean sitting in a place where you see all the infinite possibilities and pathways that can emerge from a particular point in space-time?

JOHN: I don't know if it's infinite. It's sure 360 degrees and each alternative reality was every two degrees or something like that. There were a hell of a lot of them and some that I couldn't ever imagine.

RMN: If you were conscious of that do you think you would be able to make any decisions to go anywhere?

JOHN: Well, I get conscious of all of them or none of them. So when I get out of my body I don't try to program anything because there are so many alternates possible.

DJB: What are you thoughts about the future?

JOHN: What's the future?

DJB: That which hasn't happened yet. The next micro-second, the next year, the next century and so on.

JOHN: We act as if there's going to be a year out there, but we haven't got there yet, right? And we think the sun is going to come up every morning and we count on that, we expect it. What's going to happen when it doesn't? One alternity is enough so why talk about the future?

DJB: John, on a different note, do you think there is a qualitative difference between organic and synthesized compounds?

JOHN: I don't know what qualitative means; I never was able to grasp that word. It's one of the first things that they teach you in grade school and it never made any sense. My bullshit filter said it was bullshit.

We take something that a plant or animal did and we call it pure sugar or whatever. That's chemistry, the science of separating out components which you can't reduce any further without destroying them. So what does the plant do? The plant picks up

> *Plants are chemists just like us.*

carbon dioxide and stuff from the ground and starts combining these compounds in certain ways and synthesizes them. Plants are chemists just like us. A lot of people call something natural or organic but they don't know their organic chemistry, because anything that has a carbon atom in it is organic, okay?

RMN: How do you define addiction and how do you avoid falling into the trap of misusing the chemicals you take?

JOHN: Let's see. There's drug use, drug over-use, drug abuse, drug hypo-use and on and on. There is a set of chemicals that if you take them and you don't exercise and you don't eat right, you go downhill. When you go downhill you have to take more of that chemical to substitute for the food and stuff. But if you are taken off that

> *If you're in good physical condition you can experience a hell of a lot.*

chemical without the proper stimulus you get grand mal seizures or something. That's the old-fashioned description of addiction.

What I say is, you take certain chemicals and change the chemical configuration in your brain and body. This is a very interesting process and if you stay interested and look after yourself then you can take cocaine or heroin or any of those things. Physical exercise is absolutely essential to get good changes of conscious states. If you're in good physical condition you can experience a hell of a lot. If you lose interest then you go downhill and wind up in Harlem or something.

RMN: What about people who have developed a powerful physical and mental addiction, for example, to crack and cocaine, in some cases even killing or stealing in order to fulfil their craving for the drugs.

JOHN: They'll kill and steal without the drugs; they live that way. The drug just gives them an excuse to do it. Read Freud on cocaine. He really knew what cocaine did but he was never able to say it in the presence of the psychoanalytic people. Psychoanalysis is all based on his cocaine experiences, every bit of it.

DJB: What do you think about this whole "War on Drugs" thing?

JOHN: We've been subject to the delusion that we should suppress drugs ever since Anslinger put marijuana on the narcotics list in 1937. He was enforcing the laws on alcohol and that was repealed, so he looked around for something new and found marijuana. In an interview with Anslinger the interviewer asked him, "What if you were to smoke a joint?" And he said, "I would kill three people that I know." What a belief system! And he put all that in the law, you see. It's that insanity of certain people who don't understand what's going on.

RMN: What do you think about atomic energy? Do you have any ideas about how we could solve the nuclear waste problem?

JOHN: All the atomic materials should be shot into the sun. We're playing around with something we don't know anything about. This is the stuff of stars, it's not the stuff of a planet. But it's there so we do it and then we get the illusion that we can control it. Well, that's bull. ECCO did something in 1942 that I'll never forget; it threw LSD and atomic energy at us in one go. I once asked ECCO what they did that for and they said, "Well, we're trying to test out the survivability of the human species."

DJB: So you think that there are areas then that humanity shouldn't mess around with?

JOHN: Right. Well, we've proven it with atomic energy and biological warfare, too. AIDS.

DJB: You think that AIDS is the result of genetic engineering experiments gone astray?

JOHN: Yeah, you can see it. It's fooling around with biological warfare and something's escaped. Somebody left a sink open and it went down the sewer. Les Chambers, who is head of biological warfare at Camp Detrid is an old friend of mine so I went down and talked to him about it. We went over all this and he said, "You know, someday, somebody's going to make a mistake, and one of those things is just going to go wild all over the world." He knew. AIDS is an artificial virus; it's related to the Bovine virus, but it wouldn't affect humans before. Somebody spliced it so it would.

DJB: You don't think AIDS could be a natural mutation?

JOHN: No. Natural mutations we can handle because we've lived here for three million years and the mutation rate is very slow. Our immune systems are incredible.

DJB: What role do you think science fiction plays in the development of actual scientific research?

JOHN: Well, big brains operate with science fiction and create it. What it does is free up the creative process for a look at a simulated future which may or may not exist, but it's fun making those simulations and some of them are very good. One of my favorites is *Childhood's End* by Arthur C. Clarke.

DJB: Are you familiar with Virtual Reality?

JOHN: I've just heard about it. I want to experience it. It shows us what we're doing all the time—constructing realities. You change the chemistry of the brain, you change the realities. Sometimes that can get very scary. Once on ketamine I had an experience that scared the hell out of me, and then I realized, hey, this is happening all the time! Why should I be scared of something that's happening all the time?

> *Once on ketamine I had an experience that scared the hell out of me, and then I realized..this is happening all the time!*

DJB: What do you think about the potential of using ketamine in conjunction with psychotherapy?

JOHN: They did it in Iran. One hundred patients. Got them all out of the hospital in one trip. They programmed in that which the patient feared most. Did I tell you what happened to me with that? I went and looked up the Iranian reprint at the UCLA Medical Library and the Albanian one which confirmed the Iranian study.

This whole business about keying in that which is feared most stuck out. So I came back here and took 200 mg of ketamine. Suddenly I was transported to the year 3000 by ECCO and they removed my penis bloodlessly. I screamed in terror and Toni, my late wife, came running out of the bedroom. She looked at me and said, "It's still attached." So I looked up at the ceiling and said, "Who the hell is in charge up there? A bunch of psychotic kids? And the answer came back, "Dr. Lilly, you were at the UCLA Medical Library this afternoon and we programmed in for you that which you feared most. It was in your unconsciousness."

RMN: What do you think is the purpose of fear?

JOHN: From Orthonoia to Metanoia through Paranoia. Orthonoia is the way most people think; they're creating simulations that everyone accepts. Metanoia is where you leave all that and you're experiencing higher intelligence. But the first time you do this, you're scared shitless.

On my first acid trip in the tank, I panicked. Suddenly I saw the memorandum from the National Institute of Mental Health: "Never Take Acid Alone." One investigator who tried to take acid alone got eaten up by his tape recorder.

That's all I could think of. Luckily I was scared shitless, had no idea what was going to happen and boy, that was rocket fuel if ever there was one! I went further out into the universe than I've ever been since. So the paranoia is rocket fuel to get you into Metanoia.

Before I did the tank I was frightened by water. I sailed a lot in the ocean and feared sharks. I had a continuous phobia about this. Finally I got in the tank and went through that horrible experience, being frightened to death, you know. And after that I was never afraid of water.

DJB: Do you see a similarity between lucid dreaming and ketamine experiences?

JOHN: No. Lucid dreaming is never as powerful as ketamine.

DJB: Well, one nice thing about ketamine is that you can maintain the high for as long as you want.

JOHN: When people start talking about "higher" states of consciousness I say, "In outer space there's no up or down."

DJB: It all becomes relative.

JOHN: No, it isn't even relative.

DJB: It isn't even relative?

JOHN: It isn't anything you can describe.

DJB: Now I'm thoroughly confused.

JOHN: If you stay around me long enough you're going to get a whole new language. Some people stay around me for a while and run away. I can't keep a woman here. They all get frightened sooner or later. I'm crazier than hell.

DJB: So are you writing these days? What are you doing?

JOHN: I never say what I'm doing. My analyst said it very well. I came in one day and flopped down on the couch and said, "I just had a new idea this morning, but I'm not going to talk about it." And he said, "Oh, then you understand that a new idea is like an embryo. A needle will kill an embryo, but if it's a fetus or a baby then it's just a needle-prick." So you have to allow a certain amount of growth before you talk.

RMN: What do you think is the best therapy for people?

JOHN: The best therapy for people is to hit them over the head with a hammer.

DJB: Maybe we could start running workshops at Esalen.

JOHN: I've been hit over the head several times. We had a big hot tub out here. I stood up too fast and the circulation left my brain and I fell face down. Three days before, Toni had read how to do mouth-to-mouth resuscitation in *The National Enquirer*, and she did it. So many people have saved my life, it's incredible. I finally figured out that ECCO doesn't want me to go yet. I asked them to let me go at times. They keep saying, "You've got to teach, you've got to learn what it is to be a human." So, I'm spending all my time now trying to learn this. You know, it just gets to be fun. I realized that certain humans have a lot of fun. On some day I said, "What is it to be human?" And they said, "To laugh more."

Nina Graboi

"I think of my body as my spacesuit which I will discard
once it has grown threadbare—but I will go on."

Stepping into the Future
with Nina Graboi

Nina Graboi has had a remarkable life which covers over seven decades of some of the most transformative years in human history. Born in Vienna, Austria in 1918, she fled the Nazi takeover of her country and spent three months in a detention camp in North Africa. Through a mixture of ingenuity and good fortune she managed to escape and came to America with her husband in 1941.

Arriving as a penniless refugee, she went on to become a society hostess in an exclusive Long Island community. At the age of 36 she was living what most people considered the epitome of the American Dream, yet Nina felt a great void in her life. In search of this missing link, she plunged into the study of esoteric subjects and became an avid practitioner of meditation. When she was 47 she left her husband and became deeply involved in the counter-culture of the sixties.

Nina had her first psychedelic experience in the company of Alan Watts and she frequently spent time at the famed Millbrook estate where a group had gathered around Timothy Leary to study the mind-expanding effects of LSD. She was the Director of the New York Center of the League for Spiritual Discovery, a nonprofit organization which operated to help and educate people engaged in exploring the potential of psychedelic consciousness.

In 1969 she opened a boutique in Woodstock and lived there for the next ten years. Her recently published autobiography, One Foot in the Future, *chronicles her remarkable spiritual journey and has been described by Terence McKenna as "an extraordinary tale of humor and hope." Today, Nina lives in Santa Cruz and gives talks on the relationship between the psychedelic experience and the spiritual quest. She is a frequent radio talk-show guest and is the subject of a television documentary entitled,* Voices of Vision.

We interviewed Nina on January 12, 1992, on a rainy day at Two Bat Ranch, in Malibu. Her face dramatically contradicts her 72 years and she presents the demeanor of a woman who is in the spiritual prime of her life. Nina talked with a gracious calm in the warming glow of a log fire, about the politics of sexuality, the use of psychedelics and the future of the human race.

—RMN

RMN: Nina, in the fifties, when you were living in Long Island, you had what most people would consider the pillars of success—wealth, social status, a loving family—and yet you gave it all up. Why?

NINA: When I was the woman who had everything, I realized that everything is nothing. I had been busily pursuing the American Dream, and when I had it, it tasted like ashes. I was raised in an atmosphere where success was the goal and only superstitious peasants believed in anything beyond the physical. But unless I could discover that there is more to it than being born, getting married, having children and scrambling up the ladder of success, life lost all meaning for me at that time. I felt a yearning for *more* so profound that I was ready to die if I could not find it. That was in 1956. There were others who searched as I did, but I did not know them. I was very alone. Books were my only source of information, and for the next twelve years I read my way through psychology, psychic research, philosophy and comparative religions. This brought me to Buddhism and Hinduism, and I felt I'd come home.

> *I had been busily pursuing the American Dream, and when I had it, it tasted like ashes.*

RMN: You were divorced at a time when far fewer couples than today split up. Didn't that take a lot of courage?

NINA: It wasn't a sudden decision, you know. My children were both in college, and I had planned for a long time to end my marriage once the kids were on their own. But yes, it took a lot of courage to end a marriage of twenty-seven years in those days. Aside from the emotional toll, I had no legal rights because I was the party who wanted the divorce. Feminism was still a long way off, and the fact that I'd helped build the business, raised the children, and taken care of the home, counted for nothing. As I had no marketable skills, my financial future could not have been more bleak. It took courage, but it was the only thing I could do if I wanted to continue to grow.

DJB: What kind of life did you move into?

NINA: I moved from a fourteen-room house to a one-room studio in Manhattan. I was heading The N.Y. Center for The League of Spiritual Discovery at the time —a labor of love that paid nothing, but was as rewarding as it was instructive. In 1969, a few months before the Festival, I moved to Woodstock and opened a small boutique stocked mostly with craft items that I made. Later, I ran The Woodstock Transformation Center where many of the now-familiar New Age skills like meditation, Yoga, T'ai Chi, herbal lore, nutrition, Astrology, Tarot and related subjects were taught. Like the LSD Center, it was financially unrewarding, and when my money ran out, I learned to live on whatever I could find to support myself, including house cleaning, altering clothes, organizing craft shows, and so on. I led the lifestyle of the hippies, though I was not a hippie myself—more like a den mother. I saw them as my children, my friends, my teachers. They were so wise, these young ones—they had it all in their heads and hearts, but they had not yet learned how to live it.

RMN: Did you ever miss your former lifestyle?

NINA: Never. Not once. The lavish parties were behind me. I closed the door of that home with the lovely garden and swimming pool and never looked back. Looking back isn't my style anyway. I'm generally not very interested in what happened in the past—too busy with what's going on now!

DJB: So much has been written about the sixties, it is possibly the most over-analyzed decade of this century, and yet many people, even those who were a part of it, often find it hard to express what was going on. What do you think the sixties were about?

NINA: The main characteristic of the sixties was idealism. America's youth in the Eisenhower years was dull and apathetic; all they wanted was to prepare for a safe, secure job. And then suddenly, only a decade later, youngsters who had lived in middle and upper middle-class homes were seeing that their parents in split-level homes with two-car garages were not very happy, so they said, "Screw it, I don't want to live like that!" And they burst out of their suburban homes and landed in crashpads and huts and tents. The materialistic lifestyle of their parents made no sense to them. It was the same thing that had happened to me a decade earlier. As I see it, the sixties were the beginning of a quantum leap forward in human consciousness. Customs and beliefs that had long been taken for granted were challenged by a generation that did not blindly obey authority. And simultaneously, the heavens opened and showered down all the spiritual goodies that had for so long been the secret knowledge of the few. What followed was so threatening to the existing order that a backlash had to come. Nixon, Reagan, Bush, the greedy eighties. The forces of inertia do not willingly make room for the new.

> *...the heavens opened and showered down all the spiritual goodies that had for so long been the secret knowledge of the few.*

RMN: How do you think your perspective was influenced by the fact that you were older than most of the people who were experimenting with consciousness change at that time?

NINA: I was 47 when I left my former lifestyle. Unlike the hippies, I'd had plenty of experience; my feet were firmly planted on the ground. I was enamored of the hippies, though it wasn't easy to adjust to the irresponsibility that often went along with the idealism. Still, I felt more at home with them than I had ever felt before, and my years of esoteric studies helped me to help them see the spiritual path a little more clearly.

DJB: What did you think about the sexual revolution?

NINA: I deplored it. It was another male chauvinist ploy, though that term was still unknown at that time. It was a perfect example of male domination. Most of the young women I knew did not want to sleep with everybody who came their way. In the sixties, it was considered ill-mannered to refuse to get in the sack with anybody who asked. "We're all one," they said. The boys loved it, but few of the girls did. Besides, I don't believe that freedom means license. Everybody was so interchangeable—bodies, bodies, playing musical chairs.

RMN: Tell us a little about your time at Millbrook, the psychedelic research center where you often stayed with Timothy Leary and Richard Alpert (now Ram Dass).

NINA: Well, I didn't exactly stay with them, but I saw a good deal of them on my visits to the Millbrook mansion in upstate New York. As a setting for the exploration of the psychedelic consciousness, the vast estate could not have been more perfect. The sixty-four-room mansion and other outbuildings on the estate were in sufficient disrepair to lend a note of funky eeriness to the scene. Inside, the bizarre mingled with the sublime. It was a combination of research center, monastery, country club, mental hospital and testing ground for all the New Age methods of spiritual growth and physical healing. Add Indian music, jazz, incense, beautiful people clad in loose, lovely robes—that was Millbrook. The people who lived there took LSD together in the spacious living room. They lay on mats listening to music. You know, when people think of what went on in those group sessions, they think of orgies, wild, Dionysian revelries. I'm sure that these went on in many places, but in my experience, group sessions at Millbrook appeared quite sedate. I remember a video crew from a major TV station filming a small group on acid, and all they saw were some people sitting cross-legged on the floor chanting "Om, Om, Om".

RMN: In the sixties, many individuals experimented with mind-altering substances like LSD and marijuana, and yet, as you mention in your book, you observed very few negative effects. Why do you think that was?

NINA: There were some negative effects, but the great majority of experimenters before psychedelics were made illegal had predominantly positive experiences. Some of the negative effects can be traced to the disinformation put out by the government and the sensation-hungry media, but in most cases, those who were pushed over the edge had been close to it before. It is unfortunate that there is no way to screen out people who are at risk, as there would be if these substances were legally controlled instead of criminalized.

RMN: Could you tell us about the dangers involved in taking psychedelics and can you specify who should and who shouldn't use them?

NINA: I don't believe psychedelics are for everybody. People who are already pretty spaced out need first to get grounded. Others with rigid belief systems may find themselves shaken to the core by the collapse of their valued beliefs. Then there are those with weak egos. I define the body as a spacesuit and the ego as the survival kit that contains the instructions that ensure survival on this planet. The weak ego has not developed its survival skills. It can also get inflated and believe that it needs lots of money and power and possessions to survive. Before we approach psychedelics we should understand that we are not what we think we are—we are more! We are more than our bodies. Out-of-body experiences may occur in a psychedelic session, and the unprepared person can have a profound panic reaction. Psychedelics can be used as a therapeutic tool, to go deeper into oneself; this may best be done in the presence of a therapist. They

> *Before we approach psychedelics we should understand that we are not what we think we are.*

can also be used as an aid to creativity and to problem solving. But their noblest and most ancient use is as a bridge to the ineffable—the Higher Self. The most dangerous and wasteful use is to take them simply for kicks.

DJB: How have your experiences with psychedelics affected your perspective of yourself and the life process?

NINA: One of my first discoveries when I entered the psychedelic consciousness was, "It's all upside down!" The absurdity of the things on which the world places the greatest value came home to me in Day Glo colors. I had seen it before, when I lived among the wealthy suburbanites, but now the willingness with which people enslaved themselves to a life of producing unnecessary services and consumer goods so they could buy more unnecessary services and consumer goods struck me with great force. In one of my LSD sessions, the words *real estate* came into my mind, and I laughed hysterically for half an hour. The idea of owning a piece of the planet! Do you see how ludicrous it is? On LSD, I had flashes of the cosmic consciousness of which the saints and yogis speak. I had had brief hints of it in my solitary meditations, but they didn't come close to the actual mystical experience. To *know*, not just to believe, that we are part of the stream of being and that we exist, even apart from our bodies—inevitably, this must affect every aspect of our lives. Like thousands of others, I "dropped out" of a lifestyle that seemed meaningless to live with the hippies who shared my quest and my ideas.

> *In one of my LSD sessions, the words* **real estate** *came into my mind, and I laughed hysterically for half and hour.*

RMN: Of all the major religions you relate to Hinduism the most. What is it about this religious philosophy that attracts you?

NINA: What I find particularly attractive is the lack of dogmatism in eastern philosophy. It is very broad in its acceptance of all forms of worship and all kinds of manifestations of God. Most people need to relate to a personal divinity before they can see that all is God. Hinduism has a variety of divinities and spiritual disciplines to choose from—a brilliant approach to psychology that has no equal in the West. And then there is the impressive fact that only Buddhism, of all the world religions, has never been responsible for a Holy War. There is also their approach to desire; they say that it is caused by ignorance—the ignorance of our own true nature which is no other than the Atman or Buddha nature —the in-dwelling God. In my pre-psychedelic meditations, I was shocked to discover that my mind is a chattering monkey, as the Hindus and Buddhists say. To still it even for a minute is no easy task. Today, millions know the benefits of meditation, but before the sixties, yoga was widely assumed to be no more than a set of physical exercises.

DJB: What do you think happens to human consciousness after death?

NINA: I know nothing about that except that my consciousness, when it is liberated from the body, goes into strange and unfathomable yet somehow familiar dimensions. The only certainty I came away with from my LSD studies is that I am not my body. Strangely enough, today many New Agers see this as heresy. They call it dualism. "I am what I eat. I and my body are one", they say. True, I'm no more separate from my body than from the air I breathe, or from a rock, or from a worm, or from *anything* at all. So I wind up in a cosmic goo. But we have learned to name things so we can distinguish between what's me and what's not me. I am not my body any more than I am the air, the rock, or the worm. I think of my body as my spacesuit which I will dis-

> *...I think that we are travellers, and that our journey is endless.*

card once it has grown threadbare—but I will go on. People in our culture think of death as the enemy, yet death is as natural as eating. There are two possibilities: either we die and everything is over, we're just simply, you know, gone—so what's there to be afraid of? Or else life is a spiral that is eternally ascending. We may or may not come back to this planet in physical form, but I think that we are travelers, and that our journey is endless. I don't like the idea of being in pain and all that stuff that leads up to the actual death, but death itself doesn't frighten me.

DJB: What are your thoughts on euthanasia? There is so much fear of legalizing it.

NINA: I can understand it. We're all too human, and no doubt there will be abuses. On the other hand, to be spared the agony that precedes death is a blessing that many people would welcome. As for myself, I hope to be able to end it once my spacesuit is beyond repair!

RMN: I'd be interested to know your ideas on abortion, Nina. Is it a crime from the spiritual point of view?

NINA: The crime is to bring an unwanted child into the world. I believe that the soul enters the body at birth, and that the embryo is a spacesuit in the making. I see no reason to be any more sentimental about our biological container before birth than after death. To me, it is simply matter not yet or no longer animated by life. It's interesting to note that the Catholic church is as ready to bring masses of uncared-for children into this overpopulated world as to bless troops that are going into battle. Could there be a connection, I wonder? Are these unhappy masses needed for cannon fodder? The pro-life stand of the church is a desperate attempt to continue to rule by appealing to the flock's self-righteous emotions, and in many cases, this appeal succeeds.

Former generations took it for granted that it is woman's destiny to bear children. Women were bred to be breeders, but when girls began to receive the same education as boys it became clear that not all women are cut out to be mothers. I thought that the pill and other contraceptives would generate a new approach to bringing children into the world, making the act of conception a free, conscious choice rather than a haphazard accident. Today, as in past generations, more than ninety percent of all children are the result of an accident, but even some who desire children do so for the wrong reasons. They submit to peer pressure, or they wish to have something that belongs to them, something that will give them the love they can't find anywhere else. A child is not property. It is an incoming soul—a visitor from another dimension who is entrusted to our care. The visitor needs to learn the native language and the use of the spacesuit and has to be taught, nurtured and loved. One of the best-kept secrets is that bringing up a child requires a great deal of self-sacrifice and the willingness to subordinate one's own needs and desires to those of the growing child. Parenting can't be done with one hand tied behind one's back. In the utopia I envision, people will make informed choices about welcoming a soul into this world, and they will do so in the full knowledge that their children are not their children but the sons and daughters of life.

RMN: What is your personal understanding of God?

NINA: God! You know, devout Jews will neither write nor pronounce the word G-d, holy be His name! I think they're right, because as soon as you try to define God, you're no longer talking about the omnipresent power that set all this in motion and pervades all there is. I think the Jews and the Christians are wrong about giving God a masculine pronoun. God, as I conceive it, is neither a he, a she, nor an it. God is everything, or God is nothing. Trying to put a gender on the ineffable is like trying to drain the ocean with a sieve. When you question the Hindus about God, they say, "Tat twam asi," which means, "Thou art that." Or they answer, "Not this, not that." Can we limit the illimitable by calling it this or that? My understanding of the divine is of a force that is the sum total of All There Is, which includes, but is not limited to, nature.

DJB: Why did you write *One Foot in the Future* and why did you choose that title?

NINA: The events of my life, which spans most of the twentieth century, are dramatic enough to make the book "a good read," as an English friend put it. I wanted to entice the reader to view the psychedelics in the context of the life of a mature, rational woman who used them as a means to touch the noumenon. I also wanted to try to set the record straight about the pioneers of the psychedelic consciousness. The Harvard trio of Leary, Alpert and Metzner had been re-searching consciousness long before their involvement with psychedelics, and this has remained their primary interest throughout the years. The title of the book calls to my mind the Fool in the Tarot deck. All he has kept of the past is the little bundle on the end of his stick. One foot is firmly planted in the present, on the earth, the other extends over the abyss—the unknown, the not-yet. Most of my life, I've been just half a step ahead of the crowd and have looked to the future instead of the past.

DJB: One of the things that delighted me when I read your autobiography was your undying sense of optimism, and your continual willingness to let go of your past, as you journeyed through life. Are you still optimistic about the future, and what gives you faith in the life process?

NINA: I'm no Pollyanna. I see that we've messed things up, but I believe that at this time in history we're making an evolutionary quantum leap. My view of evolution begins where Darwin's leaves off. An ancient Hindu text declares that the aim of evolution is not just survival of the fittest but the manifestation of the perfection that is already present in all of us. Teilhard de Chardin's idea that we are advancing toward Christogenesis, the Christ consciousness lived and personified by us all, appeals deeply to my intuition. My faith in the life process comes from the same source as the willingness to let go of the past. Go with the flow, we used to say in the sixties. I believe that surrender is the key to the psychedelic experience as well as to life; when we impose our will on it, we're sure to have a bummer.

> *...I believe that at this time in history we're making an evolutionary quantum leap.*

DJB: How do you feel about, and what type of potential do you see for some of the new scientific advances in technology that will influence the future evolution of consciousness, such as designer drugs, brain stimulation machines, and Virtual Reality?

NINA: Wow! The words "designer drugs" and brain stimulation machines bring all sorts of possibilities for behavior control to my mind. In the wrong hands, a sci-fi horror movie could result. I'm impressed by the practical applications of Virtual Reality, but my God, do we need more high-tech toys? We're living in a Disney world, even without TV. Does the fact that I can't wholeheartedly cherish the thought of a future laden with all kinds of toys for changing our brains mean that I now have both feet in the past?

DJB: How do you see human consciousness evolving in the future?

NINA: O.K., here goes: I believe that the knowledge that we are all eternal spirits who will continue our adventure after the body's death will bring about a profound change of values. Science has already demonstrated that what we perceive as solid matter is only a bunch of atoms that have come together for a while to form an object. In the last few decades, science and mysticism have begun to resemble each other more and more, and I don't doubt that it will eventually find the means to prove the reality of life after death. A technology that fulfills its promise of freeing us from hard labor will make an unprecedented amount of leisure time available to all. It was the financial ease of the fifties that allowed the spiritual awakening of the sixties to occur. Perhaps the poverty of the nineties will bring us back to the ideals of respect for all life, for the gifts of the earth, and for each other.

RMN: Can you explain the theory that you have about androgyny and the evolutionary end of biological sex as you see it?

NINA: I once read somewhere that long ago, when we still lived in caves, we had the ability to close our earlaps so that no insects could enter while we slept. I don't know if this is fact or fantasy, but it struck me as a good example of Nature's adaptability. When she's through with a feature, she impartially discards it. I believe that the future of mankind is wo-mankind. I think we're evolving toward androgyny, neither male nor female nor bisexual, but beyond sex. The old system of procreation is becoming obsolete. Pleasure is the carrot Nature holds up to keep us alive and reproducing, so she gave us pleasure in eating and in sex. But we have over-reproduced. Overpopulation is the biggest threat facing the human species. We cannot continue to cover the earth with our progeny. I think that we will transcend gender. An astonishing number of today's younger generation already looks neither male nor female. Nobody can watch the present volcanic upheaval in the relationship of the sexes without being aware that a gigantic reshuffling of the sexual card deck is in progress. Something new is happening. The boundaries between the genders are getting more and more blurred while the war between the sexes rages. To me, it looks like the last anguished gasp of an evolutionary dead end, the chaos before a new order appears. Perhaps in the future there will be neither males nor females, but androgynes who are complete within themselves and not subject to the eternal dance of attraction-repulsion that dominates the sexual scene. Human love, as we now know it, is possessive and exclusive. I believe that true love is possible only where no motive of self-interest is involved.

> *...we're evolving toward androgyny, neither male nor female nor bisexual, but beyond sex.*

RMN: What are you doing these days? Can you tell us about any projects on which you're currently working?

NINA: Well, actually, I'm just sitting back letting it happen—whatever it is. I wrote a scenario for a Cosmic Soap Opera. It begins with the cosmic egg splitting in two and the Divine Couple trying to come together on earth through many incarnations. I give talks about the relationship of the psychedelics to the spiritual path, but beyond that—hey listen, kids! I'm 73 years old. Don't I have a right to sit back and enjoy the breeze?

RMN: Yes, you do. You've certainly led an active and adventurous life. Looking back over it, how do you see the various stages that you've gone through contributing to the person you are today?

NINA: The person I am today...But who is that person? I'm not very self-analytical. I like what G. B. Shaw says in *Joan of Arc*: "Thinking about yourself is like thinking about your stomach—it's the quickest way to make yourself sick." I could say I'm a writer, a mother, a senior citizen, an iconoclast, a researcher of human consciousness, but you know, none of these labels really describe me. I could say I'm an energy blip in the cosmic void, or that I'm a crazy quilt of attributes, good and bad—but I'm more than that. I'm more than the sum of my parts. Trying to define oneself, I think, is an exercise in futility that can put us in the self-concentration camp. As you know, Freud was my compatriot; we both came from Vienna, but while I greatly appreciate the quality of his writings and his scholarly grasp on mythology, I can't help feeling that he was to a large extent responsible for putting great numbers of people in the self-concentration camp. His imaginative way of looking at mental dis-ease and neurosis made them seem most attractive, and people began to watch their emotions with the fascination of Narcissus beholding his own image in the lake. America fell in love with Freud's ideas years before they were accepted in Europe. When I came to this country in 1941, everybody was talking about Freudian slips and Oedipus complexes. Phallic symbols were everywhere. In the fifties, it was very "in" to have a shrink. People went back to their childhood to search for the subconscious roots of their present mental quirks, and what they found was that Mom was to blame—it was all her fault. It seems to me that when people are so busy observing their subjective feelings, they lose touch with the great big world around them.

Who I am today is who I became in the years of peeling the onion of my conditioning and attempting to relocate the center of my small self in the Higher Self. The Nina Graboi self is transitory, an instant in an ocean of being, but the Self is undying and unborn—or so the Hindus say. Let me quickly tell you, before we go on, that there is nothing any more today that I *absolutely* and *positively* believe. Everything is possible, but our ignorance is abysmal and so is our tendency to embrace belief systems that we find attractive. In an LSD session, our self-transcendent experiences seem a thousand times more real than our everyday world, but that does not mean that they necessarily embody ultimate truths, no matter how attractive they are.

DJB: To the people who know you, you appear to be a happy person. Can you tell us what your secret is?

NINA: Happy? I don't know. Content may be a better word. I think it's because I buy the Buddha's idea that all suffering is caused by attachment to the objects of desire. It makes good, practical sense to me. If this is as clear to you as it was to me when I read it for the first time many years ago, then desire and attachment will start slowly to fall away. Besides, all I am is a blip in the cosmic soup. Life is ephemeral, an instant in eternity. So why get hung up? I go with the flow, as we used to say in the sixties.

Laura Huxley

"When the body/mind has been attended to, then, as a flower
free of weeds, the Higher Self will naturally emerge…"

Bridging Heaven and Earth
with Laura Huxley

Laura Archera Huxley has received wide recognition for her humanistic achievements including that of Honorary Doctor of Human Services from Sierra University, Honoree of the United Nations, Fellow of the International Academy of Medical Preventics, and Honoree of the World Health Foundation for Development and Peace from which she received the Peace Prize in 1990.

Born November 2, 1911, in Turin, Italy, she expressed a great talent for music and went on to become a concert violinist. She played all over Europe but her American debut was at Carnegie Hall, just before World War II. She played in the Los Angeles Philharmonic Orchestra from 1944 until 1947 and then went on to produce documentary films and become an editor at RKO. During the fifties Laura worked as a psychological counsellor, a lecturer, and a seminarist of the Human Potential Movement, in which she is still involved today. She is the founder of Our Ultimate Investment, a non-profit organization for the nurturing of the possible human.

In 1956 she married the reknowned writer and philosopher, Aldous Huxley, and lived with him until his death in 1963. She has written a number of books which focus on the development of psychological freedom: You Are Not the Target, Between Heaven and Earth, OneADayReason to Be Happy *and* The Child of Your Dreams *which she wrote with Dr. Piero Ferrucci. She is also the author of* This Timeless Moment, *a book describing the life she led with her husband and a beautifully touching tribute to his genius.*

We met with Laura on April 8th 1992 in her lovely, chapel-like home in the Hollywood Hills. Her easy smile and bright-as-button eyes spoke of a serenely playful spirit. Together with her graceful posture, they revealed that after eighty years of life she has succumbed neither to emotional nor Newtonian gravity.

—RMN

DJB: What originally inspired your interest in mysticism, personal growth, and spiritual development?

LAURA: I don't know that there was one moment that it happened. It was just a natural development. You can call it whatever you want to—the creative forces, an inspiration. But all my life, and now at this very moment, I have wanted to go farther. It is so clear that there is so much more. This immensity, this beauty, this mystery all around us—and we perceive such an infinitesimal part of it. I guess it is greed to want to be more than a limited being with a limited body-mind. But you feel that the potential is so much greater than what you have actualized, and then something happens showing that you can go farther. That is a wonderful aspect of life.

DJB: So you see it as a natural extension of your own development?

LAURA: Yes. When you feel the immensity of the possible, naturally you are interested in plunging into it. When you feel good, you plunge deeper. However, at my age—I am eighty—I often am exhausted. Then I have to stay quietly—I have no choice. And then again something new happens. It may be something distressing and I just *have* to deal with it however I can. Or something wonderful happens, giving me again the overwhelming apprehension of life's renaissance forever, even when death may be around the corner.

RMN: How did your interest in psychotherapy develop?

LAURA: In 1949 Ginny Pfeiffer, my best friend, was diagnosed as a terminal cancer case. The Mayo Clinic declared with total certainty that there was no possibility for her to get well. Death would come in six months, or if a miracle would happen, in two years. It was a shock. It plunged me into all kinds of exploration. Until then, my life had first been devoted to the violin, totally. After that, I had started to work in films. I had never studied medicine, psychology, nutrition or healing. Actually, I had left school at fourteen so I could concentrate my energy on practicing and concertizing.

The doctors of the Mayo Clinic kept telling me, "Miss Archera, you must face reality. Your friend is going to die in about six months." I just could not accept what the authorities told me. And let me add that at that time at the Mayo Clinic the authorities were very kind and wonderfully supportive. In fact, I became a good friend with the Mayo family then, in 1950. But, I could not accept that death sentence. So I began to study everything under the sun. I went to lectures, and then started to actually practice on my friend. So that is the way it happened. Usually, it is a drama, a trauma that pushes us into something else, because I never thought I would be involved in psychology. It was completely out of my field.

RMN: So did it help her?

LAURA: She lived twenty-three years longer. She is written up in all the case reports.

DJB: Wow. Well, I wanted to ask you about something that you talk about in your book *Between Heaven and Earth*—a recipe for living that involves the transmutation of energy through the imagination, the will, and the body. Can you tell us about this?

LAURA: A powerful triangle: the imagination, the will, and the body. I mean the will is ultimately what is *us*. We are not speaking about that stiff will that betrays the body and does not accept the imagination, but the will that is attentive to the urging of imagination, and the needs of the body. That is a triangle that responds in all ways—because the body responds to the imagination. If you two would just imagine that there is a big tiger that is going to come right out and chew you.

DJB: The body responds.

LAURA: Immediately. Because the imagination and the body are so close, the will has to take an overview and direct it. I have exercises for this triangle in my book *Between Heaven and Earth*. The will is basic, as are the two cooperators of the will— imagination and body. The will is the conductor of the rich vast orchestra of imagination and body.

> *The will is the conductor of the rich vast orchestra of imagination and body.*

DJB: Had you heard of this model from anyone else, or did you come up with it yourself?

LAURA: No. I never heard it from anyone.

DJB: Well, I'll tell you, one time while I was in the midst of an altered state I wrote the following down in my notebook: Everything that exists comes through the imagination, is directed by the will, and expressed through the physical body. I considered it to be a profound insight.

LAURA: Exactly the same thing, and so well expressed.

DJB: Then I opened up your book and found it there several months later.

LAURA: Oh really? Well, that's extremely interesting. You and I seem to be the only people, because no one has paid much attention to this concept.

DJB: It is a good model for understanding how everything comes into existence.

LAURA: Including the placebo effect. Years ago, if a patient's symptoms could not be given a diagnostic label, the doctor would say, "It's just your imagination." As you know a certain percentage of the population is cured by taking a medicine that has no curative property; it is just a pill with nothing in it. How do these people get well? It seems to me that their will to get well directs their imagination which on its own, in turn, influences body chemistry. This is again the triangle we're discussing. I suppose that those people who are healed by a placebo have a closer connection, maybe a direct line from the will to the imagination and body.

I remember when I was fourteen years old, I read a book entitled *Things Greater Than Himself,* by an Italian author by the name of Zuccoli. It recounts the story of a fourteen-year-old boy who had fallen in love with an older woman who was hardly aware of his existence. Well, I was a fourteen-year-old girl who had fallen in love with an older man who was hardly aware of *my* existence. The boy became so sad, so desperate that he died. I became so sad, so desperate; but I did not die. And even then, I wondered: why did he die and I didn't? Now I think that maybe his connection of will (in this case the will to die) to imagination and body was stronger than mine! Actually that feeling of being surrounded, propelled, sometimes, exhausted by *things* greater than myself is often with me; by now I should be used to it! But I am not.

DJB: I know that you're fascinated with the subject of nutrition. What have you learned, in a nutshell, about how one's diet can affect one's physical or mental well-being?

LAURA: When I was helping my sick friend, I went to Rancho La Puerta, a spa on the Mexican border. Now it is a very well known, beautiful, and elegant spa. Then it was only a few houses. I think we paid five dollars a day. There was Professor Szekely—he's dead now, but his wife and son are constantly improving the spa. I learned from Professor Szekely basic elements of nutrition. I learned in 1950 what is now being discovered, a simple obvious fact of nature. *Nutrition* is a *transformer* of *consciousness* and touches every point of our lives. In fact, when I look in the Health & Cooking section of a bookstore, I can see that the subject of

> *Nutrition is a transformer of consciousness...*

food and nutrition is involved in politics and finance, in war and peace, in love and hatred.

Basically, all that has been written about nutrition from the point of view of the choice of food could be summarized in one page. I would say, buy food that is grown very near the place where you live, not something that is transported and preserved like a four-thousand-year old Egyptian mummy. Read *Diet for a New America* by John Robbins and you will learn just about all you need to know about food choices. But we must be aware that it is not just *what* we eat that's important; we must choose the food our body can metabolize. Now I don't eat any animal food, and haven't for a long time. I eat one egg once in a while, but no cheese or meat.

DJB: Is this for nutritional or for spiritual reasons?

LAURA: First of all, I know the way that animals are treated, and they're full of drugs. If I want to take drugs, I don't have to take them through a cow or a chicken. I like to choose! The animals are killed when they are full of rage, when all the adrenaline is flowing. So it is for taking care of myself first, and also to protect the way animals are treated. I wrote at length about this subject in *Between Heaven and Earth.*

DJB: So you feel that if you eat an animal that was killed in certain way, then you would be absorbing some of that energy state?

LAURA: Yes, we absorb the nutrition and we absorb the toxicity as well. Of course, the miracle is that our body eliminates much of what is harmful, but seeing the increase in degenerative diseases, even among the young, it is clear that there is a limit even to the immense wisdom of the body. I have been a few times, not very often, on a fast. After a fast, you are more sensitive and you will know pretty well what to eat. You will know that we all eat at least twice as much as we need.

RMN: We become very sensitized to what is healthy and what is not.

LAURA: Oh yes; and you will eat much less and be better nourished when you eat simple food and enjoy it.

RMN: Do you believe in vitamins?

LAURA: If you had a perfect environment, the perfect lover, and the perfect food, you obviously wouldn't need any vitamins. But the way we live, with tension and noise and pollution, supplements are necessary. I studied the megavitamin system and then I studied homeopathy, which are the two extremes. It is difficult to decide because the person and his or her situation has to be taken into consideration first. Even with vitamins, the basic question is in the relationship we have with them. For instance, when I was young, I could take niacin in large doses and it did me a lot of good. Now I can take only a little.

RMN: On the theme of mental health I would like to ask you a question about mental health institutions, which from my experience are often places for retreat and stasis, rather than transformation. Why do you think that during the past hundred years there has been so much theoretical advance in the science of psychology, yet the practical applications of psychotherapy don't seem to have advanced that much?

LAURA: Psychotherapy profits from the science of psychology but the basic difference, it seems to me, is that psychotherapy is understanding while psychology is knowledge. Psychotherapy is mainly a humanistic and artistic endeavor—psychology is involved in scientific research of actual human behavior—on the other hand the psychotherapist's premise is that in all of us there are valuable latent qualities, which, given the opportunity, can emerge and flower. Apart from psychology I am thinking of the extraordinary series of lectures Aldous gave at USC and MIT on many subjects, not only psychotherapy, but also for the ecological situation as it was in 1959. Everything he previewed is here: in other words, the ecological situation is enormously worsened. Moreover, the inexpensive, practical methods he suggested have not been taken into consideration.

It has been said that it takes twenty-eight years for any good idea to be accepted. Well, thirty-three years have passed now and prestigious conferences about ecology are happening. We have to hope. We all have had the experience of giving a simple suggestion to a friend: take a one hour walk every morning; eat an apple last thing before going to bed and another first thing when you get up. Those are simple, inexpensive Rx, but the person, rather than taking charge, chooses to get a pill or go to an expensive seminar or psychiatrist; which is also effective, but it seems to me that trying a simple thing first is to be considered. Primitive cultures sometimes use very simple means with effective results.

RMN: That's very true. In many non-technological societies, such as exist in Borneo and also in the Amazon, there are ritualized battles where very few, if any, people get killed and the tribe is offered a form of release from pent-up emotional stress. So do you think part of the problem with violent crime in the West is related to our not having a socially acceptable channel for our frustrations?

LAURA: Oh yes. Look, I was visiting Brazil with Aldous, and in Rio on a Saturday night we went to see a ritual called the "makoomba." The people would start to dance together, sing and go on and on and on and on. By 3:00 A.M., they would be sweating and breathing enormously, the frustration was gone and they would be laughing and dancing. Aldous spoke enthusiastically about "makoomba," saying how more effective and less expensive it was than lying on the psychoanalyst's couch. Now we know that while dancing, running, and swimming, the body produces chemicals called endorphins which give us a happy, elated feeling. We have our own inner chemical factory. We have to learn how to use it well.

DJB: So are you saying that the problem stems from just repressed physical energy? Would something as simple as playing sports be helpful?

LAURA: Oh that is wonderful, yes. That was the Greek idea. They used sports and emphasized the mobility and the nobility of the body. But even if you would take groups of people out in the open, near mountains or water or forests, give them just a little bit of ritualistic direction, like you were saying, it would be much more effective than giving them advice. They know it all already.

RMN: Or think they do. What do you think are some of the major psychological differences between men and women, and how can these differences complement one another rather than being a source of tension?

LAURA: Well, I think that there is not such a great psychological and emotional difference between men and women. I think that we make the differences and that if we would accept the fact of androgyny, there would be balance and cooperation, rather than competition. Each one is both: every man has some feminine elements and every woman some masculinity. When I asked Krishnamurti what is a religious person, he said (among other things) that a religious person must be both man and woman—I don't mean sexually, he said—but must know the dual nature of everything; the religious person must feel and be both masculine and feminine.

DJB: So you are saying that you see the conflict between men and women as being an externalized drama of the conflict going on inside each of us?

LAURA: I feel that it is educational and cultural, rather than basic. It seems to me that the wonderful work done by women for a more just recognition of women's talents and capacities is sometimes a bit flawed by a tendency to imitate man. A small instance: a woman can hardly buy a pair of jeans or pants without a zipper in front. Why a zipper? We don't need a zipper in front. Refusing to wear pants with a zipper in front would be a clear statement—and probably better pants.

RMN: Do you think men are beginning to get more in touch with their feminine side and vice versa?

LAURA: Oh yes, because much has been accomplished. Men can feel fairly free now to cry, dress more freely, take care of the household, and take care of their baby. It is the best thing for baby, father, and mother.

RMN: We touched earlier on the idea that the mind affects the body. This is taken for granted in a lot of places—like in Chinese and Ayurvedic medicine. But still, despite the monumental evidence to the contrary, purely physical explanations are still invoked, more often than not in the West, to explain, not only physical, but mental illness. Why do you think this is, after so much evidence has shown that the mind and body are parts of the same whole?

LAURA: Because of the great division of body and mind that has been with us for two thousand years. Two thousand years are difficult to overcome. The power of words, if coming from High Places and repeated enough times, is so powerful so as to obscure such tangible present inescapable facts as the body-mind interaction. Doctors go to school for thirty years and they are told that the body is a mechanism that you fix or you don't, and that belief has been programmed so deeply in their minds.

RMN: Why do you think it even began in the first place?

LAURA: Well Aldous said it began with Aristotle and Plato and many others.

RMN: Really, the Greeks. Blame it on the Greeks.

LAURA: Then the Catholics.

RMN: Because they wanted to control the spiritual mind.

LAURA: The belief that the body is something dirty is overwhelming.

DJB: So you think it began long before Descartes divided the mind from the divine?

LAURA: Oh yes. Before that St. Augustine condemned the body.

RMN: Have you found any one psychotherapeutic technique to be especially valuable, or does the success of a particular method vary from person to person?

LAURA: There are many psychotherapeutic techniques which are effective in the hands of a capable therapist. However, the most important factor is the relationship between the guide and the client. My strong feeling is that any psychotherapy who does not include the body from the beginning is incomplete. The medical evidence is pointing more and more to the body-mind connection. For instance, our relationship to food and cancer; how body movement, breathing, running, etc., changes one's body consciousness; how emotion and personality are connected to degenerative disease.

> *...any psychotherapist who does not include the body from the beginning is incomplete.*

In sum, it is increasingly clear and accepted that the way we treat our body-mind is the way our body-mind will treat us. The Golden Rule applies here too. It is amazing to me that the two main branches of therapies, psychotherapy and somatic therapy, are kept separate, when in fact, every state of being is either psychosomatic or somato-psychic. What else is there? I see the human being as a circle and all the points on the circle must be considered important. If you take even the smallest point out of the circle, the circle is no more a circle. The optimum is, in my view, that kind of education or therapy that contacts as many points of the circle of the human being as possible. To contact only the intellectual, emotional, or social points of the human being without involving the body through which the intellect and emotion are expressed is inadequate and the outcome is slower and not on the high level of excellence it might be.

RMN: Nowadays there is a lot of body focus and people exercising for health and vanity reasons.

LAURA: Yes, and it does them a lot of good even though it's often *mindless* exercise. What I mean is synchronizing the psycho and somatic therapy. One must be aware of how the emotions play on the body and how one can use the body to transform emotion. It is exorcism through exercise. Exorcism means casting out the devil. So consciously exercising to squeeze out, push out, move out the devils of rage, fear, sadness, and boredom from the muscle. Albert Szent-Gyorgyi, the eminent biochemist, twice Nobel Prize winner, said that the muscles are the greatest transformers of energy in the body. It is one of the ways of transformation that is clear and available—always with us—at no cost!

RMN: Is this the principle you applied in *You Are Not the Target* ?

LAURA: Yes, and in *Between Heaven and Earth* as well. And I add the dimension of service because service is what gives significance to the self by confirming its importance to the world. The relationship of body-mind and service should be addressed at the same time. In my mind, *body-mind-service* is the ideal education. I would not call it therapy— that would be an implicit agreement that a person interested and active in improving him/herself is sick. What I'm saying has

...service is what gives significance to the self by confirming its importance to the world.

been admirably and fully presented in the monumental book by Michael Murphy which has just been published, *The Future of the Body*. Michael Murphy who, with Dick Price, founded Esalen, being acquainted with all the greatest world teachers and their methods, realized that every teacher promotes a certain set of values while others are either neglected or suppressed. Murphy coins the phrase "Integral Practices," which I quote, "are practices that address somatic, affective, cognitive, volitional and transpersonal dimensions of human nature in a comprehensive way." A very important book.

RMN: Do you think there is too much attention given to the individual in our society?

LAURA: It seems to be so. Had we the kind of education just mentioned, we would realize that we are little cells in an immense, inextricably connected organism and would not pollute the very source of our life. the air we breathe, the water, the food. We would pay more attention to the way other human beings are and feel. Service gives us a chance to be aware of that. Karen, my seventeen-year-old granddaughter, just returned from a white water expedition, programmed according to the principles of Outward Bound, the greatest educational institution in the U.S.A., in my opinion. Karen told me that one day of the trip was dedicated to serve another person, who did not know who the serving person was; finding out would be the subject of the evening discussion. Karen said that she never had experienced in a group of teenagers such a profound peace, such quiet contentment. It is encouraging that a simple, inexpensive recipe is so effective; that teenagers, whose personal drama is so intense, can forget it for a day, and experience peace and contentment by serving.

RMN: What foundation needs to be laid for the spiritual to emerge?

LAURA: The spiritual dimension of the human being is ever present, but often dormant, and emerges of itself as a natural consequence when we are ready—not as a goal to be reached. Spirituality has to have space to emerge; a flower cannot grow if overcrowded by weeds. Give it space and the flower will bloom on its own. When the body-mind has been attended to, then, as a flower free of weeds, the Higher Self will naturally emerge and service is part of its expression.

DJB: So you don't draw much of a line then between the body, mind, and spirit?

LAURA: Right. It is a continuum.

RMN: Have the techniques that you discuss in your books—movement techniques and ritual—been used by psychologists or psychiatrists that you are aware of?

LAURA: In 1963, when *Target* was published, there was much demand to organize a national network for teachers. I resisted the temptation; I did not know how to organize, and above all, my life was full enough. The recipes are used by some therapists, sometimes classes are organized. Mostly people use them from the book—I had and have the most rewarding and touching reports of experiences from the letters I receive from friends I have never met who profit from the Recipes for Living and Loving.

RMN: Do you think that the methods you employ would be beneficial to a person with a serious imbalance like paranoid schizophrenia?

LAURA: The Huxley Institute and the American Association of Orthomolecular Medicine have, since 1957, conducted studies on schizophrenia and have demonstrated that specific nutritional supplements, like Vitamin B3 and B6, Vitamin C, Zinc, and others are extremely helpful and, in certain types of schizophrenia, have brought recovery. I believe that a schizophrenic person would be greatly helped by being grounded through exercise, particularly if he would understand the principle I mentioned before: to *exorcise*, to cast off devils by exercise. Often a disturbed person thinks and feels that he or she is persecuted or invaded by dangerous vibrations, enemies or devils.

A method that he can use independently not only would ground him but also would give him that power he so desperately seeks so that he himself can get rid of his persecutors. He could not only feel, but even visualize the devils coming out of his muscles—move his muscles, and since he is the only one who can, he would achieve autonomy and self-authority. Of course this would not always happen, but why not give it a trial—particularly with the mesomorphic type; the person with a prevalence of musculature might feel a liberation by using himself in a self-beneficial way; of course, alert supervision is essential.

RMN: This is going into the next question. Many psychotherapeutic techniques are considered by orthodox practitioners to be in the realm of the paranormal, even though many have been shown to be successful. Why do you think there is so much nervousness on the part of scientists to investigate, not only the paranormal phenomena, but also alternative healing techniques?

LAURA: An investment, whether intellectual or financial, gives us security. Scientists protect their investment of years of study and work. When something new and different emerges, this does not mean that the previous work loses its value. So in a way, the resistance you speak of is the fear of being wrong, is that way of thinking in separate camps, of "either/or" rather than considering what can be valuable in more than one view—normal and paranormal, orthodox, and alternative healing technique. We can use everything in this complex life we are living.

DJB: One of the things that brings the body-mind problem to attention is psychedelics. How have psychedelics affected your life?

LAURA: It was an expansion. I wrote about it in a book about Aldous—*This Timeless Moment*. It was something that gave me a larger view. Psychedelics open our hearts and minds. Sometimes we open on the aesthetic level, sometimes on the level of compassion—the feeling of compassion, and the beauty of the world, as well as the gigantic suffering in the world. This is the way in which they affected me. Probably a psychedelic emphasizes what is in an individual and amplifies it. But we are a crowd, and which one of the crowd will be amplified? We don't know.

> *Psychedelics open our hearts and minds.*

DJB: That leads to the mistake a lot of people made when they first started experimenting with psychedelics. Because they saw their own positive qualities get amplified, they assumed that anyone who did a psychedelic would become more creative, more compassionate, more loving, and it just doesn't work that way. It takes whatever is there and amplifies it.

LAURA: Yes. I remember very well when we realized that. Aldous and I were very, very surprised when we heard from Boston that there were many negative experiences. We always prepared very carefully, which makes a great difference. In general, if you take a psychedelic without preparation, it's risky. I know many kids do it, and sometimes it's okay, but then comes a time when it's not okay any more, and it's difficult for many reasons, one being that what is ingested can be any chemical mix.

RMN: Of the people who know about the benefits of psychedelics, some believe that it should be made legal and everyone should have access to it. Other people think there should be some kind of restriction imposed. What do you think?

LAURA: I think that if we had it all completely free again, abuse and damage would happen. That is why Oscar Janiger founded the Albert Hofmann Foundation, which I am a part of—so that there is some beginning, at least, in being able to use and guard from misuse. If there is a beginning, even with strict rules, then little by little, one can enlarge them. But I think that if everybody can get everything that would not be a just way of doing it.

RMN: If it were restricted to begin with, who should decide who can take the substance and who cannot? What are the qualities and qualifications such a person should possess?

LAURA: That is the question. First of all, one would have to have experienced it oneself, and one should not try to get any gain from this at all. One's own opinions and personality should be put aside, at least as much as possible. It is difficult to put them aside all together, but one can try to put them aside as much as possible. If you are asking about the role of the guide, probably it is easier to say what the guide must *not* do: not patronize, not preach, not impose, not do nothing, not come to quick conclusions, not deny intuition, not believe intuition as if it were God dictated, not deny common sense, not deny evidence, not accept evidence *only*, not be intensely personal, not be intensely impersonal, not be only masculine, not be only feminine.

DJB: Is that not the same as the role of any guide or teacher?

LAURA: Yes. However, if you refer to a period of therapy in general rather than one single psychedelic experience, I would add that, in the beginning, the guide dances with the student, imperceptibly, now and then, exchanging leadership. After a while, the guide dances the student's dance, but adds to it an higher octave and a rock-strong basso continuo. Dovetailed between the two, the student is supported and inspired in leading his own dance. Finally, strong and free, the student soars alone to new heights. Let me immediately add that all this is easier said than done, but I followed that famous quote of Browning even before I knew it: "Ah, but a man's reach should exceed his grasp, or what's heaven for?" It's a bit tiring at times to stretch like that, but it gives life a fascinating flavor.

DJB: What role do you see psychedelics playing in the future?

LAURA: That is almost like asking: what do you see for the future of this planet? We are at a point where just about anything can happen. If the negative happens, the psychedelics will have a bad role to play because many people will get sick on it. If what we tried to do—to encourage consciousness and responsibility—begins to happen, then psychedelics would be a help. Finally, it is the interplay between the outer stimuli which continuously effect us and our reaction to them—and to what extent are we responsible for our reactions? We can say I am

100% responsible, and that is a lovely thought.

But how much of the 100% is our destiny and how much is our personal will? And when do we follow our destiny and when do we follow our personal will? I think it is lucky that such a question, it seems to me, cannot be answered totally, because should I believe that I am totally at the mercy of my destiny, then I may become lethargic and be just a leaf in the wind. On the other hand, should I believe that I have full powers over my destiny, I would become a harsh judge of others who would appear to me to be just drifting. Years ago, I tried to devise a recipe entitled *Be What You Are* which was based on a line of Shakespeare. "Who is he who can tell me who I am?" I tried hard but never succeeded. I believe in the perfectibility of the human race and in the support we can give each other in evolving. But that is all I believe.

> *I believe in the perfectibility of the human race....*

RMN: Do you believe that people who have seen further, and have more awareness, have a responsibility to others?

LAURA: Absolutely yes. Those of us who have been given more gifts certainly have a responsibility for others.

DJB: If you could sum up the central message that you got from the time you spent with Aldous, what would you say that you learned from him?

LAURA: He said it himself. I can do no better than what he said. It was at this important meeting of outstanding scientists in Santa Barbara. Everyone was very serious, and they said, well, Mr. Huxley, what is your final advice after all these years of inquiry? He said, "I'm very embarrassed because I worked for forty years, I studied everything around, I did experiments, I went to several countries, and all I can tell you is to be just a little kinder to each other."

> *[Aldous] said..."all I can tell you is to be just a little kinder to each other."*

DJB: That takes a lot of learning.

LAURA: You're absolutely right. It takes a lot of learning and living and loving and suffering.

DJB: It seems obvious but it's not.

LAURA: Often the obvious things are the ones that are the most difficult to understand and appreciate. It seems obvious that we breathe. You know we do breathe, but do we understand it? Do we appreciate it? No—we only begin to appreciate it when we suffocate.

DJB: How do you think the LSD that Aldous asked for as he was dying influenced his dying process?

LAURA: It went so smoothly. He did ask for it and he knew exactly what he was doing. It is my belief that it made it very easy for him. This doesn't mean that it would make it easy for everybody else. Remember that this is, again, the process of one person—a person who had prepared himself for this event throughout his life. He asked for it at the right time, too, just six hours before he died. He asked for a big sheet of paper; he evidently knew that he could not handle small handwriting. Then he wrote his own recipe: "Try LSD 100 mm intramuscular." During the week prior to his death, I had been thinking that maybe I should mention it. I was alert as to when he was going to ask me for it. It was not until that moment, at about 11:00. Then he died about 5:00.

DJB: I read in one of your books that people seem to have two basic approaches to death. Some want to die in their sleep, and go as unconsciously as possible. Others see it as an adventure, and want to go as lucid and aware as possible.

LAURA: Yes, that's right. Probably one of the reasons is whether one is naturally afraid to be unconscious or not. It seems to me at this point in my life, when I'm feeling good, my choice would be to be very conscious, aware of this process that must be fantastic. But it is easy to speak this way when you're alive and well. It is easy to speak this way when you are not in agonizing pain, when you're not undergoing the division of the body from its vitalizing essence. So I do not know what I would say *then*. But *today* I feel this way. What is the date today? Write down the time and date, because I may change my mind.

DJB: What do you think happens to human consciousness after death?

LAURA: I think and feel that it goes on. I can't imagine that this extraordinary complex of feeling, thought, and whatever else, just vanishes. I believe that it goes on; but *how* is a mystery. Perhaps it goes on into vibrations, or into other bodies, or into something totally different and unknown to us.

DJB: I read about the medium and the bookcase experience that you wrote about at the end of *This Timeless Moment*; that suggested the possibility of contact with Aldous after he had passed on into the afterlife.

LAURA: That was extraordinary wasn't it? I never speak about that because I wrote it with such exactness. I think that if I were to speak about it, I would not remember the moment, the time, and all that exactly. What I have written is absolutely correct.

DJB: Have you had any other experiences where you felt the presence of Aldous after he had died?

LAURA: I went to one or two other mediums who also gave me a very strong presence, but not like that one. That one was...

DJB: Uncanny.

LAURA: That's right.

RMN: Would you describe yourself as a religious person?

LAURA: It depends on what you mean by religion. I don't know exactly. What does religion mean anyway?

RMN: In Latin it means "to be tied back," the idea being that one's spirit is bound to God in some way. I guess you can interpret God however you want.

LAURA: Well, I eat God every day when I have a meal.

RMN: Okay, let's put it another way. What's your personal understanding of God, apart from food?

> *...I eat God every day when I have a meal.*

LAURA: I think—I feel—that there is an immense power; something that is so incredible that we cannot even imagine it—*it* has so much more imagination than we have. So that when we imagine God, we just imagine as far as we can imagine. But our imagination is very limited when you think of all the flowers and stars. You think of a star, and you think of a cell, and it's mind-boggling.

DJB: Yeah, we can't even grasp ourselves, let alone a supreme being of cosmic proportions.

LAURA: Exactly. How can we grapple with God when we don't even understand the simplest of things? I don't even know what goes on when I speak to you, or how you hear and how you interpret what you hear and how this influences what I am going to say, etc., etc.

RMN: Why do you think that people get so hyped up about religion, which causes so much war and devastation? Why do people get so worked up about trying to prove one god against another god?

LAURA: I think that we've come once again to a basic problem: fear. Suppose that a person has been worshipping a certain god with millions of other people. That gives security. It is like saying, "Millions of us cannot be wrong; we have the best god." These persons' security is threatened by the possibility that there is another and a better god, the possibility that "Maybe I am wrong." It's again the fear, the fear of being wrong. Of course, I may be wrong; who isn't? But being wrong could be grist for the mill—the possibility of discovery. The greatest blessing of all time would be the presence of a *Genius of Love* who could diminish the Global Fear even a little bit. Fear is the most widespread, malignant, infectious disease.

RMN: Do you think you could define consciousness?

LAURA: I would equate it with life, and life has many different levels of consciousness. In general when we say "consciousness," we mean that particular consciousness of which we are aware: the consciousness that becomes aware of itself. But there is a lot of consciousness that *is*, but is not aware of being, and of which we are not aware.

DJB: To some people there is just simply consciousness and unconsciousness.

LAURA: Oh no, no.

DJB: Obviously there are many, many stages and levels.

LAURA: Yes, oh yes. I believe that's why it is so interesting to be alive—because there is just so much that we don't know, because there lies forever still another surprise. How sad life would be for the person who knows everything!

RMN: Do you think that humanity is evolving towards, to use Nina Graboi's phrase, a "species-wide enlightenment"?

LAURA: There are some good signs. The problem is that it is so slow. But if you compare what was going on in the Middle Ages—for instance, what was going on with child labor, and how people who were mentally upset were put into dungeons we see that there is an evolution. The point that my husband made again and again is that the real problem is overpopulation, which makes evolution much slower. Because there is such a large number of us, evolution is very slow. The more mass there is, the slower the evolution.

DJB: What was it that inspired you to write your beautiful book for children *OneADayReason To Be Happy*?

LAURA: Because it seemed so natural. We think that children have such a good time; but often life is quite difficult for them. The same for teachers —besides parents, they are the most underrated, unappreciated, underpaid class in America. Teachers work hard

> *How sad life would be for the person who knows everything!*

to make school meaningful for children and children should acknowledge that. So I thought that children who do not yet read and write could have the equivalent of homework everyday, in the form of bringing to the teacher and class one reason to be happy they had that day; and then if a child says, "No, I have no reason to be happy; nothing is good for me, yesterday was terrible," then all the other children have an opportunity to surround him and say, "Look, we like you just the same and it's fine." There again such a little recipe, yet it could brighten the classroom and give the children the joy of being grateful; and to the teacher a measure of appreciation as well as a look into the student's life.

DJB: I was curious about how adopting a granddaughter at the age of sixty-three affected your life?

LAURA: Oh! It affected my life! Tremendously! It is unbelievable. People sixty-three years apart are in different worlds, but it is very touching sometimes because she has this extraordinary kind of insight. Karen is seventeen now, and is just graduating from high school. She took me to all kinds of worlds that I had no idea existed. You see, I was brought up in a very conservative family in Turino, in Northern Italy—a totally different universe. Even if it were just one or two generations it would be different, but this is just so different.

I see that there is, of course, all the weight of this society which is not for a teenager to be heaped upon her. This continuous, continuous, continuous stimulation is really very difficult to deal with. I mean, I used to go to a movie, maybe once, or twice a month. Here we can push a button and have one hundred movies any time of the day or night, and many, if not most shows, identify sex with violence and vulgarity. Vulgarity is paid probably the highest amount of money. I am lucky that Karen focuses a great deal on her inner world and tries to figure out what's inside. She has remarkable insights.

DJB: Do you think that they focus too much on what's external, rather than what's internal?

LAURA: To focus internally is made almost impossible for young people. The environmental impact is overwhelming. Every day the distractions are multiplied and are more hypnotic and addictive. Like with every addiction, the dosage must be augmented—so, more TV, more noise, more guns, more advertising. In the meantime, the body is not moving, is just accepting whatever it is fed, psychologically or physically. There is an advertisement for a computer Nintendo game that I cannot forget. It represents a young boy, about thirteen or fourteen years old, lounging in an executive armchair, grinning with delight; he is holding a terminal in his hand and he is experiencing (the copy says) the thrill of racing 200 M.P.H., of climbing to the sky in his B-14 jet fighter, or parachuting, or diving under the depth of the sea. All these thrills are given to him—free and for nothing. He did not have to train his body-mind, did not have to feel fear and surmount it; he did not have to face danger.

In *Island*, Aldous has a beautiful passage about the initiation from childhood to adolescence. Young people have been trained in rock-climbing as part of the school curriculum and today they are having a test. Rock-climbing requires skill, cooperation, coordination, and facing danger. "Danger," Aldous writes, "danger deliberately and yet lightly accepted—danger shared with a friend, a group of friends, each totally aware of his own straining muscles, his own skill, his own fear, and his own spirit transcending the fear. And each, of course, aware at the same time of all the others, concerned for them, doing the right things to make sure that they will be safe."

Do you see the chasm between a youth lounging in an armchair and being spoon-fed thrillers and one who experiences his achievement through his own doing—through his dedication and courage and his concern for others, through the training of his body-mind? Which one of these two youths will have the higher self-esteem and therefore better health and more capacity to love and to be a valuable member of society?

DJB: Is that part of the education described in *Island* ?

LAURA: Yes. Instead of mainly verbal education as it is here, in *Island*, education is on all levels.

DJB: What kind of advice would you give to young people in our society?

LAURA: I would tell them: Respect your body. Focus your mind. Love your heart. Support and cooperate with anyone who wants to do the same.

DJB: What are you doing these days?

LAURA: Now that Karen is seventeen we spend less time together. I am becoming again more active on *Our Ultimate Investment*, the organization I founded in 1978 for "The Nurturing of the Possible Human." The concept is that much of the predicament of the human situation begins not only in infancy, not only before birth—a fact which is now being finally accepted—but also in the physical, psychological, and spiritual preparation of the couple *before* conception. We call it "Prelude to Conception."

The most cruel and unanswerable question that, shamefully, is now a despicable political banner: "Should I abort or not abort?" Must not exist in a culture that thinks of itself as advanced and civilized. There is more attention, time and care given to choosing an automobile than to the decision of creating the greatest miracle of all: a human being. Surely if the future parents prepare for this miracle, if they inquire into themselves and their relationship honestly enough, and then decide to have a child, the question of abortion *could not* exist. Dr. Piero Ferrucci and I have written a book, *The Child of Your Dreams*, which is being reissued by Inner Traditions International. In it we follow the future human being, *the possible human*, from the time s/he is only a thought and a desire in the mind of the parents until three years of age. It is an extraordinary voyage, the most extraordinary of all voyages if one pays attention to it.

DJB: Final words?

LAURA: Final words are not my own. When Ferrucci and I were thinking and working on "Prelude to Conception," a prayer came to me. I did not write it— only wrote it down. It belongs to everyone. Here it is:

"Prayer of the Unconceived"

Men and women who are on Earth
You are our creators.
We, the unconceived, beseech you:
Let us have living bread.
The builder of our new body
Let us have pure water
The vitalizer of our blood.
Let us have clean air
So that every breath is a caress
Let us feel the petals of jasmine and roses
Which are as tender as our skin.

Men and women who are the Earth
You are our creators.
We, the unconceived, beseech you:
Do not give us a world of rage and fear
For our minds will be rage and fear.
Do not give us violence and pollution
For our bodies will be disease and abomination.
Let us be wherever we are
Rather than bringing us
Into a tormented self-destroying humanity.

Men and women who are the Earth
You are our creators.
We, the unconceived, beseech you:
If you are ready to love and be loved,
Invite us to this Earth
Of the Thousand Wonders
And we will be born
To love and be loved.

Allen Ginsberg

"Language joins heaven and earth and joins the
mind and the body."

Politics, Poetry and Inspiration
with Allen Ginsberg

Allen Ginsberg's poem "Howl," published in 1956, caused such a controversy that it was the subject of an obscenity trial. Having received the court's "approval," it went on to become one of the most widely read and translated poems of the century. He is an extraordinarily prolific artist, having had over forty books published and eleven albums produced.

Allen's friendship and literary experimentation with Jack Kerouac and William Burroughs began in 1945, and a decade later as this core group expanded to include other poets and writers, it came to be known as the "Beat Generation." He has received numerous honors, including the National Book Award for Poetry, a Guggenheim Foundation Fellowship, National Arts Club Medal, 1986 Struga Festival Golden Wreath, and the Manhattan Borough President David Dinkins Medal of Honor for Literary Excellence 1989.

A potent figure in the cultural revolution of the sixties, he has been arrested with Dr. Benjamin Spock for blocking the Whitehall Draft Board steps, has testified at the U.S. Senate hearings for the legalization of psychedelics and been teargassed for chanting "Om" at the Lincoln Park Yippie Life Festival at the 1968 Presidential convention in Chicago.

His Collected Poems 1947-1980, were published in 1984 with White Shroud and the 30th Anniversary Howl annotated issue in 1986. Several books of his photographs and a record/CD of his poetry-jazz album, The Lion for Real, *appeared in 1989. He is a member of the National Institute of Arts and Letters, and is a Distinguished Professor at Brooklyn College and a member of the Executive Board of PEN American Center. A practicing Buddhist, Allen co-founded Naropa Institute's Jack Kerouac School of Disembodied Poetics in Boulder, Colorado.*

We talked with Allen at the house of his cousin, Oscar Janiger, in Santa Monica. He presents a very dignified and unassuming figure, his non-conforming and wildly creative persona loosely disguised in a professorial suit and tie. We asked Allen about his relationship with Burroughs and Kerouac, his thoughts on madness and creativity, and the nature of politics and revolution. This interview took place on April 23, 1992, six days before the Los Angeles uprising.

—RMN

DJB: What was it that originally inspired you to start writing poetry?

ALLEN: It's a family business. My father was a poet —his *Collected Poems* were posthumously published—they just came out recently, in fact, from the Northern Lights Press in Maine. My father was in the old Untermeyer anthologies and he was one of the standard poets of that genre of lyric poetry that included people like Eleanor Wiley, and Lisette Woodsworth Reece.

DJB: Was it something that you always knew you were going to do?

ALLEN: No, but I always wrote poetry; since I was a kid I knew poetry—my father taught high school and college, so I knew a lot of Milton, Poe, Shelley and Blake when I was five, six, seven years old. And I memorized it, or it just sort of stuck in my head. I started writing when I was maybe fifteen, or younger, but I never thought of myself as a poet. I just thought that it was something you did on the side like my father had done. But then, when I met Jack Kerouac at the age of seventeen, I realized that he was the first person I had met who saw being a writer as a *sacramental vocation*. Rather than being a sailor who wrote, he was a writer who also went out on ships. That changed my attitude towards writing, because now I saw it as a sacred vocation.

DJB: How did your mother's struggle with mental illness affect your development?

ALLEN: I've written a great deal about that in the poem "Kaddish," in *White Shroud*. I developed a tremendous tolerance for chaos, other people's illness, irrationality and contradictory behavior. I tend to throw it off like water off a duck's back, but it also dulls me to hear what people are saying when they're complaining about their troubles. I sometimes just shut off and give them a bowl of chicken soup instead of listening carefully.

I tend to be more concerned with people's comfort and welfare—like a Jewish mother—rather than trying to solve a mental problem, a financial problem or whatever. So I sometimes miss the boat. Quite often there's a tragedy happening and somebody's sinking right in front of me, but I don't see it. On the other hand I have a lot of tolerance for people who use drugs or are half mad. Sort of like how the children of alcoholics, in order to develop a kind of balance, clean up after everybody else and have a more neat and orderly life because they've seen the chaos and have reacted against it.

DJB: It seems that you would go one way or another. Whenever people are confronted at an early age with overwhelming circumstances, they either come out as a total mess or so strong that they can deal with most anything. Either you learn to become comfortable with chaos or you become overwhelmed by it.

ALLEN: I compensated by becoming more stable, probably because I realized that if everybody began disagreeing with me all at once, there was probably something wrong with my perception of the universe. So I took a more pragmatic view rather than an absolute view.

DJB: How has all the travelling you've done affected your perception of the world?

ALLEN: Well, again it's the same thing; because I've seen so much chaos, I don't really see everything. In a sense, I don't see a lot of detail and have a tendency towards abstraction. That's why I'm so concerned with it—it's the medicine for my own neurosis. I use it to help create a sense of stability. I sort of turn off the chaotic aspect of travel too and just continue in whatever work I'm doing like keeping a journal or taking photographs. You might even say I'm sort of neurotically untouched by interaction.

> *...I'm sort of neurotically untouched by interaction.*

DJB: By what's happening around you?

ALLEN: Yeah. It's maybe part of the same process with which I used to shield myself from the chaos, and it's made me sort of aloof. I'm just guessing. I mean since we started talking about one thing, I just transferred it over to the other—from my mother to travel. I might have a different answer for a different context, but since we started out with a very definite idea, I just transferred it to the other, because it's an aspect of the other, but it's not the whole story.

I mean, obviously I saw a lot of anthropological blah blah. A lot of different views, a lot of different folk ways, different ways of wiping your behind after going to the bathroom, different ways of eating, talking, different kinds of poetics, different religions, meditation practices, different primitive rituals, different takes on the universe, different nationalisms, different chauvinisms.

Experiencing a lot of different things makes your mind more wide—screened, or more tolerant. It makes you more sophisticated—or maybe less sophisticated. One of the basic things that's changed is my habit of wiping my ass with toilet paper. Now I wash my behind afterwards. I got that from North Africa and India. Kerouac has a whole book about that.

DJB: I'm curious as to how important you think it is for writers and artists to have a sense of community. How did your experience with other writers like Jack Kerouac and William Burroughs affect the style of your own writing?

ALLEN: Oh, it affected it very much. Kerouac persuaded me to stop writing rhyme poems and revising everything fifty thousand times—to just lay it out on the page in the sequence of thought-forms that arise in my mind during the time of composition. This is traditional with twentieth-century painting and calligraphy style. Shakespeare never blotted a line according to Ben Johnson.

With Kerouac and Burroughs, it wasn't so much their instruction as the whole ambience—their directive candor and informality. We were writing for our own amusement and the amusement of our friends, rather than for money or for publication. We assumed that nothing would be published from the very beginning. So the private world of my friends became the center of our artistic activities, rather than the public world of publishing, media, universities and literature.

DJB: The collaboration lowered your inhibitions, in terms of the way you expressed the creative urge?

ALLEN: Well, no. If you're just writing for yourself and your friends, then you don't have to develop inhibitions. People develop inhibitions from the commercial or social situation, they're not born with them. So in this case, since we didn't expect to succeed and we were just having fun with each other, we just never developed those inhibitions.

So as a result, we never developed the manner or style of counterfeit literalness that is characteristic of most university or academic poetry or prose. You know that Burroughs scene, the routine about the talking asshole in *Naked Lunch?* Well, it wasn't necessarily meant to be published. I mean, at that time it was considered impossible, so it wasn't thought of in that realm at all. It was thought of as being just intelligent humor between friends.

> *If you're just writing for yourself and your friends, then you don't have to develop inhibitions.*

DJB: Speaking of *Naked Lunch,* what did you think of the way that you, Burroughs and Kerouac were portrayed in the film adaptation?

ALLEN: Well, Kerouac was a good deal better looking than the character in the movie. Martin was somewhat of a wimp. I don't mind that because I'm a wimp, but I can read "The Market Section"—which was what he read over the couple fucking— much more vividly than the poet in the film. Four days before I saw the film I was teaching a graduate course at CUNY entitled, "Literary History and the Beat Generation." I didn't know that scene was in the film, but I read "The Market Section" to the students when we were discussing *Naked Lunch* to give them a sense of Burroughs as a panoramic poet.

It's one of the most beautiful passages in Burroughs, and the seed of all of *Naked Lunch* basically, as it intersects the past and future: *"In expeditions arrived from unknown places, leave for unknown places with unknown purpose.*

Followers of obsolete trades....Carriers of viruses not yet born." This is the interplanetary time-zone market.

The guy who played Burroughs did well, except when it came to doing the routines like the "talking asshole" or the "Hespano Suiza" auto blowout. Burroughs always did that much more uproariously and with such fascinating vigor that you'd roll around on the floor laughing. The guy in the movie did it in a relatively dignified monotone, so that you don't get the gregarious wildness.

RMN: Did you like the movie otherwise?

ALLEN: I thought that Burroughs' plot was better than the movie plot. The movie plot begins with the Kafka figure being assassinated by two detectives who come to hassle him. Then, in the book, when he rebels against the authority figures, the whole long novel scene turns out to have been an hallucination. So it paralleled many mystical experiences, where you suddenly realize that everything before was maya or samsaric delusion. Burroughs empowered himself, so to speak, by rebelling against Law.

It was a very important point that Burroughs was making, but that point is not made in the movie. On the other hand, Burroughs approves of cut-ups; that's his genre. So he enjoyed it, because it's an improvisation on his work, in his own style, that he might well have done himself. The bug powder comes from a book called *The Exterminator,* so they made combinations of *Naked Lunch* and this other work plus *Queer.*

Burroughs says a very funny thing. He quotes John Steinbeck when asked, "What do you think of what they've done to your book?" And he says, "They didn't do anything to my book. My book is up there on the shelf." So I think he liked the idea of them improvising on his text. I went to visit Burroughs about three weeks ago. We made thirteen ninety-minute tapes, which are being transcribed for an interview for a Japanese magazine, so we went to the movies and saw the picture.

DJB: That was the first time either of you had seen it?

ALLEN: It was only the second time he'd seen it and it was the third time I'd seen it. I liked it more watching it with him because I began to see that the hooks which interpolate the movie make a little more sense than I'd thought. It may make complete sense, but I haven't been able to figure out the very end. Is that reality, or is that unreality?

RMN: That was left unanswered.

DJB: Maybe intentionally. Tell me, how do you see the beat movement of the fifties having influenced the hippy movement of the sixties—and how do you see these cultural movements influencing events occurring today?

ALLEN: There are a lot of different themes that were either catalyzed, adapted, inaugurated, transformed or initiated by the literary movement of the fifties and a community of friends from the forties. The central theme was a transformation of consciousness, and as time unrolled, experiences that Kerouac, Burroughs and I had, related to this notion—at least to widening the arena of consciousness. For example, this world is absolutely real and final and ultimate and, at the same time, absolutely unreal and transitory and of the nature of dream-stuff, without contradiction. I think Kerouac had the most insightful grasp of that already by 1958.

> *...this world is absolutely real and final and ultimate and, at the same time, absolutely unreal and transitory...*

So that one spiritual insight—which is permanently universal—led to the exploration of mind or consciousness in any way shape or form. Whether it was Burroughs through his exploration of the criminal world, or Kerouac through his exploration of Buddhism, or Gary Snyder's meditation practices, or myself who worked with the Naropa Institute under Tibetan Buddhist auspices. Spiritual liberation is the center, and from spiritual liberation comes candor or frankness.

So from 1948 on, Burroughs was writing on the Mind, and this somehow moved on to gay liberation, although at the time it wasn't called that. You simply called it "explicitness" and "openness." In 1952 Burroughs presents his manuscript and it's *totally overt,* 100% out front and out of the closet—not even thinking he's being out front; it's just there because there never was a closet.

So that would take us to '55 with Gary Snyder and Michael McClure. The latter's major theme is biology and he had insights regarding the reclamation of consciousness which included ecological themes. It's not your traditional poetry. It's modern American folklore, and it influenced everybody. By 1950, Kerouac had already written *On the Road* which includes the sentence, *"The Earth is an Indian thing."* A very beautiful slogan.

DJB: I'm not sure I understand.

ALLEN: Well, it ain't an Empire State thing! Local knowledge of plants, geography and geology comes to the people who live a long, long time in one place without a lot of mechanical aids and who relate to the land itself. It's like bioregionalism, which comes out of a sort of Indian-type thinking.

DJB: So then do indigenous and Indian come from the same root?

ALLEN: I don't know. Kerouac also in *On the Road* reflected Oswald Speagler's view of the "Fellaheen" people living on the land near the Nile, tilling the soil and sailing their boats up and down, who were not affected by the changes of the Egyptian empire. They just stuck there, century after century, putting in whatever crop they were putting in, gathering it and pounding rice. So, the earth is an Indian thing.

DJB: Do you see the earth as being like an organism?

ALLEN: No, no, no, absolutely not. None of that bullshit! No Gaia hypothesis. No theism need sneak in here. No monotheistic hallucinations needed in this. Not another fascist central authority.

DJB: That's interesting, that you see the Gaia hypothesis as monotheistic and fascist whereas others see it as liberating.

ALLEN: Well, you've got this One Big Thing. Who says it's got to be one? Why does everything have to be one? I think there's "no such thing as one—only many eyes looking out in all directions." The center is everywhere, not in any one spot. Does it have to be *one* organism, in the sense of *one* brain, or *one* consciousness?

> *I think there's "no such thing as one—only many eyes looking out in all directions."*

DJB: Well it could be like you said earlier, about how reality is simultaneously real and a dream. Maybe the earth or the universe is many and one at the same time.

ALLEN: Well, yeah, but the tendency is to sentimentalize it into another godhead and to re-inaugurate the whole Judeo-Christian-Islamic mind-trap.

RMN: What do you think about the New Age movement?

ALLEN: I don't think all this crystal beads and channelling is spiritual. I don't want to put down the New Age, but only an aspect that seems like *spiritual materialism.*

> *I don't want to put down the New Age, but only an aspect that seems like spiritual materialism.*

RMN: Do you see it as a less valid phenomena than, say, the sixties counter-culture?

ALLEN: No. I think the New Age movement is basically a very good thing. Healthy foods, ecological understanding—that's all fine. It's just very specific spiritual materialism that seems to me to be the problem—accumulating experiences as "credentials for the ego."

RMN: In the fifties, did you anticipate that a cultural revolution was in the making?

ALLEN: Not in the fifties, no. But I think that the sixties were politically awry because of animosity. You know, the notions of rising up and getting angry, i.e., using anger as a motif.

RMN: Didn't that anger lead to a lot of positive social change, though, like in the area of human rights?

ALLEN: No, no. Things started fucking up when people got angry because they started action from that angry pride. By 1968, 52% of the American people thought the war over in Vietnam was a big mistake, but instead of leading people out of the war, seducing them out, people got out onto the streets and got angry.

RMN: Just because half the people in America thought the war was a bad idea doesn't mean that would translate into political action. It was the anti-war movement which vocalized those concerns and effectively changed government policy—whether they were angry or not.

ALLEN: No, if you do it that way you get it all wrong. You immediately open the door for crazies and the double agents to come in and fuck everything up. You need absolute discipline and for everything to be calm, otherwise where do you get to? You know that if you get excited while you're doing martial arts, you lose. You have to be stabilized, balanced and centered. The guy who gets excited becomes off-center, off-balance, and falls on his own weight. So there was this idea that if you set one blade of grass alight, the whole nation will follow suit "prairie file." "All we have to do is to get together and physically attack the police and then all the negroes and hippies in America will rise up and abraca-dabra!" Oh God! Lunatics! A bunch of lunatics! And it prolonged the war.

RMN: In the present situation, growing unrest and dissatisfaction has spread from farmers in the mid-west to the unemployed in inner cities to middle-class suburbia. Keeping in mind what we've seen in Eastern Europe, do you believe that an American revolution is possible?

ALLEN: Well, what do you mean by revolution? No, I don't think so, because if you mean violence, I don't want to be around—and it probably wouldn't be interesting. It would be just another group of jerks getting up there with their fucking gun, thinking they have this power. It happens every time. It happens endlessly. If we ever get into one of those left-wing, right-wing revolutions, it could be worse than any country on earth. The Americans are the most stupid and heartless...

RMN: And the best armed.

ALLEN: Yeah. It would be worse than Cambodia. They'll be sending junkies off to concentration camps.

RMN: With social attitudes tending to swing from openness and tolerance to discrimination and fear, do you feel there can ever be any real collective advance towards enlightenment?

ALLEN: Maybe not. Maybe the very nature of high technology imposes central- ized authority. The nature of the bomb is such that once you have created it you need to have some kind of omnipresent sur- veillance to monitor its use. You can't be open to people in other countries very much because you are constantly suspicious of their activities, maybe they're making H- bombs just like you did.

> *Maybe the very nature of high technology imposes centralized authority.*

RMN: Do you feel hopeful that someday the spirit of cooperation will overcome humanity's competitive and territorial urges?

ALLEN: I don't think that hope is useful at all here. I don't think in terms of progress, particularly in the face of the hyper industrialization, because it carries too many connotations. It is technology which imposes more and more goals. "Science is a lie," said Harry Smith.

RMN: Do you see the current hostility towards gays as a minor hiccup or as a serious regressive trend?

ALLEN: Yeah, it's a minor hiccup, but it's a classic political thing—a lot of Republicans are cocksuckers.

RMN: Looking at the general rise in fundamentalism, I'm left wondering, what went wrong? Why has it happened again?

ALLEN: Well, I think the left fumbled the ball by allowing right-wing style, close-minded aggression to be part of their policy. It's a fuck-up, but it should be seen as a fuck-up rather than something to be penalized for. Unless people get the idea, they'll just repeat it over and over again, "rising up angry," and then wondering why no permanent change has occurred. There's a small band of thieves, right and left, taking it upon themselves to be dictators and leading everybody astray. On the left they're painting "Die Yuppie Scum!" All over the Lower East Side, but nobody knows who is a yuppie—do they mean me? Everybody thinks it means somebody else.

> *They're painting, "Die Yuppie Scum!" all over the Lower East Side, but nobody knows who is a yuppie—do they mean me?*

RMN: We have witnessed the failure of communism and the inadequacies of capitalism. Do you think there is a political system which, if diligently applied by good people, could work?

ALLEN: Well, I don't think we've seen any real communism or capitalism.

RMN: Do you think there are just too many people with too many special interests to be successfully governed?

ALLEN: Well, no, it's not that. One—it's technological. *"The hyper-technology fuels the non-human within me."* Burroughs said that.

DJB: Are you sure that it's science and technology that's the problem, or is it the way that the technology is applied?

ALLEN: I think it's science and technology. Once you've got an absolute weapon, then you have to have absolute control.

DJB: Technology doesn't *have* to be used for weapons.

ALLEN: What has most of it been used for so far?

RMN: To blow people to smithereens. But still, the availability of technology on a local, private level has vastly increased people's access to information and has encouraged a decentralization of control. People are making their own TV programs, creating their own entertainment.

ALLEN: Okay, so everyone can be a communicator, electronically hooked up with one another. Still, the Central Intelligence Agency type is the very nature of the machine. I wouldn't want to be absolute about it, but there are definitely two sides to the story that the solution for the world's problems lies in the advancement of technology.

RMN: What do you think are some of the biggest practical and perceptual errors that the government has made in its policy towards drugs?

ALLEN: Well, obviously lumping all other drugs together in one category, while regarding the use of nicotine and alcohol as something apart. My proposition for drugs is: have marijuana as a cash crop for the otherwise ailing family farm. For junkies, well, it would probably be better to get off the methadone—apparently it's more addictive than heroin.

> *...the war on drugs has created a niche for military-minded demigods to prosper in.*

Then once you've separated grass and psychedelics from "the drug problem" in public consciousness as Oscar Janiger is trying to do in his work with the Albert Hofmann Foundation, then you have to deal with cocaine and crack. So the consequences of the present drug policies have been further criminalization, further prohibition, more and more police and more and more surveillance. As Noam Chomsky has pointed out, the war on drugs has created a niche for military-minded demigods to prosper in.

RMN: As history shows that prohibition does nothing to decrease demand, and as most of the money in the drugwar is being used to fight off the criminal element, why is it that so few politicians are willing to voice their support for legalization?

ALLEN: We have this vanguard of fundamentalists who don't want abortions, who don't want drugs—and they're very powerful. There's a hard nut, a residue of energetic, active, organized, networked, technologically sophisticated censors—the neo-conservatives and the born-agains. It's a composite of religious fanaticism and economic interest.

The pharmaceutical companies are among the people opposing decriminalization because they make a lot of money in the drug business. The Coors beer people support the right-wing Heritage Foundation and then you have Jesse Helms representing tobacco. So there's that combination of economic interest. Then the national and state drug bureaucracies have one of the most protective lobbies in the nation, with a twelve-billion-dollar budget monopoly, hundreds of thousands of telephones, FAX machines, PR people, resources and files. So how do we get out of that? I don't know, it's always been a source of confusion.

DJB: I'm curious about how your experiences with psychedelics affected your writing and your life in general.

ALLEN: Well, I wrote a couple of good poems on them—with mescaline, acid, nitrous oxide, marijuana and amphetamines. So those are direct influences on my writing. But aside from sixty or so pages, the spiritual effect of drugs was not too extensive in the creation of texts.

DJB: What kind of relationship do you see between madness and creativity?

ALLEN: I don't really know; it's an old stereotype. When we talk about certain states of madness, what are we talking about exactly? Somebody on a roll, who's very active and talking to himself, dominating his space and people working around him, like Picasso? Or someone in a manic phase of manic depression, which is often very creative? Or how about full-blown schizophrenia? In a lot of those states, you're cut off from the surrounding environment so it would be impossible to produce anything concrete.

DJB: Have you ever experienced the fear of going mad?

ALLEN: A couple of times, on psychedelics. I remember in 1948 I had a hell of an experience: an ominous, threatening universe. I'm sure that madness, paranoia or megalomania came in then.

RMN: I read something you once said in reference to language which was, "Man's power of abstraction dooms us to lose touch with detail." What did you mean by this? Isn't that what poets do?

ALLEN: Well, when did I say it and under what circumstances? How do I know what I said? That's a very common, almost trite, stereotypical thought. I'm sure it's in general true, but I probably never said it in those words. I probably said some general thing like that, but "man's power of abstraction"—bullshit!

RMN: I take it you don't agree with the statement.

ALLEN: Well, I'm struck just now by the vulgarity of the expression, the phrasing.

RMN: I have a problem with the first word, actually.

ALLEN: Well, so do I. *"Woman's* power of abstraction?..."Actually, I don't think that's true. I think it's a temptation to think that. I think it's *civilization's* power of abstraction, or the development of abstracted power that could lead to a loss of contact with detail, hypertechnology so to speak.

RMN: And language, in that context, plays a part in the process?

ALLEN: No. That's the semiotic, deconstructionist, Burroughsian view. That's not my view at all. It's the opposite, in fact. I think it's a fascist statement, frankly. It attacks language and it attacks people talking. It's an attack on communication, actually. I would say that language joins heaven and earth and joins mind with body. It synchronizes them through speech, poetry, and words which connect abstraction with the ground.

It is also obvious that continuous generalization and abstraction lead to mixed judgment and manipulation of phenomena in an inappropriate way; but to make a general statement as blanket as that discourages the attempt at sincere communication, or description of what you are experiencing.

By using that kind of generalization like "man's power of abstraction," the Marxists had to convince writers that they are not worthy of writing because they don't really represent the proletariat—only the abstract interests of the upper middle class or the bourgeoisie. The Catholics have convinced people to burn books and burn people because they or their work doesn't represent the true word of God. And deconstructionist, semiotic poets have used it as a way of avoiding interacting with phenomena, of interacting on a heart-felt level with their own experience of living.

That generalization has always been an excuse to hard-nosed students of their own perceptions to be cool, you know, to play it cool. That is to say, that words don't count, that this is abstract, therefore I don't want to make any comment. It's been a way of diminishing expression. In Blake's description of the Urizenic quality, "boundedness" arises. *Your Reason,* the figurative reason of the symbolic description, creates a hyper-abstraction, a hyper-rationalization.

RMN: What do you think was so special about Blake as a poet?

ALLEN: He had a good mind. From Blake's point of view, hyper-rationality, hyper-abstraction leads to the nuclear bomb, from the point of view of reason, trying to assert power over feeling, imagination and the body. If any one of them tries to take over, then it disrupts the whole balance of nature.

DJB: What do you think happens to human consciousness after biological death?

ALLEN: I don't know. The Tibetans say that some kind of aetheric electricity or some kind of impulse moves on. I think it's a good idea to cultivate an openness to the possibilities that might occur. When you're drowning, once you've stopped breathing, there's still about eight minutes of consciousness before brain death, and there have been people who have been resuscitated, so something is there. In that eight minutes, what should you prepare for? My meditation practices are on the breath, so then what happens after I stop breathing?

I asked my guru this question and he started laughing. He said that was the purpose of the advanced meditation practices, the visualization, the mantra, the mandala, all that stuff. He said, "If I were you, I wouldn't pretend this or that, openness or emptiness, I would go along with whatever made the process more comfortable." As for what happens after death, I've always been a little skeptical about anything persevering. I think the process of dying takes over, whatever you think, and goes on automatic. What you think may be harmonious with what happens, but what happens is going to happen in any case. Sometimes I think that you enter open space and become open space.

In the last moment you don't want to be pissed off, even if there's no re-birth. So it's a good idea to get into the frequency of some kind of meditative practice, in case

> *...in the last moment you don't want to be pissed off...*

there's no afterlife. In case there is, it's also a good idea. It prepares you for whatever situation. *"Do not go gently into that good night, rage, rage against the dying of the light."* You know that poem? It seems the worst advice possible.

RMN: Do you see death as an adventure, or are you afraid?

ALLEN: I'm a little scared, yeah, but I'm not afraid to admit it. I'm not quite up to the adventure yet but on the other hand...

DJB: What do you think it is about death that you're afraid of?

ALLEN: How about entering a realm where there's twenty-nine devils sticking red hot pokers up my behind and into my feet. Maybe I'll turn into a big prick with this little tiny asshole.

DJB: Do you think that the fear of death could be the fear of non-existence?

ALLEN: Well, no, that wouldn't be so bad. It would be the fear of *existing again,* in another life. Popping up again, like pop goes the weasel, and being stuck with whatever hard-on you started out with. You could have an obsession and think, oh, I should have cut that out long ago! I should have stopped lusting after pretty boys long ago! You're born into a universe with nothing but pretty boys and you get stuck there for another one hundred years until you realize, uh oh, you're going to die. Something like that.

DJB: Do you have a personal understanding of God?

ALLEN: Yes. There is no God.

DJB: There's no question about it?

ALLEN: No. It's a big mistake. It means six thousand years of darkness. It means a Judeo-Christian-Islamic control system. It means war and centralization.

DJB: What about the concept of God as a state of consciousness?

ALLEN: Too easy. Why do you need a concept of God when you've already got a concept of a state of consciousness? Why do you have to add "God" onto it? It's sneaking in a centralized state of consciousness, it's sneaking in a metaphysical CIA. In an open universe, nothing is closed in, no judgment of beliefs, just infinite possibilities of roles to role-play. If God made everything the way it is, then it's already done and it's pre-ordained all the way, so there's no movement. God means stasis as Burroughs points out. When you consider the whole notion of God, that's what it comes to, unless you redefine God so that it doesn't mean God anymore.

> *Why do you need a concept of God when you've already got a concept of a state of consciousness?*

DJB: Well, what if you define God as being the notion of a greater organism of which we're all tiny cells or parts?

ALLEN: You still have this *one* greater organism that started everything and knows where it's all going.

DJB: Not necessarily. It could be evolving itself, just as we are.

ALLEN: It ain't God, the omnipotent, omniscient.

RMN: If you don't believe in God, do you believe in love?

ALLEN: Perhaps it's a uselessly worn-out four letter word that substitutes for awareness to cover all cruel facts. But you have to first agree with people how you want to use the word. You know, a word doesn't mean anything by itself, there's no built-in intrinsic meaning, it's just how you want to use it. It's an abstraction like, "What is the truth?" It's a semantic blind alley. It doesn't have a meaning except that which you assign to it, and if people don't agree on the meaning then you're going to have endless feuds over nothing, which is what happens all the time.

A student and I spent time with Burroughs in 1944. We got into an argument about what is art? If we carved a walking stick and put it in on the moon, where nobody saw it, is that art? Or does art have to be social? So we took the argument to Burroughs and he said, "Art is a three-letter word. If you guys will agree on what you mean and how you want to use it, then you can use it. But to say that it has an absolute inherent meaning one way or an absolute inherent meaning the other way, that's a semantic problem, and it is too starved an argument for my sword."

You ask a large question using a large word which can mean anything, and then expect somebody to give you a sensible answer. Now, if you had said, what do you think of love? Or how do you see using the word "love" for the experience of wonder at the sight of a sunset? then I might be able to find an instance where it was used well, or I might not and I'd have to invent one. If I couldn't invent an instance and I couldn't remember any instance where the word was used well, I would say it's probably not the right word.

RMN: Well, I'm glad I disappointed you and got such an answer! Talking about the nature of wordplay, I read in a lecture you gave that you believe it's possible to teach inspiration. How do you do this?

ALLEN: Inspiration means breathing in The process of breathing is of course, central to meditation practice, but it's also central to poetry. You have thoughts which are

Inspiration means breathing in.

mental and impalpable, like heaven, and then you have body, which is ground or earth. So when you speak, the breath comes out as a physiological body thing but it's also a vehicle for the impalpable thoughts of the mind.

So, you could say that speech joins heaven and earth, or synchronizes mind and body. Exhalation or expiration—as in "he expired"—is the vehicle on which poetry comes out, whereas inhalation or inspiration takes in. So, you can say that certain kinds of poetry like Shelley's famous romantic poem, "Ode to the West Wind," has a certain elevated unobstructed breath about it; unobstructed intelligence, unobstructed production of images, unobstructed self-confidence, unobstructed majestic proclamation.

RMN: So you're saying that if people can learn to first breathe properly, they can then stimulate their imaginations?

ALLEN: To be a good example of what they call "poetic inspiration," is to be alive with this physiological attitude. A sense of a proclamation echoing to the outside space with no difference between the outside space and the inside space. So you teach inspiration by teaching people both meditation and spontaneous improvisation, a sense of self-confidence, the notion of unobstructed breath and also how to allow their minds to speak out loud without thinking in advance.

That's the way poetry is taught at the Naropa Institute. You can also cultivate or point out the notion of the space in the room so that somebody can talk loud enough so that the furthest person in the room can hear. You need a panoramic awareness of the space around you, rather than looking inward and mumbling. So, it's maybe hyperbole to say "you could teach inspiration." You can teach the physiological posture of it, but that's only half the battle.

One of the teachings is about proclamation—to mouth the syllables in an interesting way. If you listen to Dylan records or Kerouac's recordings, you'll hear an intelligence in the actual pronunciation which is the difference between a mumbling poet and a poet who actually enjoys the language in his own mouth. If you listen to the recordings of Ezra Pound you'll hear that sense of elegant imperial mouth.

RMN: William Blake actually sang a lot of his poetry.

ALLEN: Yeah, he actually sang "Songs of Innocence."

RMN: You put that to music, didn't you?

ALLEN: Yeah. There was a record in 1969 called, "Songs of Innocence and Other Experiences." It's out of print now, but it's going to be re-issued next year.

DJB: Cool. What else have you been doing?

ALLEN: Well, I collaborated with Philip Glass on an Hydrogen Jukebox opera, putting together poetry and music. I'm working on a record with Hal Wilner and with Fransco Clemente on a series of books. I'm teaching at the Naropa Institute in Boulder, Colorado and at Brooklyn College, and I'm writing a lot of poems. I've just about got another book ready and am also coalescing my journals from the fifties. Another project called *Literary History of the Beat Generation* drawn from my lectures over the years.

I'm also trying to raise money for the Naropa Institute, the Buddhist school formed in 1974 by Chögyam Trungpa. Within it is the school of poetry. We thought about calling it the *Jack Kerouac School of Poetics,* but it sounded a little boring. So then we said, well, he's dead, so he's disembodied. So now it's *The Jack Kerouac School of Disembodied Poetics.* And then will people misunderstand? Yes, well, that's permissible. They'll just have to ask what it means.

DJB: Do you still feel guilty about not doing enough?

ALLEN: Always. It's a workaholic problem.

Stephen LaBerge

"In the lucid dream you look around and realize
that the whole world…is all something that your
mind is creating."

Waking the Dreamer
with Stephen LaBerge

Stephen LaBerge is the first scientist to empirically prove the existence of the phenomena of lucid dreaming. His work has developed this technique into a powerful tool for studying mind-body relationships in the dream state and he has demonstrated the considerable potential for lucid dreaming in the fields of psychotherapy and psychosomatic medicine. His books on the subject, Lucid Dreaming, Exploring the World of Lucid Dreaming *and his more academic* Conscious Mind, Sleeping Brain *have received enormous popular interest.*

Born in 1947, he obtained a B.S. in mathematics from the University of Arizona. At the age of 19 he began graduate studies in chemistry at Stanford University, but in 1968 took a leave of absence to pursue his research interest in psychopharmacology. In 1977 he returned to Stanford to begin studies on dreaming, consciousness and sleep, and received his Ph.D. in Psychophysiology from Stanford's Graduate Special Program in 1980.

He has taught courses on sleep and dreaming, psychobiology and altered states of consciousness at Stanford University, the California Institute of Integral Studies in San Fransisco, and San Fransisco State University. Currently, Stephen is a Research Associate in the Department of Psychology at Stanford University, and Director of Research at the Lucidity Institute; a center he founded to further explore the potential of lucid dreaming. Here he is developing user-friendly technologies such as the DreamLight® to help people to learn the art of lucid dreaming and disseminating information on the conscious dream-state through a quarterly newsletter.

Stephen's energy and enthusiasm for his work is highly contagious and he has a way of dissecting information so as to always speak to the heart of the matter. His large eyes and animated features reveal an impish, child-like spirit and at the same time, an extremely sharp and analytical mind.

This interview began at the Lucidity Institute on July 8, 1992, and was completed on the evening of the same day, in the impressive grounds of Stanford University. In the evening after-sunset glow, Stephen addressed the questions of why we sleep, where we really are when we think we're out of our body, and the spiritual implications of taking responsibility for our dreams.

—RMN

DJB: What was it that originally inspired your interest in lucid dreaming?

STEPHEN: I had been interested in lucid dreaming, in a way, since my childhood experience. When I was five years old they had these adventure serials and I would go to the matinees. I had the idea, after a particularly fun dream where I was an undersea pirate, wouldn't it be fun to go back to that same dream and continue it as in the serial? Nobody told me you couldn't do that sort of thing, so that night I was back in the same dream, and I remember doing that for weeks. I would have the experience of seeing the surface of the ocean far above me and thinking, I can't hold my breath this long! Then I'd think, but in these dreams I can breathe dream-water. That was all, at that point, that I made of the lucidity, in the sense that I knew it was a dream and that I could have fun in it.

It wasn't until my early twenties that I became interested in the mind. At that point I was interested in the natural world and assumed I was going to become a chemist or something like that and when I came to Stanford in 1967 I was a graduate student in chemical physics. Being in the Bay Area in those days, you can imagine what kinds of things I got interested in which told me that there was a world inside that was of as much interest as the world out there.

I took a workshop from Tarthang Tulku, a Tibetan Buddhist, at Esalen and I was surprised at the topic of the workshop, which was essentially asking us to maintain consciousness throughout the twenty-four hours. Tarthang's English was limited at the time, he'd just arrived from India, and he would repeatedly say nothing more than "This dream!" And laugh. He was trying to get us to think of our current experience as a dream and to see what it had in common with the nocturnal experiences and the day experiences. After focusing my mind in that way over the course of this weekend, I noticed on my way back

...he would repeatedly say nothing more than "This dream!" and laugh.

to San Francisco that I felt high. I associated it with the exercise and the expansion of awareness that came from thinking of my waking experiences as a dream and trying to maintain a continuity.

A few nights after I came back from the workshop at Esalen, I had the first lucid dream I could remember since my childhood. I was climbing K2 dressed in short sleeves, going up the mountain through the snow drifts. I had the thought, look how I'm dressed, how could I be doing this? It's because this is a dream. And at that point in my youthful folly, I decided to fly off the mountain and dream big. Personally, sitting here now, I would like to see what it's like to climb to the top of the second highest mountain in the world.

So that piqued my interest in the topic of lucid dreaming and it gradually developed over the next five years, and along the way I had an experience that convinced me that developing lucid dreaming could be something of great value to me. I had a dream in which I was going up a mountain path, and had been hiking for miles and miles. I came to a very narrow bridge across an immensely deep chasm, and looking down I was afraid to go across the bridge.

My companion said, "Oh, you don't have to go that way, you can go back the way you came," and he pointed back an immense distance to the long way around. And somehow that just seemed the hard way of doing this, and I had the thought, if I were to become lucid, I would have no fear in crossing that bridge. Then I sort of noticed the thought, became lucid and crossed the bridge to the other side. When I woke up I thought about the meaning of that and saw that it had an application to life in general. Life is, in a sense, a kind of bridge, and what causes us to lose our balance is fear of the unknown, death, the meaninglessness around us, whatever it might be. Yet if we maintain the right awareness and context, it *is* possible to cross the bridge.

About that same time I decided that I'd finished my seven years in search of the Holy Grail in hippydom and that I should get back to being a scientist. It occurred to me that lucid dreaming could be a dissertation project and that it could be scientifically researched. The experts at the time said it was impossible but I had thought of a way which it could be proven that it *was* possible.

RMN: Tell us about the experiment you did with Lynn Nagel, which first empirically proved that lucid dreaming existed.

STEPHEN: Lynn Nagel was a research associate at Stanford in the sleep center when I had the idea of doing something with lucid dreaming. Without Lynn, it might never have happened. He helped me set it up, and taught me how to do sleep recordings. In our first studies Lynn stayed up all night while I slept as the subject. The basic idea of proving lucid dreaming was a simple one. It was based on earlier studies that showed that, if a person in their dream happened to be watching a ping-pong game and they're looking from left to right, the eyes of their sleeping body would show a corresponding pattern of eye-movement activity.

So I had thought that, since in a lucid dream I can volitionally do whatever I want, why not make a signal that we could agree upon in advance; a pattern of eye-movement signals that could then be used to prove that I had a lucid dream and that I knew I was dreaming while I was in the dream? We could also use that to establish in what stage of sleep lucid dreaming occurred. I thought it would be REM sleep just because that was when most dreaming occurs.

DJB: Are the eyes the only part of the body that will correspond to physical movements in a dream?

STEPHEN: No. What happens is that for any muscle group that you move, there will be small twitching activity. Some parts of the body are much more paralyzed than others and the main muscles that are strongly paralyzed are the muscles of vocalization and locomotion. The large muscles of locomotion could cause you to fall out of a tree while you're in the midst of a dream. Also you obviously want to suppress vocalization in the middle of the forest at night, so that you don't cry out, "Hungry tiger, come and get me!" Things like that. Or, "I'm glad there are no tigers around here!"

So those muscles are very strongly paralyzed, but the eye muscles can do us no harm. You can't wake up by moving your eyes and evolution hasn't developed any connections to inhibit them. There are a few other muscles that are not very inhibited and some that are not at all, for example, respiration. You don't want voluntary respiration muscles inhibited during REM or you don't wake up!

So, anyway, Lynn and I did experiments in the beginning where we were trying to press a micro-switch. So in my dream I would be pressing my dream-thumb down "here," but there wasn't any micro-switch in my dream-hand so it was a little funny and I could never do that. We did find muscle twitches in the arm that corresponded to that effort, but the problem is that most of the muscle fibers are not firing when my brain commands them to and only a few impulses get through in the same pattern. So we made up some eye movement signals; the one that we use now, most typically, is two pairs of left-right eye movements which are very easy to see in the context of other eye movements and it's also easy to do. After a few false starts where he did things like waking me up at the beginning of the REM period to *remind* me that I wanted to be lucid, he finally let me alone. Then I had the first lucid dream in the laboratory in which I made eye movement signals, and sure enough, there they were on the polygraph.

RMN: You say you had a hard time getting your results published, let alone accepted. Why do you think there is so much skepticism in this field?

STEPHEN: Basically, people were thinking of the dream as a product of the unconscious mind, and of Freud's idea that the dream is the royal road to the unconscious. From that they seemed to develop the mistaken idea that dreams are themselves unconscious somehow, but they're not; they're conscious experiences, otherwise, you couldn't report them. It's true that the *source of dreams* is largely unconscious and we don't know why things happen in the typical dream. In that sense much of the dream content is unconsciously determined but that doesn't mean that the *experience* is unconscious.

> *...dreams are ...conscious experiences, otherwise, you couldn't report them.*

One is given to speaking very loosely about saying somebody's conscious or unconscious and we would sometimes hear people describing sleep as being unconscious. If you tighten up the language a little, you'd say what you mean is a sleeping person is unconscious of the *environment*. It's not the same thing as being absolutely unconscious. When we say, a person is "conscious," that is a shorthand for is "conscious of *x*." What's the "x"? What is consciousness? That's a very difficult question.

A much better way of putting it is, what is the difference between a conscious and an unconscious mental process? So it's kind of a philosophical problem that people were having. They just thought it was plain impossible. So when we brought forward scientific evidence, in 1980, their first conclusion was that we obviously must have made some mistake because it just doesn't make sense. I think where people's minds had a change was from presenting the material at conferences to the colleagues who had the opinions about these things. There they see it, and have their opportunity to say, "Well what about that?" And you answer, or you don't, to their satisfaction.

So most people by 1983 who were going to believe it, believed it, and then there were some people who weren't going to believe it no matter what. One skeptic, when he saw the data in 1983, said, "Well, it's all very nice, but it's not dreaming." So I said, "What kind of evidence which you haven't seen so far could prove this to you?" And he said, "There isn't *any* kind of evidence." Admittedly this was after a few beers that he said that.

DJB: What was his definition of dreaming then?

STEPHEN: Something that's *not* lucid dreaming. In other words the problem was that people's concept of what dreaming and what sleep was was too limited. In fact when REM sleep was first discovered it was called "paradoxical sleep" in Europe because the characteristics of it were so unexpected, and it's still called that. Basically it looks like wakefulness, and in my view we're seeing the same story all over with lucid dreaming. Lucid dreaming shows that under some circumstances the sleeping brain can sustain very high levels of reflective awareness and function very much like in the waking state. That's not the typical dream to be sure, but it shows it is possible, and therefore one shouldn't say dreams are necessarily single-minded, non-reflective and hallucinatory.

DJB: What do you think the function of a dream is and why did it evolve?

STEPHEN: I don't know whether dreaming has a special or unique evolutionary function. I'd say the answer to why we dream is simple; it's the same reason that we've got brains. Brains are primarily evolved to produce models of the world, to be able to simulate the environment and to predict what's going to happen so that we can get what we want and avoid what we don't want. That's a strong pressure driving the evolution of nervous systems, in particular primates and humans, to a very high level at which we simulate the environment so well that we're unaware that we're simulating.

We look out and we see the world. That's the common sense way of viewing reality; but what I see when I look out at the two of you and the tape recorder on the table and the room that we're sitting in here is not the world, unless I'm referring to my world, *my* mental world. I'm seeing a simulation of my brain that is based on sensory input that I'm receiving, plus other patterns of expectation having to do with all kinds of other things I expect to see and am ready to see. Sensory input is great evidence but also memory and expectation is good evidence too.

RMN: So you're saying that we dream as a habitual function of what we do during our waking state and dreams don't have any particular purpose?

STEPHEN: It's the same constructive process that we're using now under the special conditions of sleep. So if the brain is activated in REM sleep, if it's turned on enough to be making a world model, it makes a world model, but it's not making it out of sensory input anymore. Now it draws on the other sources that may have been secondary in the waking state, the expectation, the motivation, those biases that bias perception. So it constructs a world that shows us what we expect, fear, wish for, need and all that.

RMN: So it's not necessarily a way to assimilate our experience?

STEPHEN: No. It may serve a value, but we didn't evolve a dream in order to do something, we evolved *brains* in order to do something. Surely, dreaming serves some function, but in a way, almost accidental to the evolution of the brain. There's no doubt that REM sleep facilitates memory consolidation but we don't know for sure whether that has anything to do with the dream content or not.

RMN: What do you think is the purpose of sleep?

STEPHEN: No one knows for sure, but there may be multiple purposes served by sleep. On this planet we have a strong twenty-four-hour dark-light cycle, and almost all creatures are adapted to being active in one of those two phases. Humans are active in the light as we are strongly dependent on vision but suppose you didn't sleep, instead you're awake in the middle of the night in the jungle. Are you *more* likely to get what you want or what you *don't* want, wandering around the jungle in the dark? You see? So it makes more sense to have an enforced period of inactivity during the phase of the dark-light cycle at which you're at a clear disadvantage.

There are perhaps other energy conservation purposes and other specific functions that sleep serves, but that seems a sufficient argument to me of accounting for why it happens. So one idea about REM sleep is that it's something that's designed to maintain active enough brains so that if you need to get up for some reason, you can, and when it's time to get up in the morning you can do that. That's perhaps one of the reasons why REM sleep increases later in the night and becomes more frequent and more active. So given that we've got an active brain in the context of sleep and no sensory input, then you get dreams, not because it serves a function, but because—why not?

RMN: You've talked about using fear and anxiety in a dream as a catalyst to propel you into a lucid state; tell us more about this?

STEPHEN: Anxiety certainly seems to stimulate reflectiveness and there may be a biological basis for that, that conscious processing in general seems to have evolved as a special problem-solving feature. It's not just fear; by the way; fear is not enough for you to become conscious. Fear is: here you are in the jungle and there's a tiger. What do you do? You run. That's what fear motivates you to do— avoid and escape.

So let's say you climb a tree and the tiger starts to climb up after you. Now you feel something new, which is anxiety, which is fear *plus* uncertainty and that causes an increased scanning of the environment for alternative actions. What else can I do? What new combination of things? Oh yeah, look, a coconut! Which you throw at the tiger, you see? So in the origins you can see the rudimentary consciousness being very strongly associated with anxiety and the re-framing, the re-formulation, the re-scanning of the environment for new ways of getting out of a problem you're in. You see that same thing in less threatening ways in everyday life.

RMN: So when you're dreaming and you experience anxiety, it's an opportunity then to check out your options and change the outcome. What, to your knowledge, was the earliest documented account of lucid dreaming?

STEPHEN: Aristotle talks about lucid dreaming. He doesn't use that term but he says that sometimes during sleep there's something that clearly says to us, this is in your mind, this isn't really happening. Then you see accounts here and there throughout history where somebody talks about this, usually a philosopher. Yet there's very little research in the West until the nineteenth century when Hervey de Saint-Denis published a book on dreams and how to guide them based on thousands of lucid dreams he had. Fredrik van Eeden, in the late nineteenth century coined the term "lucid dream," largely from the psychiatric sense of lucid as in "lucid interval," where an otherwise normally mad person will come to his senses for a moment.

RMN: What about other cultural awareness of lucid dreaming, the Hawaiians and Native Americans and the dream-time of the Aborigines?

STEPHEN: In regard to the Aborigines there may well be a correlation. In terms of primal cultures in general, dreaming is usually the business of the professionals; your everyday person doesn't get involved in these things. I have wondered to what extent shamanistic experiences are related to lucid dreaming, they sound similar in many ways. In Native American cultures you see something like what I'd call the *opposite* of the lucid understanding of the dream. Let's suppose I had a dream last night in which the two of you wrecked my Porsche, so I now expect reparations, so pay up.

> *In terms of primal cultures...dreaming is usually the business of the professionals...*

RMN: They took dreams completely literally.

STEPHEN: Right. In other words they viewed the dream as the supernatural version of what *must* be, and that, in my view, is the worst way to take dreams because it takes the freedom of them away. Instead of being able to imagine anything with no constraints from physical reality, whatever you imagine you have to make physically true. On the other hand, in this culture, dreams are considered *nothings*, you know, things to be forgotten and ignored.

DJB: *Just* a dream.

STEPHEN: Right. Where you *do* see this developed to high levels however, is in Tibetan Buddhism, since they've been practicing lucid dreaming probably for a thousand years.

RMN: It seems that the criteria to be a successful lucid dreamer is similar to that for being a successful Buddhist, but Dzoghen, one of the branches of Buddhism which practices lucid dreaming, sees it as a very advanced technique only to be embarked upon after a great deal of preparation.

STEPHEN: Some practices of Buddhism indeed regard it in that way. The Nyingmapas don't tend to; they tend to say, "Well, give it a try!" So in some cultures this had been taken to great extremes and today we still don't know how far Buddhist practitioners of this art are able to take lucid dreaming and I'm hoping to be able to do some research on that some time in the future.

RMN: Have you found any correlation between people who practice some kind of meditation and the ability to have lucid dreams?

STEPHEN: There's a study by Henry Reed based on some ten thousand dream reports, in which people were asked whether or not they had meditated the day before the night that they collect those dreams on. Then the percentage of lucid dreams occurring on nights following meditation the day before was measured. The difference was seven percent versus five percent, so that's two percent difference with people who meditated the day before. We don't know what kind of meditation, how much or anything of that nature, so there are a lot of questions about it, but the point is there is a small difference.

DJB: It can also be the type of person. The type of person who would be interested in meditation would be more aware of alternative realities and that sort of thing.

RMN: Have you found any other criteria such as age or even sex which makes someone a successful lucid dreamer?

STEPHEN: We've asked about all of those things and have not found any way of predicting to any large extent whether or not a person will report lucid dreams, except for one thing, and that is, how often you remember your dreams. Frequent dream recallers are more likely to have lucid dreams. If you ask do you recall your dreams at least once a night, or find the median split on dream recall, then you'll find *twice* as many lucid dreams in the group that reports more dreams in general. You can see why that makes sense, because if people don't remember their dreams they don't ever reflect on them in the waking state. Also, what determines dream recall has a lot to do with the habits of what you do in bed. So if you wake up while lucid dreaming, that's one thing; if you wake up thinking it's time to get out of bed then you're not going to remember dreams.

> *Frequent dream recallers are more likely to have lucid dreams.*

RMN: You talk in your book about a woman, Mary Arnold Forster, who was teaching lucid dreaming to children at the beginning of this century. That sounds like a very wonderful thing. Do you think that children may be more receptive partly because they don't have so many fixed beliefs about what can be?

STEPHEN: Exactly. That's something I'd very much like to see—more children learning about this. I think it could be of great value to them considering that most children have extremely little power; they're basically at the mercy of what everybody else tells them to do. So here's a world in which they can be the master.

Also, in this society, we have various problems with drugs that are associated with children. I think children as adolescents are the people *least* likely to benefit from drugs. Certainly psychedelics can be useful to *some* people at *some* circumstances in their lives but I'd say that hardly ever applies to ado-

...I think there could be real value in developing lucid dreaming as a kind of drug-abuse inoculation.

lescents who already have plenty of change and structures that are in flux going on. It's most valuable for people who have rigid structures that have built up over the years and who need them loosened up.

So the problem is that our current approach to this seems to be "Just Say No," and the idea that the only reason that kids ever take drugs is peer pressure. Let's realize that there may be other reasons. They may want something else, something new, something that's fun, something other than the routine they're used to, and lucid dreaming could provide that for them, in a way that is safe and legal and harmonious with their development. So I think that there could be real value in developing lucid dreaming as a kind of drug-abuse inoculation.

DJB: What kind of techniques, do you think, are the most effective for dream recall and actually producing lucid dreams.

STEPHEN: If you were to say, I want to become a lucid dreamer, how should I go about it? I would say that means you've got some extra time and energy in your life, some unallocated attention that you could apply to working on this. If you're somebody that's so busy that you have hardly time to take a walk, you're not going to have the time and energy to do this.

We have developed a course in lucid dreaming that is designed for people to use at home. The first lesson in there is about how you develop dream recall. After you've got a sufficient level of dream recall you start studying your dreams for the dream signs; what's dream-like about them? You then start doing exercises that use your focus in your mind on your typical dream content, becoming more reflective and developing your ability to have specific intentions that you carry out in the future and so on.

The course in lucid dreaming right now is something you can use either with or without a DreamLight®, which is a device we developed primarily in response to people's requests for methods to help them have lucid dreams. It's a mask that you wear while you're asleep and it flashes a light during REM, not so much as to wake you up but enough to remind you in your dream that you are dreaming.

RMN: A lot of people hear about this phenomena and then have a lucid dream for the first time; it happened to me when I first read your book. How much do you think that *realizing* this is possible is linked to the ability to lucid dream?

STEPHEN: That's clearly important, and what you've just described happens very frequently. Part of what you learn when you learn how to have lucid dreams is that *you can do it.* However, if you're thinking, "I'm not sure I can," that "I'm not sure I can" is a barrier. The problem is, since it rarely happens for most people, then it gives you the idea that it must be difficult, instead of thinking that it rarely happens simply because you never have the mental set where you're thinking I *want* this to happen, and I'm intending to do this.

RMN: What are some of the benefits that you've observed and experienced from developing this skill?

STEPHEN: The applications of lucid dreaming range from the poor man's Tahiti, the adventure and exploration and thrill part of it, to the mental rehearsal, the practice, trying things out in the dream state that you've learned. You can also develop motor skills or work on overcoming shyness, overcoming nightmares, dealing with fears and of course there's the mental health aspect of it that might have extensions into a broader sense of health.

> *we've found that when you dream, you do something to your brain that's as if you've actually done it.*

On the basis of mind-body experiments that we've done at Stanford using the signaling technique, we've found that when you dream, you do something to your brain that's as if you've *actually* done it. So there are very strong relationships between dream content and physiological response which we think could be used for facilitating healing, facilitating the function of the immune system in some way.

DJB: Have you done any studies on that?

STEPHEN: No, but in the book *Exploring the World of Lucid Dreaming,* we published anecdotes of people doing some kinds of healing. These are all uncontrolled in that they decide at some point in time that they're going to have a lucid dream in which something is healed and sure enough it gets better, but we don't know if it would have got better on its own or at what rate and so on.

RMN: What about the potential for incorporating lucid dreaming into an educational program in the sense of sleep-learning?

STEPHEN: The most important kind of sleep-learning that you can do is not having a tape recording and trying to pipe *more* factual information into you.

Sleep time is not a very good time for taking in information, but lucid dreams are an excellent opportunity for experiential learning, for finding out about the wisdom of life—having an encounter with a dragon, for example, which you won't ever have the opportunity for in the waking state. You

> *...what you can learn from your experiences in the lucid dream state are things that can apply to your waking state.*

have to have the courage to resist the fear that you'll actually feel, to say this dragon is a mental image—a mental image can't hurt me, and then to act on that. I would advise having a conversation, making friends with the dragon.

The point is that what you can learn from your experiences in the lucid dream state are things that can apply to your waking state. When you learn that when you face your problems and fears you overcome them, and things turn out better than they do when you simply try to avoid them, that generalizes and you have more sense of self-confidence that you can do things. Your security can improve as you realize that you can handle difficult situations if you keep your head about you.

DJB: It actually sounds real similar to Virtual Reality.

STEPHEN: Right. To put it in terms of Virtual Reality, I would say that lucid dreaming is high resolution Virtual Reality with appropriate technology *now*. The best computers we can get are our brains. If you look at the pluses and minuses of the two approaches, you see with lucid dreaming that you have something which is not directly shareable; I can't record a lucid

> *...lucid dreaming is high resolution Virtual Reality...*

dream and say here, you try it. The Virtual Reality with an external computer that generates everything has the potential of doing that, but it's just like a playback; it's more like watching a videotape than it is actually doing something.

Jaron Lanier has complained about VR not having that unexpectedness and intuitive surprise, and of course there's plenty of that in lucid dreaming. Clearly the lucid dream state has much more *felt* reality. At this point no one has anything near to a solution of how you can be embodied in VR. If you're driving a car, or flying, you know, that's easy to represent because all you see is, here's the wheel and there's the picture out there - and that feels real. Yet the moment that you want your body to be walking, you see the picture move, but you don't feel like your doing it.

DJB: Well, in North Carolina they've developed treadmills that simulate the sensation of walking with tactile sensors.

STEPHEN: Okay, suppose you want to go to the lab? Sorry you can't, you can only walk *this* way.

DJB: It actually has a steering column that allows you to change direction.

STEPHEN: Well, okay, the point is, at this stage the technology is limited.

RMN: In terms of the difference in the potential for empathy between VR and lucid dreaming, have you explored the possibility of conscious dream sharing with another person? I've read about Alaskan shamans who claim to be able to visit their shaman buddies in their sleep.

STEPHEN: I haven't really experimented with that. I consider it to be theoretically possible, but it's not something that I felt was of developmental value first of all. There are many aspects of dream control that I haven't pursued. I've emphasized instead controlling myself and my responses to what happens, instead of making it magically different, because I've wanted something that would generalize the waking state. In this world we don't have the power to magically make other people appear and disappear.

There have been a few people who've said, "I can visit you in your dream," and I've said, "Okay do so." But I've never experienced an unequivocal success that I remember.

I think the problem is that we tend to bring mental models from the waking state into the dream state. So we have expectations in the dream, especially in a lucid dream. Here it is, it's all so real, and so hey! You two people look perfectly real to me so you'll remember this conversation later, right? Now why would I think you'd do that, any more that I would think this table would remember this conversation?

One of the things you have to do in developing skill with lucid dreaming is to be critical of your state of mind. So you wake up from a lucid dream and you think, did I make some assumptions that were inappropriate or do something that didn't make sense? So you can therefore refine and clarify your thinking and build up mental models that are appropriate to the dream world.

I dreamed in a lucid dream that I was flying above the San Francisco Bay, and I had the thought, my body is asleep over there, I'll go visit it. And I woke and said, What? This is a dream! Your body's not in there or you'd be in trouble if your body's asleep in your own dream; how could you wake up? People who don't make that extra effort don't tend to learn.

RMN: Some inventions have come about through lucid dreaming—for example, the sewing machine and part of Einstein's equations. Have you found a link between creativity and lucid dreaming?

STEPHEN: We have anecdotes from people who've used lucid dreaming for creative problem-solving or artistic creation of some kind. It's surely a state where you can get a great many ideas; the problem is that not every idea you get is good. I think the major value of lucid dreaming is in giving people the sense that we live in a much wider world than we might imagine.

DJB: So becoming lucid in a dream can be analogous to what people call a spiritual awakening?

STEPHEN: Yeah. Giving people the idea of what life would be like if we realize that everyday life is sleep-walking and that there can be a further kind of awakening.

RMN: It seems that lucid dreaming can do much to help people broaden and develop their sense of themselves. Do you see lucid dreaming becoming a successful part of a psychotherapeutic program?

STEPHEN: Oh yes, very clearly. I think that's one of the strongest applications we have, what I think has the most definite proved value so far. There are a few psychotherapists who are using it, but it has been slow to catch on. Lucid dreaming is the most obvious approach to overcoming nightmares, telling people that they are imagining fears and they just have to exercise courage to face it somehow.

I'd say that the great value of lucid dreaming is as a means of self-development, a sort of self-therapy. This would apply to people that have an interest in getting to know themselves better and becoming more whole. I would think that people who are interested in something like Jungian analysis would be good candidates for this kind of thing, where they can take responsibility for the individuation process and help to further it in the dream state.

> *...the great value of lucid dreaming is as a means of self-development, a sort of self-therapy.*

DJB: Has your experience with psychedelics influenced your research?

STEPHEN: In a way. It was one of the things that inspired me to take an interest in the mind and before that, as I said earlier, I had no interest in the mind, I was interested only in the outside world. At first I wanted to make analogs of tryptamine molecules. I thought that if I could modify these molecules then they would really work by telling you *all* instead of telling you *almost* everything. That was my naivete, not realizing that the problem wasn't the molecule; the problem was the *mind*.

Going from the ordinary state of perceiving the world to an extraordinary state of perceiving the world, I would think so this is what it's *really* like! Of course the next day when I was back in the usual state, comparing the two, I realized, of course, *that* wasn't what it was like and *this* is not what it's like. They're *both* mental models or simulations. It's something that was very important for me in terms of understanding the power of the mind and seeing how just changing some of the operations paramenters in the perceptual system could lead to a radically different view of the world. I think it's shocking and a tragedy what's happened with the illegality of these substances, preventing scientific research and therapeutic use and I look forward to the day when that changes.

RMN: There seems to be a correlation between psychedelic consciousness and lucid consciousness in the dream state.

STEPHEN: There's a lot in common between the two states. In fact people can, in the dream state, take a dream "psychedelic" and have it produce an effect.

> *...people can in the dream state, take a dream psychedelic and have it produce an effect.*

DJB: Terence McKenna says that he smokes DMT in his dreams and then has the full experience.

STEPHEN: And what that shows is that what prevents us from having these experiences is not the chemical, it's the mental framework. So in a way psychedelics can be a kind of guide in revealing some of the potential in the mind. I think they have limitations in terms of taking us to the visions they show us. One can take the mistaken path of saying, well since I had the taste of it with the substance, if I keep taking it I'll eventually get the whole thing because more of the same should help. It doesn't seem to work that way.

RMN: Do you think that lucid dreaming is a more valid approach to personal development than psychedelics in as much as it can become more of a yoga, or do you think they're equally likely to have a long-lasting beneficial effect on someone's life?

STEPHEN: Well, I would say almost any experience can be valuable to a person if they're prepared to make use of it, and psychedelics or lucid dreams can be very useful if a person heeds the lessons that experience brings. It's not what happens to a person that matters, it's what they make of it. In a way lucid dreaming requires more of your own responsibility in making it happen and dealing with it. It's easy enough to take a pill and that can put you in a relatively passive role.

DJB: But you can take an active role in it.

STEPHEN: That's right, the question is: what do you do with this state? Do you direct it in a way where you seek for what you're looking for inside yourself? So it can be used in the same way.

DJB: Have you noticed any correlation between people who use psychedelics and a propensity towards lucid dreaming? Every time I've done a psychedelic, within a couple of days I'll almost always have a lucid dream.

STEPHEN: Yes, that is probably due to biochemical changes. Taking psychedelics will produce changes of neurochemical levels which will intensify REM sleep. Basically what you've done is you've altered the regulation of the system and so you've pushed it away from the equilibrium and it's going to come back and perhaps oscillate for a while until it gets back into its new equilibrium. So it's not surprising that in the next couple of nights you're going to have variations in REM sleep.

RMN: What is known about the chemicals given off by the brain in REM sleep?

STEPHEN: Relatively low levels of norepinephrine and serotonin, high levels of acetylcholine.

DJB: How in the world did they figure that out?

STEPHEN: Cat brains.

DJB: How about out-of-the-body-experiences. Do you think they're related to lucid dreaming?

STEPHEN: It's a complicated topic and I devoted an entire chapter to it in *Lucid Dreaming* because it's something you have to deal with carefully. I think they're not what people naively think they are, which is literally that you're leaving your physical body in some *ghost* body in the *physical* world. Let's take what happens in an out-of-the-body experience (OBE). Typically people are lying in bed, awake—at least they think they are. Next thing they know, they feel themselves separating from that body as if they have a second body that floats out of the first one, and then they may look back down and see what they take to be their physical body. So let's just examine that idea for consistency.

Now I'm floating up here, and then I look around at the bedroom and I notice that there's a window where there shouldn't be or there's no window where there should be and so I say, "Oh, I guess that wall there is not exactly a physical wall, maybe it's an *astral* wall, and of course then that's an *astral* floor, an *astral* bed—and what's that down on the *astral* bed that a moment ago I thought was my *physical* body?" It's an *astral* body or a dreambody. Therefore, what happened to the assumption that I'm moving in *physical* space? It's suddenly evaporated. The reason people find it so compelling is that it *feels like* you leave your body, and since it feels like it, that's what you believe is happening.

In our experiments in the laboratory, out of about 100 lucid dreams that were recorded, about 10% of those had out-of-body phenomenologies. So we analyzed the physiology associated with the out-of-the-body-experience-type lucid dream compared to the other lucid dreams to see if there's some character-istic that predicts that a person is likely to have a dream in which they think they are out of their body. And what we found was that there was much more likeliness of a brief awakening *before* the experience.

Now, I think the way the OBE takes place—in the typical form, which is in association with sleep—is, you're lying in bed, you wake up, you're awake. It's from REM sleep, so you're now in the context of going back into REM sleep and what happens is that you fall asleep without knowing it. Suddenly the sensory input is cut off and you've got now the *memory* of the body instead of the sensory perception of the body.

A moment ago your body had weight but now that gravitational force has been cut off; there's not sensory input for it, so it suddenly disappears and, I propose, the same thing happens as when you pick up an empty carton of milk. Suddenly your body flies upwards and you *feel* as if as there's a force going up that compensates for your mental model of your body-weight. When you per-ceive that the weight is less than expected by your mental model you explain that as an upward force.

DJB: What do you think about near-death experiences, when people feel they're leaving their body?

STEPHEN: Another factor that can produce an OBE is the capacity to dissoci-ate. There are some people who can much more readily than others detach themselves from their current experience. Once you detach it's possible then to reconstruct a view of reality that involves you outside the situation somehow. For most people, for that to happen, they either need the context of REM sleep, or they're falling off a mountain, or they've just been declared dead, or something. That's quite an emotional shock and it's enough to produce dissociation which then allows you to reorganize the experience.

Now you hear stories about people in near-death experiences seeing things that they shouldn't be able to see and that sort of thing. Well, I don't deny them that; there may be some paranormal information transfer occasionally in these experiences, but I think we underestimate how much knowledge we have about our surroundings through other senses. I don't buy the account that we leave in some second body. That second body, does it have a brain in there? What are the fingers for? If you pulled an eye out, would it look like an eye or is it just a mental model of an eye? It seems clear that that's what it is.

It's one of those ideas that people are very attached to for some reason and I think it's a misplaced sense of the value of individual survival. They think "this proves that I survive death because I was there!" Yet I don't think that's what we *want* to survive death. Why would we want these funky monkey forms to persist forever?

DJB: What do you think happens after biological death and has your experience with lucid dreaming influenced your thoughts in this area and about the nature of God?

STEPHEN: Let's suppose I'm having a lucid dream. The first thing I think is, "Oh, this is a dream, here I am." Now the "I" here is who I think Stephen is. Now what's happening in fact is that Stephen is asleep in bed somewhere, not in this world at all, and he's having a dream that he's in this room talking to you. With a little bit of lucidity I'd say, "This is a dream, and you're all in *my* dream." A little more lucidity and I'd know you're a dream figure and this is a *dream*-table, and this must be a *dream*-shirt and a *dream*-watch and what's this? It's got to be a dream-hand and well, so what's this? It's a *dream*—Stephen!

So a moment ago I thought this is who I am and now I know that it's just a mental model of who I am. So reasoning along those lines, I thought, I'd like to have a sense of what my deepest identity is, what's my highest potential, which level is the most real in a sense? With that in mind at the beginning of a lucid dream, I was driving in my sports car down through the green, spring country-side. I see an attractive hitchhiker at the side of the road, thought of picking her up but said, "No, I've already had *that* dream; I want *this* to be a representation of my *highest* potential."

So the moment I had that thought and decided to forgo the immediate pleasure, the car started to fly into the air and the car disappeared and my body, also. There were symbols of traditional religions in the clouds, the Star of David and the cross and the steeple and Near Eastern symbols. As I passed through that realm, higher beyond the clouds, I entered into a vast emptiness of space that was infinite and it was filled with potential and love. And the feeling I had was— *this is home*! This is where I'm from and I'd forgotten that it was here. I was overwhelmed with joy about the fact that this source of being was immediately present, that it was always here, and I had not been seeing it because of what was in my way. So I started singing for joy with a voice that spanned three or four octaves and resonated with the cosmos with words like, "I Praise Thee, O Lord!"

There wasn't any I, there was no thee, no Lord, no duality but, "Praise Be" was sort of the feeling of it. My belief is that the experience I had of this void—that's what you get if you take away the brain. When I thought about the meaning of that, I recognized that the deepest identity I had there was the source of being, the all and nothing that was here right now, that was what I was *too*, in addition to being Stephen. So the analogy that I use for understanding this is that we have these separate snowflake identities. Every snowflake is different in the same sense that each one of us is, in fact, distinct. So here is death, and here's the snowflake and we're falling into the infinite ocean. So what do we fear? We fear that we're going to lose our identity, we'll be melted, dissolved in that ocean and we'll be gone; but what may happen is that the snowflake hits the ocean and feels an infinite expansion of identity and realizes, what I was in essence, was *water!*

> *...we feel only our individuality, but not our substance...*

So we're each one of these little frozen droplets and we feel only our individuality, but not our substance, but our essential substance is common to everything in that sense, so now God is the ocean. So we're each a little droplet of that ocean, identifying only with the form of the droplet and not with the majesty and the unity.

RMN: Do you believe that the soul then reincarnates into another form?

STEPHEN: There may be intermediate states where—"to press the metaphor"— the seed crystal is recycled and makes another snowflake in a similar form or something like that, but that's not my concern. My concern is with the ocean; that's what I care about. So whether or not Stephen, or some deeper identity of Stephen survives—well, that'd be nice if that were so, but how can one not be satisfied with being the ocean?

DJB: If I were able to, through nanotechnology, completely replicate every atom in your brain, identically down to every last trace—would that be you?

STEPHEN: That would be "Stephen," if that's what you mean. I don't see a reason why we couldn't transfer the information in our brain to some other structure. It may be, for example, if you had something like you just described with nanotechnology, or a digital computer that was sufficiently complex, you'd still need some kind of substrate to sustain the different informational states and for all we know the vacuum of space itself may have an infinite amount of structure in it that could easily sustain a mind.

DJB: We interviewed Nick Herbert, the quantum physicist, and he described how there are mathematical models that leave a lot of latitude for things like parallel universes and other dimensions. Have you ever entertained this as a model for lucid dreaming, that there actually really are other dimensions or places that are not just mental simulations or constructs?

STEPHEN: I think of those as skew, not parallel, universes. Seriously, I've never liked that model; it seems tremendously inelegant to require that, every time you make a quantum decision, the thing you didn't decide on is still there in some way. It seems like a *reductio ad absurdum* of quantum theory. People think quantum theory is about the world but it's not; it's about *descriptions* of the world. What's the world really like if you don't make a measurement? Well, making the measurement *is* making the world—the world is interaction.

In other words, as a thought experiment, let's think about an object. Here it is right here on the table. I just pointed as if the space encloses it. Well, let's say, not only is it invisible as you can see but it doesn't interact in any way with any other thing in the world—is it a part of the world? No. What is the universe? The universe is a collection of objects that interact in some form with the other objects of the world.

DJB: Can you tell us about the Lucidity Institute and any current projects you're working on?

STEPHEN: The purpose of the Lucidity Institute is to sponsor and support research on human consciousness and what we're focusing on now is primarily lucid dreaming because that is one capacity of the mind that we feel is useful. If we knew more about the physiology of lucid dreaming we will be able to make it happen more readily, to find other mental techniques or physiological interventions, perhaps some drug effects that could make the state much more accessible and stable.

To help people make more viable decisions about what they're going to do in life, to get more experience out of the world, but basically to understand that life can have many more possibilities than we ordinarily think of. In the lucid dream you look around and realize that the whole world that you're seeing is all something that your mind is creating. It tells you that you have much more power than you'd ever believed before—or dreamed—for changing the world, starting with yourself.

Glossary

Algorithm: A recipe outlining the steps in a procedure for solving a problem; often used to describe key methods used in a computer program.

Androcratic: See "Dominator Society."

Attractors: A term used in modern dynamics to denote a limit towards which trajectories of change within a dynamical system move. Attractors generally lie within basins of attraction.

Axons: A thin neuronal branch that transmits electrical impulses away from the cell body to other neurons (or to muscles or glands).

Basin: A supporting element and/or foundation in a mathematical equation. In fractals these are the areas of dense information.

Bell's Theorem: A mathematical proof derived from physics demonstrating that whenever two particles interact, they are thereafter connected in a mysterious faster-than-light way that doesn't diminish with time or distance and can't be shielded. Also known as the "mechanism of non-locality."

Bifurcation: The splitting or branching of possible states that a system can assume due to changing parameters.

Chaos Theory: A new perspective emerging out of the study of dynamics that is discovering and mapping a high level of order and pattern in what has long been thought to be random activity.

Chaotic Attractor: Any attractor that is more complicated than a single point or cycle.

Copenhagen Interpretation: Physicist Niels Bohr's notion that an unmeasured atom is, in some sense, not real, and its attributes are created or realized through the act of measurement.

Cybernetics: A term coined by Norbert Weiner, meaning the study of communication, feedback, and control mechanisms in living systems and machines.

Dendrites: Tiny tree-like branchings at the electrical impulse-receiving end of a neuron.

Differential Topology: The study and mapping of changing surfaces.

Dimorphism: Biological division of structure in a species, such as for sexual reproduction.

Directed Panspermia: Francis Crick's theory to explain the origin of life on earth. He hypothesizes that spores traveling through space on the back of meteorites seed planets throughout the galaxy.

DMT: Dimetyltryptamine— an extremely powerful, short-acting hallucinogenic molecule found in the South American shamanic brew *Ayahuasca.*

DNA: Deoxyribonucleic acid— the long complex macro-molecule, consisting of two interconnected helical strands, that resides in the nucleus of every living cell, and encodes the genetic instructions for building each organism.

Dominator Society: A type of society in which one sex, or one group, dominates or rules over another. Also known as "Androcratic."

Dynamical Systems Theory: Mathematical models devised for understanding the processes of whole systems.

Dynamics: The study of systems in motion, which overlaps both physics and mathematics, and seeks to devise mechanical models used to understand processes.

ECCO: John Lilly's acronym for the Earth Coincidence Control Office. A hypothetical hierarchy of entities who manage coincidences in a fashion intended to accelerate the motion of human beings along their psycho-spiritual evolutionary pathways.

EEG: Electroencephalogram— electrical potentials recorded by placing electrodes on the scalp or in the brain.

Field: A region of physical influence that interrelates and interconnects matter and energy. Fields are not a form of matter; rather matter is energy bound within fields.

Fractal: Computer-generated images corresponding to mathematical equations, that repeat self-similar patterns at infinitely receding levels of organization.

Gaia: A model for interpreting the dynamics that occur on planet earth as being part of a single self-regulating organism.

Genome: The complete set of genetic material or genes for a single organism.

Gylanic: See "Partnership Society."

Holographic: The condition upon which the information for creating a whole system is stored in each of its parts.

Hypnogogic: The twilight state of awareness, characterized by vivid dream-like imagery, that occurs as one is falling asleep.

Hypnopompic: The dream-like state of awareness that occurs as one is waking up from sleep.

Information: Non-predictable patterns that carry a message.

Information Theory: A branch of cybernetics that attempts to define the amount of information required to control a process of given complexity.

Ketamine: A dissociative anesthetic agent with profound psychedelic properties.

Left Brain: The left hemisphere of the human brain associated with the processing of symbolic information in a linear, analytical mode.

Limbic System: A region of the brain believed to be important in the processing of emotions.

Lucid Dreaming: The phenomenon of being conscious and aware that one is dreaming, while one is in the process of dreaming.

Mechanism of Non-locality: See "Bell's Theorem."

Meme: A term coined by Richard Dawkins, who defines it as "a unit of cultural inheritance, hypothesized as analogous to the particulate gene and as naturally selected by virtue of its 'phenotypic' consequences on its own survival and replication in the cultural environment."

Metaprogramming Circuits: A hypothesized part of the brain that is responsible for over-riding social and cultural conditioning.

Morphic Field: Defined by Rupert Sheldrake as "a field within and around a morphic unit which organizes its characteristic structure and pattern of activity. They underlie the form and behavior of holons or morphic units at all levels of complexity. This term includes morphogenetic, behavioral, social, cultural, and mental fields. They are shaped and stabilized by morphic resonance from previous similar morphic units, which were under the influence of fields of the same kind. They consequently contain a kind of cumulative memory and tend to become increasingly habitual."

Morphic Resonance: The influence of previous structures of activity on subsequent similar structures of activity organized by morphic fields.

Morphogenesis: The coming into being of form.

Morphogenetic Field: A non-material region of influence that guides the structural development of organic forms.

MRI: Magnetic Resonance Imagery— A scanning technique that creates a visual image using electro-magnetic fields to see inside the body.

Nanotechnology: Atomic engineering—the ability to devise self-replicating machines, robots, and computers that are molecular sized.

Natural Selection: Charles Darwin's theory of biological evolution, based on the survival and replication of the fittest and most adaptable genes, through competition over limited natural resources.

Neural Network: An interconnected system of brain cells.

Neurophysiology: The physiological study of the nervous system.

Non-linear Dynamics: The study of chaotic processes.

Noosphere: A term coined by Teilhard de Chardin, defined as a non-material sheath that surrounds the earth, containing all of humanity's cultural achievements.

Paradigm: A cognitive model for explaining a set of data.

Paradigm Shift: A change in the perception of information.

Paranormal: Phenomena that are out of the realm of that which is explainable through conventional science.

Partnership Society: A type of society in which both sexes and all people have complete equal rights and representation, and live together in peaceful cooperation. Also known as "Gylanic."

PCP: Phencyclidine— an analgesic-anesthetic compound with powerful hallucinogenic effects.

Peptides: A compound consisting of two or several amino acids.

Phase Portrait: Images that display the state of a system at a moment frozen in time.

Phenome: The smallest linguistic unit.

Quantum Physics: The scientific study of sub-atomic reality.

REM: The phase of the sleep cycle where there are "rapid eye movements," and dreaming occurs.

Right Brain: The right hemisphere of the human brain which is associated with pattern-recognition and nonlinear holistic thinking.

Selfish Gene Theory: Darwin's theory of natural selection applied at the genetic level, which proposes that the unit of selection in evolution is not the species or the organism, but the gene.

Separatrix: The threshold between attractors in a dynamic system.

Sociobiology: The biological study of social behavior in animals, based upon the understanding that social behaviors can be genetically encoded and evolve through the evolutionary process of natural selection.

Space-time Warp: A crinkle, tear, or bend in the space-time continuum.

Strange Attractor: The orbital point in the mathematical mapping of a dynamic system that is neither fixed nor oscillating, but rather spirals inward.

Tangles: Diagrams that map the skeletal structure of a dynamical system.

Teleology: The study of ends or final causes; the explanation of phenomena by reference to goals or purposes.

Theory of Formative Causation: The hypothesis that organisms or morphic units at all levels of complexity are organized by morphic fields, which are themselves influenced and stabilized by morphic resonance from all previous similar morphic units.

Topological Manifold: A multi-leveled surface area.

Unified Field Theory: The Holy Grail of physics, which would mathematically unite all the known forces of the universe under a single comprehensive framework.

Virtual Reality: Interactive technology which totally controls sensory input and creates the convincing illusion that one is completely immersed in a computer-generated world.

Bibliography

Ralph Abraham
Transversal Mappings and Flows (with J.Robbin), Addison Wesley, 1967.
Foundations of Mechanics (with J.E.Marsden), Addison Wesley, 1978.
Manifolds, Tensor Analysis, and Applications (with J.E.Marsden and T.Ratiu), Addison Wesley, 1983.
Dynamics, the Geometry of Behavior: (with C.D. Shaw)
Volume 1 - Periodic Behavior, Ariel Press, 1982.
Volume 2 - Chaotic Behavior, Ariel Press, 1983.
Volume 3 - Global Behavior, Ariel Press, 1984.
Volume 4 - Bifurcation Behavior, Ariel Press, 1988.
Trialogues on the Edge of the West (with T.McKenna and R. Sheldrake), Bear and Co., 1992.
Eros, Gaia and Chaos (soon to be published).

Riane Eisler
Dissolution, McGraw-Hill, 1977.
The Equal Rights Handbook, Avon, 1978.
The Chalice and the Blade, Harper/Collins, 1987.
The Partnership Way (with D.Loye), Harper/Collins, 1990.

Allen Ginsberg
Howl and Other Poems, City Lights, 1956.
Kaddish and Other Poems, City Lights, 1961.
Empty Mirror, Totem/Corinth, 1961.
The Yage Letters (with W.Burroughs), City Lights, 1960.
Reality Sandwiches, City Lights, 1963.
Airplane Dreams, Anansi/City Lights 1968.
Ankor Wat, Fulcrum, 1968.
Indian Journals, City Lights, 1970.
The Gates of Wrath, Four Seasons, 1972.
Iron Horse, Coach House, 1972.
The Fall of America: Poems of These States 1965-1971, City Lights, 1973.
Allen Verbatim, McGraw Hill, 1974.
The Visions of the Great Rememberer, Mulch, 1974.
Gay Sunshine Interview (with A.Young), Grey Fox, 1974.
Chicago Trial Testimony, City Lights, 1975.
To Eberhart from Ginsberg, Penmaen, 1976.
Journals Early Fifties Early Sixties, Grove, 1977.
As Ever: Collected Correspondence Allen Ginsberg & Neal Cassady, Creative Arts, 1977.
Mind Breaths, Poems 1971-76, City Lights, 1978.
Poems All Over the Place, Mostly '70's, Cherry Valley, 1978.
Composed on the Tongue, Grey Fox, 1980.
Straight Heart's Delight: Love Poems & Selected Letters, (with P.Orlovsky) Gay Sunshine, 1980.
Plutonium Ode: Poems 1977-1980, City Lights, 1982.
Collected Poems 1947-1980, Harper/Collins, 1984.

Howl Annotated, (with A.Young) Harper & Row, 1986.
White Shroud Poems 1980-1985, Harper & Row, 1986.
Your Reason and Blake's System, Hanuman Books, 1988.

Nina Graboi
One Foot in the Future, Ariel Press, 1990.

Nick Herbert
Quantum Reality, Doubleday, 1985.
Faster Than Light: Superluminal Loopholes in Physics, New American Library, 1988.
Elemental Mind: Human Consciousness and the New Physics, Penguin USA, 1993.

Laura Archera Huxley
You are Not the Target, Farrar, Straus & Giroux, 1963.
This Timeless Moment , Mercury House, 1991.
Between Heaven and Earth, Hay House, 1991.
OneADayReason to be Happy (with Dr. Piero Ferrucci), Metamorphous Press, 1991.
The Child of Your Dreams, Inner Traditions International Ltd, 1992.

Oscar Janiger
A Different Kind of Healing, Putnam, 1993.

Carolyn Kleefeld
Satan Sleeps with the Holy, Horse & Bird Press, 1982.
Climates of the Mind, Horse and Bird Press, 1979.
Lovers in Evolution, Horse and Bird Press, 1984.
Songs of Ecstasy, Gallerie Illuminati, 1990.
The Sixth Dimension (soon to be published).

Stephen LaBerge
Lucid Dreaming, Tarcher, 1985.
Conscious Mind, Sleeping Brain, New York, 1988.
Exploring the World of Lucid Dreaming (with H.Rheinglold), Ballantine, 1991.

Timothy Leary
The Interpersonal Diagnosis of Personality, John Wiley, 1957.
The Psychedelic Experience (with R. Metzner and R. Alpert), University Books, 1964.
Psychedelic Prayers From the Tao Te Ching, University Books, 1967.
The High Priest, NAL-World, 1968.
The Politics of Ecstasy, Ronan, 1990.
Jail Notes, World-Evergreen, 1971.
Confessions of a Hope Fiend (with J. Leary), Bantam, 1973.
The Curse of the Oval Room, Starseed, 1974.
Terra 11 (with J. Leary and L. W. Benner), Starseed, 1974.
The Intelligence Agents, Peace Press, 1979.
Changing My Mind—Among Others, Prentice-Hall, 1982.
Mind Mirror (software), Electronic Arts, 1986.

What Does WoMan Want? Falcon Press, 1988.
Info-Psychology (Revision of *Exo-Psychology*), Falcon Press, 1987.
Neuro-Politics, (Revision of *Neuro-Politics,*with R. A. Wilson and G. Koopman), Falcon Press, 1988.
Timothy Leary's Greatest Hits, Knoware, 1990.
Flashbacks, Tarcher, 1990.
The Game of Life (with R.A.Wilson), Falcon Press, 1992.

John C. Lilly
Man and Dolphin, Anchor/Doubleday, 1961.
The Mind of the Dolphin, Anchor/Doubleday, 1967.
Programming and Metaprogramming in the Human Biocomputer, Crown, 1972.
The Center of the Cyclone, Crown, 1972.
Simulations of God: The Science of Belief, Simon & Schuster, 1975.
Lilly On Dolphins, Anchor/Doubleday, 1975.
The Dyadic Cyclone (with T.Lilly), Simon & Schuster, 1976.
The Deep Self, Simon & Schuster, 1977.
Communication Between Man and Dolphin, Crown, 1978.
The Scientist, Ronin, 1988.
John Lilly, So Far (with F. Jeffrey), Tarcher, 1990.
The Dolphin in History (with A. Montagu), University of California Press, Berkeley.

David Loye
The Healing of a Nation, Delta, 1972.
The Leadership Passion: A Psychology of Ideology, Jossey-Bass, 1977.
The Knowable Future: A Psychology of Forecasting and Prophecy, Wiley, 1978.
The Sphinx and the Rainbow: Brain, Mind and Future Vision, Ediziono Mediteranee, 1987.

Terence McKenna
The Invisible Landscape (with D. McKenna), Scabury Press, 1975.
Psilocybin: The Magic Mushroom Grower's Guide (with D. McKenna), Lux Natura, 1986.
Food of the Gods, Bantum, 1992.
The Archaic Revival, Harper, 1992.
Trialogues on the Edge of the West, (with R.Abraham and R.Sheldrake), Bear and Co., 1992

Rupert Sheldrake
A New Science of Life, Tarcher, 1982.
The Presence of the Past, Vintage, 1989.
The Rebirth of Nature, Bantum, 1991.
Trialogues on the Edge of the West (with R. Abraham and T. McKenna), Bear and Co., 1992.

Robert Trivers
Social Evolution, Benjamin-Cummings, 1985.

Colin Wilson
The Occult, Random, 1973.
Mysteries, Putnam, 1980.

Afterlife, Doubleday, 1987.
C. G. Jung: Lord of the Underworld, Borgo, 1988.
Aleister Crowley: The Nature of the Beast, Borgo, 1988.
The Sex Diary of a Metaphysician, Ronin, 1988.
The Desert (Spider World series), Ace Bks, 1988.
The Misfits: A Study of Sexual Outsiders, Carroll & Graf, 1989.
The Philosopher's Stone, Jeremy Tarcher, 1989.
The Fortress (Spider World series), Ace Bks, 1989.
The Tower (Spider World series), Ace Bks, 1989.
The Delta (Spider World series), Ace Bks, 1990.
The Outsider, Buccaneer Bks, 1990.
A Criminal History of Mankind, Carroll & Graf, 1990.
Religion and the Rebel, Ashgrove Press, 1990.
Music, Nature and the Romantic Outsider, Borgo, 1990.
Beyond the Outsider, Carroll & Graf, 1991
Beyond the Occult: A Twenty Year Investigation into the Paranormal, Carroll & Graf, 1991.
Written in Blood, Warner, 1991.
Ritual in the Dark, Ronin, 1992.

Robert Anton Wilson
Cosmic Trigger I: The Final Secret of the Illuminati, Falcon Press, 1986.
Cosmic Trigger II: Down To Earth, Falcon Press, 1991.
Quantum Psychology: How Brain Software Programs Yourself and Your World, Falcon Press, 1990.
Prometheus Rising, Falcon Press, 1983.
The New Inquisition, Falcon Press, 1986.
Sex and Drugs—A Journey Beyond Limits, Falcon Press, 1987.
Coincidance, Falcon, 1988.
Ishtar Rising, Falcon Press, 1989.
Wilhelm Reich in Hell, Falcon Press, 1987.
The Illuminatus! Trilogy (with R.Shea), Dell, 1975.
Schrodinger's Cat Trilogy, Dell, 1980-81.
Masks of the Illuminati, Dell, 1981.
Reality Is What You Can Get Away With, Dell, 1992.
Right Where You Are Sitting Now, And/Or, 1983.
The Earth Will Shake, Bluejay Books, 1983.
The Widow's Son, Bluejay Books, 1985.
Nature's God, Penguin Books, USA, 1991.
The Illuminati Papers, And/Or, 1980.
Playboy's Book of Forbidden Words, Playboy Press, 1972.
The Sex Magicians, Playboy Press, 1973.

Addresses

To find out more about *Stephen LaBerge's* work with lucid dreaming write:
Lucidity Institute
P.O. Box 2364
Stanford, California 94305

For further information on *Terence McKenna's* sanctuary in Hawaii for endangered species of ethnobotanically and ethnomedically valuable plants from around the world contact:
Botanical Dimensions
P.O. Box 807
Occidental, CA 95465

To get involved in *Riane Eisler* and *David Loye's* organization to create a partnership society write:
Center for Partnership Studies
P.O. Box 51936
Pacific Grove, CA 93950

To receive *Robert Anton Wilson's* newsletter *Trajectories* order from:
Permanent Press
P.O. Box 700305
San Jose, CA 95170

To find out more about *Carolyn Kleefeld's* artwork and publications contact:
Atoms Mirror Atoms
P.O. Box 221693
Carmel, CA 93922

Laura Huxley's foundation for "the nurturing of the possible human" can be reached at:
Our Ultimate Investment
P.O. Box 1904
Los Angeles, CA 90028

To find out more about *Oscar Janiger's* information center dedicated to the scientific study of human consciousness write:
The Albert Hofmann Foundation
291 S. La Cienega Blvd. #615
Beverly Hills, CA 90211-3325

To find out more about *John Lilly's* work with dolphin communication write:
Human/Dolphin Foundation
11930 Oceanaire Lane
Malibu, CA 90265

David Jay Brown and *Rebecca McClen Novick* can be reached through:
Brainchild Productions
P.O. Box 1101
Topanga, CA 90290

About the Authors

Silvia Utiger

David Jay Brown is the author of the science fiction novel Brainchild *(Falcon Press, 1988). He attended eight different universities throughout the United States and Europe during his formal education, earning his B.A. in psychology from USC, his M.A. in psychobiology from NYU, and then completed a year of post-masters training in USC's doctoral program in behavioral neuroscience. At NYU his research into the positive and negative reinforcement systems of the brain was compiled into a master's thesis entitled "Paradoxically Motivating Effects of Electrical Brain Stimulation Delivered Via a Single Electrode." He has written for such publications as* Mondo 2000, Magical Blend, Critique, High Times, The International Synergy Journal, The Los Angeles Reader, *and* The Sun. *He co-wrote a chapter in Terence McKenna's book* The Archaic Revival *(Harper), and some of his photographic work appears in Nina Graboi's autobiography* One Foot in the Future *(Ariel Press). His research background in the study of learning and memory at USC, and his fascination with experimental psychopharmacology, made him a natural spokesperson on the "smart drug" phenomena; he appeared on such popular television shows as* A Current Affair *and* The Montel Williams Show. *He oriented and worked with isolation tank and brain machine users at the Altered States MindGym in Los Angeles, and therapeutically, he has worked for years with the mentally ill in psychiatric hospitals and other treatment centers—primarily with the extremes of schizophrenia, suicidality, manic-depressiveness, and multiple personality disorder. He currently lives high on a mountain overlooking Topanga Canyon in Southern California, where he is working on* Virus, *his new science fiction novel.*

Renny Novick

Rebecca McClen Novick is a freelance journalist, writer and award-winning poet whose work has been published in numerous magazines and journals. Born in England, she specialized in psychology and travelled extensively through Europe and the Middle East in her late teens, studying cultural anthropology and the history of religion. She teaches reading and writing to dyslexics and is involved in making television documentaries. Currently she is working on a children's book. She lives on a ranch in Malibu with her artist husband, dogs, cats, horses, chickens, peacocks and other critters too numerable to mention.

The Crossing Press

To receive our current catalog, please call
TOLL FREE 800/777-1048